IN COLD
WATER

IN COLD WATER

Mike Humphreys

authorHOUSE®

AuthorHouse™ LLC
1663 Liberty Drive
Bloomington, IN 47403
www.authorhouse.com
Phone: 1-800-839-8640

Published by AuthorHouse   06/24/2013

ISBN: 978-1-4817-5738-6 (sc)
ISBN: 978-1-4817-5739-3 (hc)
ISBN: 978-1-4817-5904-5 (e)

Library of Congress Control Number: 2013909814

This book is dedicated to my friend Tom Kop,
who taught me that swimming is mostly about friendship
and who left this world and my life way too early.

Prologue: A Delayed Finale, July 2008

July 23, 2008

After four years of training and one failed attempt to swim the English Channel in 2006, my swim across the Channel was finally underway and going as planned.

I was about nine hours into the swim and already in French waters—about three-quarters done. To stay faithful to English Channel-swimming tradition and abide by the rules, I was wearing nothing but an ordinary racing suit, a swim cap, and goggles. The water was about sixty degrees Fahrenheit, about twenty degrees colder than the average swimming pool.

I'd swum past sunrise and high noon. I'd heard from my crew about other Channel swimmers who had started at the same time but been forced to abandon their swims. I had seen ships going south on the UK side of the Channel and north on the French side, and I had watched as thousands of jellyfish floated semi-aimlessly in the Channel's separation zone, where the south and north sides of the Channel meet and the water is slack.

Now came the hard part: the final miles to France and the finish.

I was shivering, which was odd. I didn't feel cold, but I was vibrating like a hummingbird. I looked around in confusion and saw that the sun had disappeared behind a layer of thin, flat, gray clouds that continued all the way to France. Was that enough to make me shiver so violently?

Besides the shaking, I was starving. I found myself daydreaming about the real food I knew was on board my pilot boat, the *Seafarer II*, which was idling slowly about ten feet to my right. As is customary in open-water swimming, I'd been feeding exclusively on specially formulated liquids for the past nine hours. Now, my stomach was craving something solid, something I could chew. On my next feed, I drank deeper and longer, trying to quench that hunger. This filled my stomach, but I could see that the crew was alarmed when they saw my shivering up close while I fed.

Ten minutes after my feed, my crew waved me back to the *Seafarer II*. I swam over and hovered off the port side. "Here's something to warm you up," my friend Lynne Smith said, throwing me a bottle of warm feed. Lynne, a champion triathlete and Annapolis graduate from Oklahoma whom I'd met in 2006 when in Dover for my first Channel attempt, was a successful Channel swimmer in 2007. She was in charge of my feeding.

I took a swig and felt delicious warmth cascading down inside me like a hot rock sinking in snow. I couldn't drink much, though; my stomach was still processing the deep slurp I'd taken just a few minutes earlier. My lips were shivering full speed, and my hands had joined the tempo. I was worried. Fighting off hypothermia is a war of attrition, and I knew it would be tough to overcome. I swam away from the boat, pointed myself toward France, and resumed swimming.

I don't remember everything that happened next.

A bit after 1:04 p.m., I'm told, the pilot noted that I was making good progress and was on the verge of leaving the French shipping lane in favor of the inland waters around France.

Soon after that, I swam over to the boat and just stopped. "What's wrong, Mike?" Lynne asked.

I was lost, cold, stunned, confused—clearly hypothermic. "I don't know, I don't know," I mumbled.

Lynne, already in a swimsuit, stepped out of her warm-ups and jumped into the Channel.

"Hey, Mike, let's swim to France," she said cheerfully.

I hung in the water, dumb, incoherent, and unresponsive. Lynne swam over and asked me something—I don't remember what. I flipped over, trying to swim. I couldn't. I gave up and hung facedown in the water, floating, giving in to my fate. I was waiting to sink.

Someone on the crew yelled, "He's done!" and all hell broke loose.

Lynne tried to flip me over and pull me to the *Seafarer II*, but she was finding it hard to complete the maneuver in the choppy Channel. She managed to get me on my back and hold me face up as she treaded water. One of the captain's mates, Keith, stripped to his skivvies and jumped in. Together, Lynne and Keith dragged me to the *Seafarer II* and hauled me unceremoniously onto the transom.

Violent whole-body shivers overtook me as I lay prone, dancing between consciousness and oblivion, woozily attempting to replay what had happened.

After some time, perhaps fifteen minutes, I regained full consciousness and found myself on the deck of the *Seafarer II,* being warmed by crew members spooning me on both sides. I tried to stand—no luck. The maneuver was the last straw for my stomach, which started working backward. I spoiled the carpet on deck as I retched uncontrollably, still shivering violently.

We were headed back to the starting line, and two or three hours later, Dover Harbor welcomed us impassively as I thanked everyone for keeping me safe.

"I talked to Chris, and he has spots open on tides for next summer," Lynne said with a grin.

So much for my English Channel swim of 2008. I may not have made it, but I got twice as far as I had on my first attempt in 2006—and I'd done it faster.

Still, I'd failed when it came to withstanding the cold waters of the Channel, and I'd almost sunk. Not so good.

I was forty-five years old that summer, and I knew the English Channel wasn't going anywhere.

I'd go back.

Chapter 1

Dover, England, and the English Channel

Everyone has dreams, and for much of my adult life, mine has been to swim the English Channel. The process of moving from daydreaming to doing began with my 2001 move to Seattle, a city with access to abundant and inspiring open-water swimming venues. I began to train for the Channel in earnest in 2004 and made my first attempt in 2006.

I failed because I was underprepared. Having badly miscalculated my feeds, I vomited over the course of five hours until I was drained of energy and my body shut down. I was forced to quit halfway across.

In 2008, much better trained and prepared, I made another attempt. This time, I moved smoothly and relatively comfortably into the French inland waters—until hypothermia slammed into me like a cyclist on steroids.

Surprisingly, I still had a passion for the challenge—or maybe it was an obsession. Nothing if not goal-oriented, I never seriously considered giving up. I was going back.

I wanted to swim the Channel—all of it. I wanted to see France in the distance from a beach in Dover and swim until it wasn't just a shadow on the horizon, tasting the salt along the way, watching the jellyfish, waving at ferries. I wanted to watch the French seabed rush up to meet me and feel French sand in my toes as I stood and walked for the first time in hours. I wanted to climb out of the water and turn to wave back at Dover, now twenty-two miles in the distance, and yell *"Vive la France! Je suis navige La Manche!!"*

Why? Swimming the Channel had been a lifelong dream, yes, but that wasn't all. To me, the history and logistics of the enterprise were absorbing, and the people involved in the sport were fascinating, compelling. On top of that, after a couple decades of regular travel to London, I was an Anglophile and swimming the Channel was just so . . . British.

To fully understand why I (or anyone) would want to undertake such an enterprise, though, you probably need to understand Dover, where all Channel swims begin. So I'll start there.

Dover is a beautiful yet gritty little town, small and intimate. It's personal but touristy, with a history that stretches back further than that of the Romans. Its layout is long and relatively narrow, and it's situated in a series of valleys surrounded by hills and cliffs. Stretching back from the Channel waterfront, Dover reaches inland a few miles until it dissipates into County Kent.

Whenever I go, I have a similar experience. I step off the train at Dover Priory, and fifteen seconds later, I'm outside the small, uncomplicated train station collapsing into a cab—easy as that. I tell the cabbie I'm staying at Victoria House, and we're on our way; providing the address is usually redundant. As the driver flings us down twisted and tortured roads, around structures new and ancient, I roll down my window to take a deep breath of Dover. The Channel is a couple of miles away, but the salt and wind tickle my nose and throat. The seagulls are singing, howling, screeching . . . and I feel at home.

Dover isn't a shopping mecca, but everything you need can be found on High Street. There's a sporting goods shop and a Marks & Spencer (where I replenished after Delta Airlines lost my luggage in 2008). WH Smith, the local newsstand, will keep you informed, and the Eight Bells Pub, where

I've downed countless pints, burgers, and pies in the friendly company of Dover's finest citizens, is the spot for sustenance. On a small side road off of the High, you can check out the Dover Mangle, a public laundry that's been a mainstay for me since 2004, when I first started Channel training in Dover. It was in the Mangle that I got a crash course in the colorful local slang when a young couple burst into an obscene shouting match while their baby munched happily through sweets in his carriage. Dad was wearing a full set of motorcycle leathers, and Mom, about six or seven months pregnant, sported a bright teal T-shirt that warned, "Hands off the bump!"

Beyond the High, over by the new Cooperative Food market, you can wander through Pencester Gardens, a verdant public park. It seems there's always a carnival at Pencester during my visits, complete with rides and contests of skill. I love walking there, absorbing the rhythm of Dover as it talks and laughs, argues, reconciles, and flirts. It's like walking through a live episode of the beloved BBC soap opera *Eastenders*. There are kids everywhere, teens gossiping and text messaging, moms with prams, conservatively attired retirees, pierced skateboarders, and cheerful dads having a fag and a bit of sun.

The cabbie whips us past the Dover Museum on our left, the Channel itself winking to our right through waterfront buildings, and we lean a hard left around the main roundabout. If we'd gone south toward Folkestone instead of north toward Dover Castle, we'd pass the local-hire car shop. Most years, I rent some conveyance or the other to explore the surrounding villages during downtime, while I'm waiting for clear, wind-free weather. Deal is a particularly pretty town, like an oversize Victorian ice cream shop with lots of retirees. Canterbury is justifiably renowned for its colorful Church-of-England history.

Above and behind the hire car shop, up on the famous White Cliffs of Dover, are gun bunkers left over from World War II, now gazing empty across the Channel. On the waterfront side of the street is Dover Marina.

3

I've met my Channel crews at the marina twice in the wee hours of the morning for Channel swim attempts. Each time, I've returned earlier than planned, dejected. On other occasions, I've waited at the marina to meet friends coming back from their own Channel attempts. Whether they're jubilant or defeated, they always look rough, with sunburned faces, lips bloated from saltwater, skin chafed raw. They are shuffling very slowly, ready for a bath and sleep, often unaware that the swaying aftereffects of the Channel's chop might not leave their bodies for days. Their crews typically are just glad to be back on solid land.

Barreling along the A20, parallel to Dover Harbor, the left-side cab windows fill with the brooding hulk of Burlington House, an abandoned complex the Dover Council can't tear down because it's the only structure high enough for the community's radio antennas. The central part of the complex is County Hotel, a gray and gritty edifice that would make a fine setting for a Stephen King novel.

Next to Burlington House is the site where a three-thousand-year-old seafaring boat was found years ago, one of the oldest such finds in the world. You can go check it out at the Dover Museum and then walk through a diorama showing the stages of Dover's development from before Jesus walked the earth. In a typical juxtaposition of old and new, the museum sits on the town square where the National Olympic Committee installed a massive outdoor TV for community viewing of the 2012 Olympics; it was left in place afterward for the town to continue to enjoy.

The cabbie persists, and we're getting closer to Victoria House. He's a colorful fellow in long, bright-yellow shorts and a blue plaid shirt, who hollers out his window at another cabbie, "You'll soon need a whip for that piece of shit!" mocking the aging Skoda that is giving the other cabbie grief. As he chats amiably with me in his thick accent, I'm not entirely clear what he's saying but I'm willing to bet it's something cheerfully cynical about the Dover Town Council and their inaction that leaves the Burlington brooding over Dover year after year after year. Out the right window, an apartment complex ruins the view of the Channel for anyone who isn't in a helicopter, leaving only a wink of it viewable through a walkway set in the middle.

First by smells, then glimpses, the Channel reveals itself slowly, as if mocking my obsession. She's patient. She's been there for more than 250,000 years, and she's not going anywhere soon.

Up ahead, high on the White Cliffs, is Dover Castle, overlooking the harbor and guarding all it surveys. The castle's history spans from the Romans to Henry VIII, through the Napoleonic wars to Churchill's finest hour. The stories soaked into its walls, keeps, chapels, and tunnels would fill volumes.

As the taxi flies around a left corner onto Maison Dieu Street, it passes Dover Leisure Center, where I cross-train occasionally. In 2008, I enjoyed the patronage of a large lady swimmer there. It was chaotically crowded, and she very deliberately cleared a path through the other swimmers for me, like a broom through sawdust.

Up a bit farther, we turn onto St. James and continue past the White Horse Pub, an establishment very well-known in Channel circles. For years, successful Channel swimmers have engraved their names on the walls there for posterity and a congratulatory pint. The swimmers memorialized on the walls and ceiling of the White Horse are ordinary people who decided to do something extraordinary—teachers, photographers, retired corporals, IT consultants, homemakers, and such. These everyday athletes trained dutifully, carving out time around their jobs and family obligations without benefit of sponsorship deals, entourages, yellow bracelets with their names embossed on them, reporters, or PR people validating their egos. All they had in their corners were family and friends, appropriately proud.

5

A moment later and a fiver for the cabbie, I'm standing on Bill and Audrey Hamblin's front steps at Victoria House. As always, Bill has hung an American flag outside to show his respect for his American guests. My many visits to this place have all begun the same way. I drag my suitcase inside, past a painting of her majesty Queen Victoria, and tap lightly on their salon door. Audrey welcomes me in the same warm tone that I use with my sons and that I'll undoubtedly use with my grandchildren. I crack open the door, and Audrey smiles happily at me from the sofa, where she is watching cricket. Bill is standing by his computer, one hand or both perched on his waist, grinning broadly. Bill is like a five-foot-eight lighthouse, strong in the base and beaming at the top. Audrey warmly defines *motherly*. They've been married since 1955, eight years before I was born.

"Hallo, Mike!" Bill says as I lean down for a hug from Audrey.

We catch up for a while, sharing tales of family, friends, and the Channel community as the cricket match continues in the background. To be clear, cricket is *always* playing in the background. Audrey manages the impressive feat of watching her beloved cricket peripherally while we catch up. Occasionally, her mouth twitches at a bad play, but she hides it well; it took years for me to notice. I finally excuse myself and go crashing up the stairs with my bag, past Queen Victoria to my favorite room, the Balcony Room. Audrey has mentioned that she managed to withhold the Balcony Room from the clutches of another Channel swimmer only because of my two-years-in-advance booking; I grin at that as I open the door. I drop my case on the floor, toss open the glass doors to the balcony, and look out over Dover proper and the Channel beyond. The seagulls are screeching, and since it's a clear day, France taunts me.

After I get settled, I take a walk around to reconnect with Dover. Usually that means making a hasty beeline to Dover Harbor for some long-awaited reflection. I'm not hurrying because Dover has a glamorous beach, because it doesn't. It's a crescent moon of round pebbles that hurt your bare feet, a boardwalk whose appeal has worn thin since it was designed a century ago, and patronage that suggests you leave valuables elsewhere. None of that matters, though, as I head for where the action starts: Channel Swimmer's Beach.

I plop off the paved walk onto the pebbled beach, shuffle awkwardly to a vantage point, and sit down and stare out at my beloved English Channel. The harbor is like a very large U: the ferry docks form its left wall, and Prince of Wales pier forms the right. Capping the U is a seawall about a mile out from the beach where I sit. France is dead ahead, through the harbor gates—mocking me. Out beyond the seawall, whitecaps are crashing in the Channel. The water in the harbor itself is a light pea-soup green with bits of foam floating in places. I can taste it from twenty-five yards away. The seagulls' squawks have reached a crescendo, and some of them are taking potshots at me, taking turns diving and evacuating in my direction.

I reflect on the Channel—my obsession. The first swimmer to conquer it was Matthew Webb, who in 1875 took twenty-one hours and forty-five minutes to manage the feat. He swam breaststroke, popular in his day, though much slower than freestyle. Channel swims since Captain Webb have averaged about fourteen hours.

Captain Matthew Webb was a retired Royal Navy officer who'd helmed the steamship *Emerald*. His Channel swim was a major milestone in the development of swimming, and within years of it, there was a great explosion in the number and popularity of public swimming pools in Britain. Webb enjoyed years of acclaim and worldwide fame until, in 1883, he tried to swim the Niagara Rapids from Canada to America and drowned in the chaotic waters. A monument to him now stands in his hometown of Dawley, bearing his words: *Nothing Great Is Easy.*

Indeed it's not.

It took another thirty-six years before anyone managed to duplicate Webb's successful Channel swim—Thomas Burgess finally did it in 1911—and it wasn't until August 1926 that Olympian Gertrude Ederle became the first woman to swim the Channel. With her feat, Ederle broke the world record by two hours, completing her swim in fourteen hours and thirty-one minutes. As Webb had, Ederle enjoyed worldwide fame, and she was feted in New York with a ticker-tape parade, but she struggled for years afterward, her career badly managed and not sustained. Her hearing had already deteriorated thanks to a bad bout of childhood measles, and she lost it entirely a few years after her swim. She was subsequently abandoned by her fiancé. Despite her reverses, she lived a long life and passed away quietly in a New Jersey retirement home in 2003, at the age of ninety-eight. Like Webb, Ederle is a beloved figure in Channel history, and to commemorate her, there's an annual seventeen-mile memorial swim between New Jersey and Manhattan.

Since the early days of Channel swimming, many souls, challenged by its reputation as the ultimate test of endurance, have attempted to duplicate the feats of Webb and Ederle. Some have managed to make it more than once. Alison Streeter, the reigning champion of the Channel, swam the distance forty-three times before she retired and became a Channel boat pilot, helping others follow in her wake. Over the years, alongside the successes, there have been fatalities. The Channel pushes a body to its limit—sometimes beyond—and there's no respite in the water. In response to the deaths of swimmers in 1988 and 1999, the French barred swimmers from beginning a crossing from their side of the Channel, so all swims now start from England.

As I gaze out at the water and daydream about my own impending adventure, the Channel's history spins and eddies in my mind like foam in seawater. I replay past swims: the starts, sights, smells, feeds, fish, and friends of each. Why I failed and what I'll do differently.

I'm excited to be on Swimmer's Beach and can't wait for my Channel-swimming friends to join me. But for the moment, I'm alone in my thoughts, staring into the warm embrace of my beloved English Channel.

Anticipating.

Chapter 2

How It Works

After my failure in 2008, I awoke shivering madly, freezing cold, and crushed at my second disappointment. The hypothermia passed, but the crushing frustration never did. I was going back to try again.

In the summer of 2009, I was a two-time failure, yet more experienced and better trained. I was fatter yet fitter. I had more aches and pains, yet I was more patient. I was grayer yet . . . older. This last fact was brought home by a cheerful question from a concession-stand owner at the Seattle beach where I was training that June.

"Hey," he said, watching me materialize from the water, "I bet you were some kind of swimmer in your day, huh?"

My day? The mental picture I'd been entertaining until his comment was, "Channel swimmer emerges vigorously from training swim."

Before plunging ahead (as it were) into my own story, a bit of background on the sport's technicalities is in order.

Like Everest climbers carefully scheduling their ascent, Channel swimmers usually plan their swims during the more favorable tidal periods in the Channel, called "neap tides"—when the least amount of water is moving through the Channel, thus minimizing the effects of tides on the swim. During neap tides, the sun and moon are at their farthest points from each other, so their gravitational pull on our waters is at its weakest. There are two neap tides per month, lasting seven to nine days each. Most Channel swimmers have heard and accepted this explanation for swimming on neap tides. Many aren't aware that there's another reason. The earliest Dover boatmen to pilot Channel swimmers across were fishermen. Neap tides were more difficult tides to fish than the alternating Spring tides, so they scheduled Channel swim attempts on the neaps for their own convenience. Today, Channel swimmers still tend to swim on the neaps, although in recent years more are attempting the spring tides.

Neap tides happen all year long, of course, but the Channel's cold water confines swimmers to the warmest months, July through September. Even in summer, the Channel isn't exactly the Caribbean: water temperatures remain around the sixty-degree mark. That's cold enough to kill—which the Channel does from time to time. Although swimmers do make attempts in June or October, there are basically six to eight tides each year during which most Channel aspirants make their attempts.

Favorable tides don't necessarily mean favorable weather; wind is the primary culprit ruining the fun. When wind blows across Channel tides, it creates chop and waves that aren't fun to swim through. Anything over seven to ten knots, and your boat pilot will suggest you settle into a Dover pub to wait for another day. Waiting like that isn't fun, by the way, but if you wanted relaxation, you'd probably have gone to Club Med. On the other hand, you're better off than the poor bastards waiting on Everest for the right moment to attempt a climb. They're in crappy little tents peeing in a cup, while you are lounging on a barstool, drinking tasty ales to put on extra body fat and telling exaggerated versions of your favorite swimming exploits.

The Everest guys have the edge in numbers, though: the mountain has been summited more than five thousand times, while the Channel has only been vanquished by fewer than half that many. Everest climbers end up with cooler souvenir photos too, with dashing-looking climbers posing on the top of the world with the sun beaming in the background. Most of the photos of Channel swimmers show zaftig swimmers overflowing their Speedos, their lips swollen to double their normal size and slightly blue.

So, once you've got the tides figured out and you're keeping an eye on the weather, what else do you need to take care of? A pilot boat, for starters. The Channel is the busiest shipping lane in the world, with hundreds of vessels making the crossing every day, right in your intended path. Most of them can't see swimmers way down in the water, and could smear you across their bow in a New York minute—so you need a boat to run interference for you, as well as to help you navigate. Even in neap tides, you can easily get pushed up toward the tulips of the Netherlands or down toward the tapas of Spain before getting a glimpse of France. To my knowledge, every Channel swimmer who has tried the feat without a pilot has died. So, scrape up about six thousand USD and hire a good Channel pilot.

There are two associations that monitor Channel swims: the Channel Swimming & Pilots Federation (CS&PF) and the Channel Swimming Association (CSA). The CSA is much older, but the CS&PF has managed the majority of the swims in recent years. Between the two associations, there are about fifteen Channel pilots that are duly approved by the British and French Coast Guards and skilled at monitoring a Channel swim attempt. There aren't a lot of Channel aspirants (only a hundred to two hundred per year) but the pilots book up early so you have to plan ahead. Each pilot books four swimmers per neap tide, and the swimmer who books first gets first choice of good weather days, the second gets second choice, and so on. Being in third or fourth place often means there are *no* good weather days left; you are quite likely to go home without even getting wet. Which really sucks. So if you're the type who buys Christmas presents on December 24 or picks up last-minute spousal birthday flowers in the local market on the way home from work, this endeavor might not be for you. On the other hand, if you have a log of every workout you completed over the past thirty years, started planning for your retirement in your twenties, and get irritated when your spouse launders an uneven numbers of socks, you might have the obsessive personality for Channel swimming.

I started working on booking a date for each of my Channel attempts the day after my previous failure.

In 2006 and 2008, my pilot was Chris Osmond. Chris is a friendly retired attorney who looks like an absent-minded professor who's done a lot of fishing. He's also very British when it comes to economizing on conversation. After I vomited for hours without end during my 2006 attempt and then quit, he gave me a pat on the shoulder and said, "Nice try." After I was dragged limp and hypothermic from the water in 2008, he came over and gave me a quick hug and instructed me to "Get fatter."

So I did. In 2010, I would be hoping for a "Good show" from Chris.

You've got the neap tide and pilot sorted out, the weather is cheerier than Thomas the Tank Engine, and you're ready and waiting in Dover. But isn't there something else you need? How about a crew? The helpful pilots notwithstanding, you're supposed to bring your own team on the boat, made up of friends and family to feed you, watch over you, and cheer you on when you start to think, *Why the hell AM I DOING THIS?* They'll also holler at you like banshees when you start to get close to France, things like, "Get your bloody ass away from the boat ladder, you pathetic lazy wanker; I didn't spend twenty hours vomiting on this bloody boat while mixing your goddamn feeds so you could quit two miles off the French beach!". And "You're not getting on this boat until you admit you're a complete and pathetic failure three times loudly!"

Nice, huh? Those are actual quotes.

So that's it, those are the basics about how it works.

I was booked for another Channel attempt in 2010. By spring of 2009, I'd restructured my feeding system and layered up my body fat. I'd analyzed and reanalyzed my failures dozens and dozens of times. I'd logged thousands of training miles since 2004, in waters ranging down to forty-six degrees Fahrenheit, and I'd swim hundreds more before the big day.

I was ready.

Now I needed to get *more* ready.

Chapter 3

My Favorite Swim

I've done many open-water swims in spectacular locales, but my favorite swim isn't in a waterway, a lake, or even in the English Channel.

My favorite swim is anywhere I can manage to swim alongside my friend Dale.

Picture this. The sun has yet to rise over beautiful Bellingham Bay. I stand with my feet slightly apart and just submerged at water's edge. I shiver. My lips are vehemently blue, and I'm looking dubiously at the glacial water circling my feet, hoping salvation might present itself and I'll be able to scurry back to my warm and welcoming car.

"Quit stalling and get in the damn water," barks Dale with a laugh, floating and waiting impatiently in her inflatable Zodiac a few feet off my stern. While she's waiting, she's also pulling up her galoshes, waking up her tired Nissan outboard motor by hammering it with a large wrench, and trying to find a comfortable position on the hard wooden seat that she'll be occupying for the next two to three hours while we cross the Bay together.

I grin and bow comically to acknowledge that in that moment, her discomfort might be even greater than mine. I take five quick steps into Bellingham Bay, drop down onto my knees to get wet up to my neck, and dive deeply under the surface to complete my acclimatization to the cold. I come up stroking, and the first thing I do is look off to the right to find

Dale, who is reassuringly puttering alongside. She's squinting with a look of satisfaction and checking the impending weather on some electronic gizmo in her lap. If there's a speedboat or Jet Ski running nearby, she'll be preparing to yell, *"Slow the hell down; I have a swimmer in the water!"* at them.

Dale has spent the last seven years selflessly helping on my quest to bridge the English Channel under my own steam. Seven years!

I spend the day swimming back and forth across Bellingham Bay, usually from Marine Park to Eliza Island. Dale feeds me my carbohydrate drinks, while the time on the water feeds her soul. When I look up to breathe, she reminds me of a character from a Hemingway novel (albeit one in a much smaller boat than her oversize personality warrants).

This is it; this is why I'm an open-water swimmer, this is why I love training for the English Channel. There is no group of people better than those in the worldwide community of open-water swimming: my friends. They're all over the world, and I gained their friendship simply because we met fit, fat, and friendly on a beach somewhere. We stood side by side, either stripping down to get into some God-awfully cold water, or hurriedly throwing clothes back on afterward. We bonded over our mutual passion, our shared shivering, and stories of seals underneath, eagles overhead, and jellyfish in and among us.

We don't usually compare times, training routines, power outputs, or anything resembling a "metric." And it's not about anyone beating anyone else. It's about lingering, laughing, and taking care of one another. It's "Where are you from?" "How was your swim?" and "Are you cold, do you need help?"

It's about Freda Streeter and her beach team, coaching hundreds of Channel swimmers over decades and decades in Dover. It's about Mike and Angela Oram, using their free personal time for twelve years to found and administer the Channel Swimming and Piloting Federation so that swimmers from everywhere can realize their dreams.

It's about the people who've swum with me, fed me, laughed with me, and supported me when I shook with frustration: Dale McKinnon from Bellingham, Lynne Driscoll from Virginia, Bryan Wilkinson from Wokingham, Brent Hobbs from Kelowna, and Ishii and Miyuki from Japan. It's about Bill and Audrey Hamblin at Victoria House in Dover taking care of me year after year after year.

It's about my sons and my partner Barb, supportively giving weeks of their time to follow me to England again and again.

I spent a lot of years pursuing other sports. I started running at twelve, took up swimming competitively at fifteen, and added cycling when I was in my early twenties. Running and triathlons were my playground for many years. I'm not particularly gifted, but I have managed to squeeze out a few genuinely impressive 10ks, marathons, and bicycle centuries over the years. But every result, every race, fast or slow, every personal record, left me looking for something else.

I found that something else the first time I walked up to a group of open-water swimmers at water's edge and asked tentatively, "Hey, can I join you guys?"

Chapter 4

Bowen Island, July 2009

After my unsuccessful Channel attempt in 2008, I'd taken the autumn and winter off to recover and slowly ramped up my swimming starting in the spring of 2009. By the time July of that year rolled around, I was ready to begin training in earnest for my third Channel swim, which I'd booked for September 2010. Using what I'd learned from my failure, I made critical changes to my training plan, and everything was going pretty well. I was as injury-free as any forty-six-year-old training to swim the English Channel could expect to be, and I was comfortable and confident.

Changes to my training included implementing suggestions and ideas from friends and other successful Channel swimmers. Following in the footsteps of Brent Hobbs, a friend who'd made it across the Channel in 2008, I planned a swim around Bowen Island in British Columbia, Canada, in July. Brent told me that only three people had ever swum around Bowen, so I was shooting to be the fourth and the first non-Canadian.

Bowen Island is a small splotch of land northwest of metropolitan Vancouver, dropped into Howe Sound like a dollop of warm green paint in a sea of frigid blue. The island is six kilometers wide and twelve long and about thirty-three kilometers in circumference. It's lightly populated, with only about 3,500 permanent souls, but its appeal as a vacation and weekend destination swells that number significantly in summer months. The island offers a number of popular swimming beaches, including Sandy

Beach, Tunstall Bay, and Bowen Bay, and is serviced by sixteen daily ferries between Horseshoe Bay in West Vancouver and Snug Cove on Bowen.

Brent, a warm and friendly swimmer I'd met in 2007, with the barrel-chested build of a strong swimmer and the bespectacled mien of the health services manager that he is, had suggested that I do Bowen about a week after my failed Channel swim in 2008 and offered his services as crew. The Bowen swim appealed on a few levels. First, it had worked for Brent as a dress rehearsal for his Channel swim; he'd gone on to do a very fast ten-hour Channel swim. Second, it was a compelling challenge in its own right. I instinctively knew that I needed some sort of goal for the year off between my disappointing 2008 swim and the Channel attempt I was planning for 2010.

As the date for Bowen approached, though, I was concerned about being undertrained. I'd been training regularly, but the realities of juggling care of my youngest son, Connor (eight years old at the time), combined with the challenge of finding boaters to accompany me on long swims, had hampered my training. I'd also spent the spring and early summer focused on helping my father, whose debilitating stroke-related dementia had progressed through day care, full-time care, a slip-and-fall accident, and finally his passing on June 25, 2009. It was just plain difficult for me to focus on training when I was making school lunches, juggling work at a demanding company, and preoccupied with memories of the last time I saw my father, as he was being rolled from the hospice toward a hearse.

I hadn't been able to go for long swims often enough. I'd only managed two three-hour swims in Lake Washington and a single four-hour swim in the pool at my club. Brent and I expected the Bowen swim to take about eleven hours—so the situation was disquieting.

I wasn't prepared to call it off, though, so I forged ahead.

Come July 24, the day before the swim, my partner Barb, son Connor, and I drove a three-hour run up Interstate 5 from Seattle to Vancouver. It's a pretty route that leaves Seattle's congestion behind in favor of Skagit Valley's tulip fields, Bellingham's mountains and lakes, the Canadian Border's Peace Arch monument, and finally, a sweeping view of Vancouver as you cover the last few miles into town. Not knowing the waters around Bowen and still feeling undertrained, I worried recurrently about the swim as we drove north, but determined to attack it as best I could. One of the reasons for going ahead with the enterprise was my feeling that Bowen was just a training swim that could be aborted if something went wrong. Although I had every intention of finishing, Bowen didn't feel as if I had anything meaningful riding on it other than a good workout.

My more-focused friend Dale McKinnon had a different level of commitment in mind.

Dale is a semiretired writer and property manager in her mid sixties who has racked up more life experiences and knowledge than a Wikipedia contributor on Red Bull. I first met her in 2005, after I'd placed an ad with a kayaking association for a boater to accompany me on long swims. Dale's colorful response was intriguing:

> Hi, I am the woman that rowed from Ketchikan to Bellingham in 2004. Rowing twenty miles is not a problem for me. In addition, I can carry a lot of equipment comfortably . . . gallons of water, a lot of food, electronic equipment, photographic equipment, and I cruise about four knots in slack water. I can carry a passenger. I would be more than happy to help out during Sound swims.

Twenty-mile rows? Alaska to Washington State? I had to meet her even if we never swam a stroke together.

Anyone who knows Dale is familiar with a couple things. The first is the warmth of her smile; the other is her laugh, which is loud enough to singe the hairs off your eardrums. On cue, she belts it out with enough magnificence to make an opera singer weep with envy. After I learned more about her six-week Alaska-to-Bellingham row, I often wondered if she perfected it for rowing on foggy nights. And Dale clearly defines *friendship* as whatever a friend needs doing. Case in point: She was coming along to crew for me at Bowen.

By the time Barb, Connor, and I had settled into the Vancouver skyscraper that was our hotel and unpacked Connor's stuffed animals, books, Pokémon, and other paraphernalia, it was late. I had to get up at 3:30 a.m. to make my final preparations for the swim and meet my crew at 5:00 a.m., so Barb and I were hurrying Connor into bed. Once in his pajamas, like any eight-year-old might, he started delaying bedtime by carefully reviewing the pay-per-view menu, tourism flyers, free soaps, and all the light switches, and generally inspecting everything in the room. We finally got him to sleep—at which point I collapsed onto the bed and fell asleep in an instant. I spent a fitful night tossing and turning, though—worried about sleeping in an odd position on a strange bed and waking with back spasms or some other ache that would debilitate my swim. At forty-six years of age, that happened more and more regularly.

I was downstairs in the ornate hotel lobby at 5:00 a.m. to meet Dale, who'd driven up from Bellingham that morning. Barb and Connor had slept through me showering, stumbling around, and leaving the room. Since a marathon swim isn't a barrel of laughs for a young kid, if for no other reason than the fact that an undulating boat equals a lot of nausea, they were going sightseeing later that morning. Barb had a full day planned for Connor, knocking around Vancouver's sights and sounds. We planned to meet after the swim and find a great place to eat my recovery meal (i.e., "the best part of open-water swimming").

Dale and I chatted while driving the well-lit canyons of downtown Vancouver, a beautiful and vibrant waterfront city with the international flavor of Hong Kong, maybe a result of the large migration of Hong Kong citizens before the 1997 handover of British Hong Kong to the People's Republic of China. We arrived at Mosquito Creek Marina, on the Mission Indian Reserve at the northern end of the city, a scant few minutes before the rest of the crew. Along with Dale and Brent, the crew included Rod Craig, another Channel aspirant, and Dustin Henderson, a swimming friend of Brent's. Rod is a tall, sturdy-looking drink of water that you'll suspect will use the Canadian "Eh?" a lot (although he doesn't—that's actually Brent's distinction); Dustin is a more average-looking swimmer, quiet in demeanor and appearance. While we waited for the boat and pilot, we nervously caught up and chatted about the swim ahead. Brent was in a cheerful mood, while I was more apprehensive and my stomach churned as it usually does before long swims. I don't think I'm the only endurance athlete thus afflicted: every marathon I've ever done has had a line longer than airport security outside the portable toilets immediately prior to the start.

Once the pilot, Clyde Ellens, arrived with his boat, the *Salty Catch*, we stowed our gear on board and did intros all around. The craft was a comfortable twenty-six-footer with a line of fishing poles sprouting off the back like hair plugs on a politician. Rod and Brent were eying them appreciatively. I began to wonder if the swim was the reason for the outing or just an afterthought.

I started premixing my feeds as Dale watched intently.

In the course of my research after my 2008 Channel attempt, I'd realized my feeds were more than partly responsible for my hypothermia and failure. A marathon swimmer's body can't function and heat itself without a precise balance of calories, fluids, and electrolytes, and I hadn't experimented enough to get that right. The result had been a loss of energy, slowing pace, and a drop in body temperature. I was determined to experiment until I got my feeds right for my swim in 2010. At Bowen Island, I was trying a higher hourly calorie count than I'd used in the Channel in 2008, and fully delegating control of my feeds to Dale. Like many endurance athletes, I'm a bit of a control freak, so the second aspect of the experiment would be the more difficult for me by far. It was also the only way I'd make it across the English Channel.

We puttered the *Salty Catch* out of the marina's no-wake zone into the Burrard Inlet and absorbed the sunny crisp morning air as we drifted past Vancouver's iconic Stanley Park. Two beautiful bald eagles with white markings stood and watched impassively from the tall white mast of a tug berthed at the mouth of the marina. I took their presence as a good omen despite my fear that one day an eagle would mistake my shiny silver swim cap for a fish and sink its claws into my head.

Burrard Inlet, Vancouver's jugular, is achingly beautiful, like most waterways in the Pacific Northwest. A long, relatively wide waterway leading to the sea, Burrard is bursting with bulldog-like tugs pushing and pulling at ships, red-hulled oil tankers, blindingly white Alaska cruise ships, Gore-Tex-clad kayakers, personal pleasure boats galore, and the occasional lunatic swimmer sharing the environment. The shoreline is alternatingly rocky, grassy, tree-covered, or claimed by some industrial or residential structure of various shapes and sizes. The sun was out to accommodate us, and the wind was relatively light.

We reached Bowen in thirty minutes. Once we'd settled on a start point for my swim, the boat pilot held the *Salty Catch* steady while I got my gear and myself ready. We were floating just outside of Snug Cover, a deep trench that nature bit out of the east side of Bowen Island eons ago that has more recently been exploited by ferry companies as a gateway to and from metro Vancouver. The view of the island presented acres and acres of brilliantly green trees, while the surrounding water was a crisp light blue, exhaling a cold breeze across the deck of the boat.

We dropped a thermometer into the Sound: the water was sixty-three degrees Fahrenheit. All around the *Salty Catch,* harbor seals popped up to check us out and grin. Rod donned disposable kitchen gloves and smeared me with sunblock and a mix of Vaseline and lanolin to help with chafing—and just like that, everyone was looking at me because it was time to start. I jumped off the back of the *Salty Catch* into Snug Cove, and Brent—in his role as official observer—clicked his stopwatch crisply and said something nonchalant like, "Go."

I was off and swimming, headed counterclockwise and northwest around Bowen Island. The water felt cold on initial entry, but my body knew what to do and began shunting blood from the cold parts toward my working muscles, and toward my core to protect my internal organs from failure. As a cold-water swimmer, it's comforting to know that my body is trained to do this instinctively to protect me—but that doesn't mean the initial cold experience is pleasant.

Unlike swimming from point to point across a channel somewhere, swimming around an island is an exercise in swimming from one point on the shoreline landscape to another, another, and so on, all the while swimming slightly left (or right). The first point we aimed for was the north edge of Snug Cove. It looked to be about seven hundred and fifty, maybe one thousand yards away, but it took a few more minutes to reach it than I expected, perhaps thirty minutes. My distance perception was typically lousy. The water still felt chilly but wonderful, like slipping into my own house after a long time away. I did wish I could see the harbor seals trailing us, but they were visible only to my crew.

I'd been aiming myself at an outcropping of rock on the north edge of Snug Cove. We reached that and continued past a shallow inlet, behind which was a small lagoon. As we rounded each corner of the island, I looked up slightly, found another visual cue to target, and began swimming toward it. In this way, the swim was a more manageable series of shorter, targeted swims than the challenging mental exercise of knowing I had thirty-three kilometers of cold sea ahead of me until I could climb back on the boat and declare victory. Once we passed the small lagoon, there was some intense fishing getting underway from the *Salty Catch's* transom. I took my first feeds while worrying slightly about getting tangled up in fishing line or bait, but Dale had the feeding routine well-organized and waved me over at the proper spot. I sort of hoped the guys on the *Salty Catch* could find a way to attract one of the orca pods that frequented the area, but I was destined to swim bereft of whales that day.

The water looked and tasted clear, the sky was brilliant, we were among friends, and there was all day to swim and fish. It was a day among days.

At about ninety minutes into the swim, Rod and Dustin got into the water and started sightseeing along the waterfront as I plodded along farther out at sea. They were having a grand time cannonballing off the shoreline rocks and posing for pictures. I wanted to join in, but my task was to swim around the island, so I contented myself with watching, breathing exclusively to my left to get a good view. I'm a bilateral breather when I swim, which means I can breathe comfortably to either side. This is a useful skill that is less common among swimmers than you might expect. It allows a swimmer to balance the muscle load, versus turning one's head solely to one side four thousand times per hour. It also makes it possible to swim on either side of the pilot boat and still be able to follow alongside—a key advantage when weather whips up and one side or the other, port or starboard, can provide a bit of shelter from the wind. Despite the advantages of bilateral breathing, many swimmers start out as one-side breathers and have a difficult time becoming ambidextrous.

Rod, Dustin, and I swam parallel to the thick Douglas firs and beautiful homesites lining Eagle Cliff road on Bowen until we reached the top end of the island, at about the two-hour mark. There, at the northernmost crown, was a tiny island smaller than Hansel and Gretel's cottage, stuck in the water just off the island's coast, that we had to navigate around. A seawater river of sorts washed back and forth between the tiny island and the Bowen mainland as the tide inhaled and exhaled. Brent and the boat pilot took the *Salty Catch* around the outside of the island, while suggesting that Rod, Dustin, and I swim through the passage. I soon discovered why the *Salty Catch* had elected to go around, as the passage became shallower and shallower until it was only about one foot deep. To avoid breaking generally accepted open-water swimming rules, which stipulate swimmers must not touch land until they clear the water at the end of a swim, we breaststroked very shallowly for about ten minutes across the passage. We looked ridiculous, of course—three Lycra and swim cap-clad men crabbing and sliding through a slurry of sand and seawater while grinning inanely—but it was good fun.

We finally cleared the shallows and continued around the top of Bowen. We were now swimming between Gambier Island to the north and Bowen in the heart of the Howe Sound. Ferries were plotting courses around us, and it was picture-postcard perfect. It was obvious why Bowen had been chosen as the setting for such diverse movies as *Intersection*, *Bird on a Wire*, and *The Russia House.*

Rod and Dustin quit goofing around and started swimming along companionably. Rod was faster than I, while Dustin and I were well-matched. At my three-hour feed, still disappointed that no orcas were tailing us, I was rewarded with a consolation prize from a beach house about a half mile away, on the north shore of Bowen. While I was slurping down my feed, we heard a splash and were surprised to see a golden retriever paddling out to us. He covered the half mile at an admirable pace and amiably sniffed and licked us as we fed and congratulated him on his swim.

The puppy was a fun break, but there was still a lot of swimming to do. Rod volunteered to return the retriever to his owners and swam the dog back while I continued toward the passage between Bowen and Keats Island, on the west side of Bowen, headed toward the Georgia Strait. The Strait of Georgia is a 150-mile-long, naturally occurring waterway between the British Columbia mainland and 290-mile-long Vancouver Island off the coast, which houses the provincial capital of Victoria. It was also the part of the swim we expected to be the roughest and coldest, given that it was farther out into the Pacific than the east side of Bowen Island.

We were adhering well to the schedule we'd plotted relative to the tides. The water had become slack, aiding our progress as planned through the Bowen-Keats passage and into the open Georgia Strait. We timed things so that the tide flooded into Howe Sound for the first part of my swim, aiding my progress up the east side of Bowen. Now it would stop awhile before the tide turned and began to ebb out of the Howe Sound. If we'd timed it right, the ebbing tide would begin in earnest as I headed down the west side of Bowen and give us a bit of assistance.

But nature can be cruel, and though we were in tune with the tides, the wind began to blow northeast, across and against the ebb tide, causing rough water. A confused sea of whitecaps pulled and shoved us for the next few hours. It was hard going, and about fifteen minutes after the wind picked up, a couple of rogue waves seriously tweaked the legacy injuries in my right forearm and shoulder. I was most worried about my shoulder; a lingering problem there could plague my training right up through the 2010 Channel swim.

My Bowen swim turned from pleasant to painful quickly. Thirty minutes went by, and I began to question the wisdom of continuing. When I'd originally injured my shoulder and forearm, both injuries had taken more than six months of rest to heal. Doing the math, reinjuring could mean I'd be out until January, forcing a late start at Channel training—perhaps too late.

It was a mistake, but I began to fixate on whether to get out.

Brent joined Rod and Dustin in the water and began playing around. This was about the three or four hour mark for them and the five or six hour mark for me. Relative to other swims I'd done, it wasn't that long, but my injuries had changed things considerably. I couldn't comfortably raise my arm overhead to stroke, and the lower part of my right forearm felt like it was being pinched by a giant lobster.

I suspect Brent figured out I was hurting and decided to try to divert my focus. He dove down behind, grabbed a starfish, and came up underneath me suddenly, waving the thing in my face, scaring the hell out of me.

"What the . . . ? Hey, it hurts starfish when you pick them up," I protested.

"It's purple," he explained defensively, with a goofy grin.

"Yeah, no kidding, I see that," I said, too irritably.

We continued. I was still working the math on whether to get out when Brent and Rod disappeared around a corner in the rocky cliff we were circumnavigating. I sensed something interesting and was in need of a mood lift, so Dustin and I followed them instead of continuing to swim directly down the coast.

Brent had somehow found a private cave in the side of the island, reachable only by water. It looked awesome, and the cave-bound water sparkled like Tinker Bell dust—I'm not sure why. It lifted my spirits. We lingered a few minutes and then turned and continued. Rod was ready for a break.

"I'm getting out at my four-hour mark," he said, rubbing his shoulders.

I was more or less looking for justification to quit, and at that moment, Rod's comment was enough. It wasn't his fault I was wavering, but it doesn't take much when I fall into a negative mood. I swam on, nonetheless, and it felt better for the next hour, knowing that the other guys were also tired; I didn't think they'd think too badly of me if I quit to preserve my arm and shoulder. My shoulder was getting worse, and I couldn't stroke properly on my right side any longer.

We continued for a while. Rod and Dustin had gotten back onto the *Salty Catch* for a few minutes, but they and Brent were in and out, enjoying the water and playing around. We passed a beach with some picnickers on it, and Brent swam over to ask if they had a cold beer. They were clearly surprised to have their picnic interrupted by a swimmer popping out of the open ocean. Everyone else was having a good time, but for me, the swim had developed into the Bataan Death March. The water was washing-machine-on-steroids chaotic, and my shoulder was getting painfully pummeled with every stroke. It was like angrily swimming against the fish during salmon spawning season, with one arm tied down.

Rod swam up alongside me. "Hey, my sister lives around that point, and you've got a cheering section waiting for you!"

Great, I thought. *I can sink and drown right in front of them.*

We rounded the turn in the island around which they lived and spotted Rod's family floating in a small bay—waiting, as promised.

Rod's kin had graciously put US and Canadian flags out on their waterside deck for us. Some of his family were also on the water in kayaks and a rowboat, cheering us on. I was praying one of them would just put me out of my misery by whacking me with an oar, but instead, we did introductions all around, almost as if we were up on the deck having a barbeque. I looked up at the deck wistfully and *wished* I was up there having a barbeque.

We continued, to my chagrin.

Finally, at about seven hours, with my shoulder immobile and in deep pain, I was over at the boat for a feed. Dale had thrown my bottle out and was watching me over the back of the boat.

"Nice!" she said

"Yeah, whatever . . . hey, I'm getting out. I tweaked the shit out of my shoulder back there, and I can't pick it up anymore."

"You're what?" she asked incredulously.

Never in my life have I seen a look of disgust that explicit directed right at me. And I'm a divorced father of three sons, so that's saying something. Dale was not happy.

"Uh, I can't stroke with my right arm anymore, and at the end of the day, you know, this is just a training swim," I said, not sure what to expect but hoping for sympathy. Instead, I got the look Charles Manson gave the jury during his murder trial. Dale stared at me, clearly revolted.

Dale had been training with me selflessly since 2005, and I owed it to her to try just a little bit more—and to show her somehow that I really needed to stop. I figured I could continue awhile by stroking with my left arm and doggy-paddling with my right. I swam away from the boat doing the best stroke I could under the circumstances and came upon Brent in the water.

"I gotta quit, Brent. My right shoulder is toast."

"Hmm," he said. "Okay, just swim breaststroke for a while," and with that, he swam away.

I was floating there getting no sympathy. Nobody gave a crap that I was hurting. After a momentary pity party, I accepted the only choice I felt I had: to just drag myself across the water as best I could.

So I got on with it.

Progress was slow, and everyone in the crew knew I was hurting. Rod, Dustin, and Brent took turns swimming alongside me.

"Hey, Mike, you're swimming strong, I had a hard time catching up to you," Rod said.

That was an *extremely* generous line of bullshit that I nonetheless appreciated.

"Uh-huh," I replied.

We swam from point to point, rock to rock, tree to tree. The pain was about as bad as it could be, worse than anything I'd experienced in any endurance event. That said, my right arm had somehow loosened up, and I was actually swimming again; no more dog-paddle.

From the eighth hour on, Brent and Dale conspired to never let me near the boat for a feed. They knew that being close to the tempting stairs hanging off the back of the boat was just too great a temptation, so they simply kept the boat well offshore and Brent swam back and forth with my feeds like a St. Bernard. I didn't know about their conspiracy but loved getting my feed bottle handed to me at water level—even though reaching for it was excruciating, as if somebody was setting my shoulder aflame each time.

Rod was in the water from about eight or nine hours right through to the end.

"Hey, Brent," he said during one feed, "next time, bring me some of that fried chicken and a banana."

"You want me to? No problem," Brent agreed cheerfully.

Sure enough, for the next feed, Brent swam out with a plastic bag filled with food for Rod and himself. It looked unappetizing to me, but it was so ridiculous that I couldn't help it—it lifted my spirits.

Hours eight through ten proceeded in that manner: cheerful feeds interspersed with excruciating swimming that was getting me slowly but surely around Bowen. I thought about quitting constantly, but that option just wasn't open to me. The boat was too far away, and none of my crew would even entertain the topic.

At about nine and half hours, Brent said he thought it would be a ten-hour swim—which I thought was great. Ten hours was what I'd been dreaming about. There actually would be an end to the pain—a good end. I fixated on the next point on the island and swam toward it, figuring Snug Cove was right around the corner, within sight.

We passed the turn, though, and it didn't look like Snug Cove. We passed another point, and another. And . . . another.

Hmmm.

I swam on. We passed another point. Then we passed a long straightaway with no trees on the rocky outcropping. Then another point with rocks but no trees. After this last outcropping of rock, Brent said, "There you go, Mike, five hundred meters," and pointed. I looked up. Was I really looking at Snug Cove, or was this more charitable bullshit from my crew? If that point was "only five hundred meters," I was an Olympian on the podium. But at least I could see the end—some end.

That "five hundred meters" took about a half hour—four or five times slower than my usual five-hundred-meter pace. We rounded the corner . . . and Snug Cove wasn't there.

Brent said, "Okay, Mike, just a few hundred more meters—over there!"

Now I was just pissed off. I turned around in the water to Rod and snapped, "Brent keeps moving the fucking goalposts!"

Rod burst out laughing.

Despite my foul mood, I had to grin along with Rod. I looked over where Brent was pointing and thought to myself, *Well, sooner or later, he's going to be right; it's a damn island with a start and, inevitably, a finish.* I put my head down and swam where Brent told me. And . . . I finished.

I had gone thirty-three kilometers in ten hours and thirty-five minutes, in an average of sixty-five-degree water. Lots of seals, no orcas, one golden retriever.

Getting into the boat was the final challenge. I couldn't pull myself up, so the crew had to drag me aboard.

After a few minutes of backslapping and hugs, we headed back toward Vancouver. As I started to reflect on the swim, I realized something important. Two failed English Channel swims, and it took the swim at Bowen to start to teach me the most important lesson of marathon swimming: just don't stop until you're there.

The next day, I learned another. I was stiff when I woke up, but my shoulder was mostly back to normal and my right forearm felt fine—minimal pain.

My shoulder and arm were okay; the drama had been in my head.

All in my head.

Chapter 5

The Chairman

I'm just outside 12 Vale Square in Ramsgate, about twenty miles up the English coast northeast of Dover, unbolting a thick, well-worn gate. Surrounding me is a neighborhood that sprang up around the storybook cottage at 12 Vale in the three hundred and fifty years since it was built. Access to the house is through a sturdy front door bordered by an ornate doorframe, and up top is a traditional thatched roof, its carefully trimmed wood rushes protecting the inhabitants better than modern roofing materials can. As I secure the gate behind me, I pause a moment to reflect on the neighborhood—a leafy, warm community of attached homes oriented in a semicircle around a common garden. As I walk to that ornate front door, I notice a seagull intently pulling a bit of thatch from the Orams' roof for use in a nest somewhere nearby.

I knock and almost immediately the imposing door opens on Mike, who smiles and takes my hand warmly. His handshake is a two-handed affair, one gripping my palm and the other my forearm. He squints down his nose through his perpetually sliding spectacles, and his cheeks are rosy and weather-beaten from the sea. Without breaking his grip on me, he leads me gently yet firmly into his home, as if despite running multiple businesses in addition to his Channel-swimming responsibilities, he's been waiting all morning for me to stop by.

Mike is an imposing figure, shaggy with beard and casual in attire. His personal style seems appropriate to his experience and expertise: if you'd never met Mike but were to see him across a public square, your first thought would be something like, *Hey, there's a sea captain over there!*

"Hallo, Mike, you found us!" he says, heartily.

"Not without a few slight detours around Ramsgate," I answer with a laugh, describing my encounter with a white-haired Ramsgater after my third lap of the waterfront.

"Well, that *will* happen," Mike says, still beaming. "Come in, come in." Mike's office is inside a well-lit nook in a suite of home offices on the west side of the cottage. Mike's office suite encompasses a conference room with a heavy wooden table surrounded by framed seamanship certificates. Just past Mike's office is Angela's, a tidy space with work materials and books lined up precisely. Mike's space is . . . a bit less tidy.

Interviewing Mike Oram is like trying to windsurf in a cyclone. You hold on, manage what you can, and hope for the best. On this particular day, the sixty-four-year-old icon sits at his desk, surrounded by dozens of books, eight computers, and various nautical devices with lots of blinking lights, beeping, and knobs. In the midst of all of it are piles and piles of paper, notes, and books. Mike himself sports a faded Tasmanian Devil T-shirt that's working diligently to contain his imposing physique. His beard is neat but still somehow seems a consequence of not bothering with a razor.

After a quick tour, Mike stands facing me at a slight angle, smiling and waiting for my questions.

I had gotten to know Mike when I first connected with the Channel swimming community in late 2004. The founder of the Channel Swimming & Piloting Federation (CS&PF), which sanctions Channel swims, and its Honorable Secretary, he was the man to call if you wanted to book a Channel swim. Mike was also known to me through his active participation in the online Channel chat room, where aspiring swimmers ask the advice of Channel veterans. Mike's posts were always colorful, with subject lines such as *"Advice—probably CRAP, but it's all mine!"*

A British Army officer's son, Mike was raised all over the world, from England to Egypt to Germany and back again to England. Despite (or perhaps because of) the strict society of British Army bases, Mike reached adulthood with a mind of his own. Surprisingly, his father fostered this natural contempt for authority, and Mike's severe dyslexia also made him naturally see the world around him differently. Jackie Stewart, the world champion race-car driver and a fellow dyslexic, once said something about the condition that applies to Mike: "Dyslexics have an advantage over 'clever' folk because all the clever folk go down the same avenue, and it's very congested."

Mike Oram is comfortable going his own way.

All of these factors, combined with the enforced segregation of being an officer's son in a class-regimented organization, allowed Mike the freedom to explore a breadth of pastimes in his youth. Cycling, diving, fishing, kayaking, motorcycles, auto racing, shooting—he tried it all.

Competitive swimming happened to be among those interests, mostly for the social appeal of being on a swim team. (This was something Mike and I had in common. My own local swim team's reputation for throwing great parties was what initially drew me to the sport.) Mike swam competitively from an early age, focusing on freestyle and backstroke. His swimming career was spread across multiple clubs in Suffolk, Essex, and Surrey. He was fast and enjoyed the competition, but was stopped from going too far by his father, who preferred that he focus on school versus races. In addition to club swimming, Mike trained in open water, but there wasn't much open-water competition to be found in the 1960s and 1970s. The sea would ultimately call Mike in other ways.

To pay for his hobbies, Mike was entrepreneurial early. Harvesting and selling cooked cockles (a shellfish) plucked locally off the seabed was a favorite income-earner, and he spent time working on ferries and trying whatever other jobs struck his fancy.

Mike's mother was from Deal, a seaside town about ten miles up the coast from Dover. Although the family continually moved around, Deal, or more accurately, the Kent seaside, was home base. The family's annual home leave in England was often spent there, and Mike studied for his A-levels at Canterbury, less than twenty miles from the sea.

The common denominator in many of Mike's interests was the sea—and that led him inevitably to boats. He started by owning canoes and kayaks, and things escalated from there: at seventeen, he bought his first fishing boat. Ultimately, he became a Dover Boatman *(traditionally, a fisherman based in Dover)*.

It was being a Dover Boatman that eventually, inevitably, brought Mike to English Channel swimming.

Mike has been escorting Channel swimmers since 1982. He's accompanied over seven hundred Channel crossings and has the best pilot track record—the most successful crossings—in the history of the sport. Notable swims under his stewardship include the last three world record holders: Christoph Wandwatsch's in 2005 (seven hours, three minutes), Peter Stoychev's (six hours, fifty-seven minutes) in 2007, and Trent Grimsey's in 2012 (six hours and fifty-five minutes flat). Mike also piloted Yvetta Hlavacova's fastest crossing by a woman (seven hours, twenty-five minutes) in 2006, two three-way swims (by Phil Rush and Alison Streeter), swims by the oldest man and woman, a four-way relay swim, and many other notable crossings. In recent years, his success rate has soared over 75 percent.

In recognition of his lifelong efforts on behalf of Channel swimming, in 2005 Mike was inducted into the International Marathon Swimming

Hall of Fame (IMSHOF), recognized for both his success in piloting and his work on the administrative side of Channel swimming as the founder and Honorable Secretary of the CS&PF.

Mike's impact on the sport extends beyond just the swimmers that he pilots. He introduced his son, Lance, an exceptionally successful pilot, to Channel swimming and has trained or worked with all of the CS&PF pilots save one: the pilot I had booked, Chris Osmond.

As Mike and I chatted throughout the morning, something changed for me. Under the spell of his passion and expertise, I found myself wanting him to pilot my swim. Don't get me wrong: Chris was qualified and experienced, and had successful crossings—if not nearly as many as Mike has. But I'd had misgivings about him even before talking to Mike, based on stories I'd heard in interviews for this book, stories from people more experienced than I was. Stories of stopping marginal swimmers early instead of supporting or driving them as far as they could go. I'd dismissed my doubts because Chris had taken me aside after my 2008 swim and, in a quiet moment, promised to do whatever it took to get me across. That promise had been the determining factor in booking with him again.

Was that the right decision?

As Mike and I continued to talk about Channel piloting, worry took root and sprouted.

Chapter 6

Reading the Coast

There's a lot of planning and preparation behind successful Channel piloting, and that's what I was at Mike's cottage to learn more about. I put aside my worries about Chris and asked Mike to help me better understand how it worked.

Bookings for Channel swims start early, sometimes as much as five years early, and build until by December of any given year, Mike and his son, Lance, are scheduled to pilot about thirty-five swims. Some of those bookings inevitably fall away, as the swimmers realize they have bitten off more than they can chew.

"I had forty-three dropouts this year," Mike said. "People sign up but later realize they can't do it, or they get made redundant at work and can't afford it, or they get pregnant . . . they drop out for all sorts of reasons. We lose a lot of money when people drop out and we aren't able to rebook the slot, but I wouldn't be doing this if I didn't love it. There are other easier ways to make money."

Preparations for the season begin early, too. Mike starts by assessing the equipment on his boat, the *Gallivant*. Safety is the first concern, and budget is generally not the primary consideration if there's a piece of equipment or an upgrade that might improve conditions for his crew or swimmers.

"We have a laptop on board with a GPS device," Mike explains, "and we use something called an AIS system and trackers that allow all of the other boat traffic in the Channel to see us on their screens. Even better—the system makes it possible for friends and family to follow the swimmer's progress online. We have an automatic log that records our route, and of course, an official CS&PF observer is always on board, keeping records manually. We also have a chart plotter that's linked to a dedicated GPS that we use to plan the swim. And we have an autopilot system, two depth meters, a wind meter, and a printer for all of the forms required by either the English or the French Coast Guards."

"Geez, that's a lot of stuff," I said—genuinely amazed. "What else could you possibly need?"

"Bacon sandwiches," Mike answered evenly. "It's a long day out on the Channel."

In addition to the equipment refresh, Mike's boats are meticulously maintained. "Paint, new side rails, engine servicing, new seals, lockers refitted," Mike explained. "And this year we installed a brand-new aft deck to better support the swim crews. It all needs to be absolutely spot-on, like a Formula 1 car. After all, it's the Channel!"

The Gallivant can make about eight and a half knots at full throttle (a knot is about 1.1 land miles per hour, measured years ago by dragging a knotted rope in the water behind the vessel), but Mike has to keep things much slower with swimmers—the fastest of whom can manage less than three knots in perfect conditions. The shortest distance across the Channel is between Shakespeare Beach and Cap Griz Nez: eighteen nautical miles, or about twenty-two land miles. Crossings start in April and go through late September, sometimes later. And not all crossings are swims; Mike also pilots rowers, kayakers, and various others in their attempts to cross the notorious Channel.

Over the years, Mike and Lance have captured video of most of the relevant English and French coastline and they know the coast very well, but Mike admits there is no such thing as really *knowing* the coasts as they change every year due to weather and other factors. So the Orams go out annually with video cameras and reshoot anything of note. They toddle alongside the cliffs slowly and closely study what's happened. The French side is sandier and shifts more than the English side—which for the most part experiences rockfalls and not shifts—so France gets a bit more attention.

The weather is the final determinant of what constitutes a proper day to make an attempt. There are multiple sources of weather forecasts, some reliable, some less so. Mike, like many pilots, is an expert in reading the weather himself. There are a lot of factors involved, but wind is the most closely watched overall. The direction of the wind and that of the tides need to be in tune, or at least not violently clash (because that's what creates breaking waves out in the open Channel), but generally, it's wind strength that is scrutinized most carefully. It's gauged on the *Beaufort Wind Force Scale*, named for Sir Frances Beaufort, a Royal Navy officer who developed the system in the early 1800s. It looks like this:

Beaufort Wind Force Scale

Force	Wind Speed (knots)	Description	Sea Conditions
0	< 1 knot	Calm	Flat
1	1-2 knots	Light Air	Ripples with Crests
2	3-6 knots	Light Breeze	Small Wavelets
3	7-10 knots	Gentle Breeze	Large Wavelets
4	11-15 knots	Moderate Breeze	Small Waves with Breaking Crests
5	16-20 knots	Fresh Breeze	Moderate Waves of Some Length
6	21-26 knots	Strong Breeze	Long waves, White Foam Crests Frequent
7	27-33 knots	High Wind—Moderate Gale—Near Gale	Sea Builds Up, Foam from Breaking Waves, Airborne Spray
8	34-40 knots	Gale—Fresh Gale	Moderate High Waves with Breaking Crests, Foam Blown Along Wind Direction, Considerable Airborne Spray
9	41-47 knots	Strong Gale	High Waves with Crests, Dense Foam Blown Along Wind Direction, Large Amounts of Airborne Spray
10	48-55 knots	Storm— Whole Gale	Very High Waves with Crests, Large Patches of Foam Give Sea White Appearance, Waves with Heavy Impact, Large Amounts of Airborne Spray
11	56-63 knots	Violent Storm	Exceptionally High Waves
12	> 64 knots	Hurricane Force	Huge Waves (Go Home!)

Swimmers and pilots tend to look for Force levels of 0-2, but conditions are often unpredictable in the Channel. Swims that start at a suitable Force level can sometimes end in Force 4, 5, or even 6—at which point, the decision must be made about whether to continue the swim.

When the wind and weather are kind, the average swim is about fourteen hours. If the swimmer knows what he's doing or requests a minimum of interference from the boat crew, Mike leaves him be and sticks to piloting the *Gallivant*. Most swimmers need and want to avail themselves of Mike's expertise, though, so he's often involved in much more than pointing the boat in the proper direction. Mike assesses all of the swimmers by the end of the first hour to determine at which point during the swim they're going to have difficulty.

"It takes them an hour to settle down," he told me, "and then I can really assess their stroke. Many are too stretched out for cold water, or they get sick from too many electrolytes in their feeds or cramp up from too much potassium. Mostly, the crews they bring along are family members who are too close to the situation and won't tell the swimmer the hard truths when needed. But in any case, the women swimmers can't be egged on—they have to want it. The men, however, are generally doing it for ego, so you can taunt them into continuing," he finished with a crooked grin.

The trickiest part of every swim is the last five hundred meters. At that point, the swimmer knows he or she is going to make it to France and often stops following directions—at which point Mike loses control of the swimmer's safety. He needs swimmers to land somewhere stable, and then, believe it or not, they have to swim quickly back to the boat, but they often just land at the spot they think best and stand there, adding time to their swim and putting themselves at unnecessary risk.

"We used to send a dinghy in, but we don't send it with them anymore because we often just can't get the boat onto the beach—it's too dangerous. The swimmer's adrenaline stops flowing when he lands, and then he's in danger standing there. He's been prone in the water for many hours and can experience real health problems if he gets vertical too rapidly. Or his blood starts circulating normally again, and he gets very cold very quickly." As he explains all this, Mike's brow furrows in concern. "I need him to swim back to the boat from the beach so we can take care of him properly if something happens."

The best part of an average Channel swim?

"Eating bacon sandwiches on the boat."

"Really?" I asked with a smile.

Mike took a moment and said, "The nicest thing about Channel swimming is the friendly atmosphere on the boat, the sense of shared purpose and camaraderie."

He reflected quietly for another moment and added, "Channel swimming is a stepping-stone in life. It changes you. It makes you think differently. Your attitude, everything is different. It's the Channel."

I clicked off my recording device, put down my reporter's notebook, and thought about that while Mike and I gazed quietly at each for a moment.

It sounded better than a bacon sandwich.

Chapter 7

Rostislav and Tomislav

In August 2009, I was scheduled to be in Dover for swim training and also to be an official CS&PF observer on someone else's Channel swim. According to the official rules, an observer is a person appointed by the CS&PF to "be in sole charge of the timing of the swim, and be responsible for observing compliance with the rules, subject to ratification by the Committee." In other words, the observer is in command of the clipboard and stopwatch. He or she stands near the crew, tracks the swim time, records specific events in the official swim log, adds a few related notes ("Swimmer swimming okay, but complaining about nausea, covered with jellyfish stings, and begging to the Almighty to be allowed to get out"), and enforces the rules.

Mike Oram had helped me get the gig—I'd known I wanted to be in Dover that summer to train and had asked him if I could come on one of his swims as the observer. He was amiable enough to accommodate me, though I was a novice. I was nervous. What if I dropped the clipboard into the water or tossed my cookies over the side of the boat during a critical feed and ruined somebody else's big day?

I called Mike when I arrived in Dover, just as if I were doing a swim myself, to let him know I'd arrived and was ready to go. He asked me to call back a few days later, the evening before the weather was supposed to clear and allow the scheduled swim. I obliged, and he said to be at Dover Marina the next morning at 4:00 a.m. for a world-record attempt. Olympian and

FINA Open Water Swimming Grand Prix racer Rostislav Vitek from the
Czech Republic would be vying for the fastest time across the Channel.
The then-current record, six hours and fifty-seven minutes, had been set
by Petar Stoychev of Bulgaria in 2007, also with Mike O as pilot.

This would be a treat.

Observing a swimmer of that caliber make a world record attempt is like
being a weekend golfer invited to caddy at the British Open. I could pick
up tips and skills, or at least come away from the experience in better
appreciation of how crappy a swimmer I truly was. A side benefit of
observing what would surely be a fast swim was that I'd be in the boat a
shorter time. I wasn't sure how my stomach would react to the experience
(it wasn't like being in the water, after all), and it was nice to know it'd be
over more quickly than an average Channel swim, which requires about
twenty to twenty-two hours of boat time.

We met at the Dover docks at 4:00 a.m. and traded introductions all
around. Communication was spotty due to our language differences, but
we managed. Despite the early hour, Marcia Cleveland had come down
to the marina to see off the swim. Marcia was the chairwoman of the
Open Water Committee in the US Masters Swimming organization and
had been a successful Channel swimmer circa 1994. She was staying at
Victoria House, down the hall from me, with her son, and had asked
enthusiastically the prior evening if she could come along to wave us off.

Rostislav, a world-class swimmer, was relatively slight and approximately
five-foot-eight, with sharp facial features, closely cropped hair, and intense
eyes. He was accompanied by his wife and four crew members. They were
all friendly and very obviously confident—cocky, even. It was just another
day at the office for these guys. I'd always assumed that I'd finish my
Channel swim and then collapse at Victoria House, not to be disturbed
for a couple days or longer. These guys looked like they'd swim back from

France and then enjoy a relaxing game of squash at the club later that evening, followed perhaps by a nice evening out on the town.

Also in attendance at the start was another swimmer with his crew: Tomislav Soldo, from Croatia. Tomislav was there to help pace Rostislav by doing a simultaneous Channel swim. He'd be piloted off of a separate boat by Lance Oram, Mike's son, and would leave the beach minutes after Rostislav to help drive the pace. This confused me a little, as I knew that having a crew member pace a Channel swimmer was against the official rules, and this didn't seem that different. But there wasn't a moment to ask Mike about the subtleties, so I just set about performing my observer responsibilities.

Derek Carter, a longtime member of Mike's crew, materialized and led all of us to the *Gallivant* and *Sea Satin*, Mike's and Lance's boats. Derek is an interesting character who'd crewed for Mike since his retirement after a long career as a globe-trotting aerospace engineer. As we got settled, Mike and Lance conferred about the course, departure time, location, and other piloting logistics. After a few moments, Mike started talking to the crews about the swims. The swimmers were both elite athletes with significant open-water swimming experience in freshwater, but Mike wanted to know more about their background in the sea, where the tides, waves, saltwater, and wind make long-distance, open-water swimming especially challenging. Open-water swimming in the English Channel is very different from swimming in lakes and other open-water venues (including the oversize swimming pools they use in the Olympics). Mike needs to understand exactly how his swimmers will perform as he views a Channel swimmer as an extra engine driving alongside and tethered to his boat. He needs to gauge the swimmer's pace, strength, and characteristics if the boat's trip is to be successful.

Language difficulties made the interview with Rostislav's and Tomislav's crews a little tricky. Mike asked whether the swimmers could breathe bilaterally and how often they'd swum in tides and wind. Given Rostislav's intention of breaking the world record, every minute counted. Mike needed to plan and plot a course that was exactly right for his skills and experience. Hampered by the language barrier, the conversation went something like this:

"I need to understand how you swim."

"Yes," said Rostislav and his coach, in unison.

"Have you swum in waves before?"

"Yes."

"Where?"

"Yes."

"Do you have experience breathing bilaterally?"

"Yes."

"It's important, because we can swim you on the right side of the boat if the wind kicks up from the north."

"Yes."

At that point, Mike turned to Derek and Lance, a frustrated grin hiding beneath his eyeglasses, which were perpetually sliding down his nose, and said something like, "Bloody hell." Derek, Lance, and Mike conferred quietly and came to some sort of a consensus, which they didn't explicitly share with the rest of us. A few minutes later, we were off to Shakespeare Beach for the start.

The beach, just a little bit south of where we'd met up and affectionately known as "Shakey" in the Channel community, is so named because the Bard used the cliff looming above it in a pivotal scene of *King Lear*.

Once we were floating offshore, Rostislav swam in to the beach, raised his hand to signal his start, and unceremoniously started his swim. Tomislav ended up leaving about fifteen minutes later.

Derek was still explaining the paperwork and forms I'd have to complete when Rostislav waded back into the water. I had to scramble to mark the time of day and record it properly in the log that was still in Derek's hands. The boat cockpit had a dozen computers for various purposes, and I wondered aloud why, with all that automation, the CS&PF reporting itself wasn't computerized. Mike and Derek looked at me and laughed.

Rostislav's swim was actually uneventful because he swam like a pissed-off marlin: fast and easy. He was swimming at about twice my normal pace, which is a relatively average two miles per hour. He made stroke and glide, stroke and glide look very easy. He was also stroking more quickly than the average Channel swimmer, which helps keep you warm in cold water when you're slight of build.

His feeding was timed at about every fifteen to twenty minutes during the first four or five hours, every seven to eight minutes after that. And he was feeding quickly. A good but average open-water swimmer takes twenty or thirty seconds to feed; Rostislav was feeding so fast that I had difficulty timing it—but it was definitely in the one to two second range.

To feed, most Channel swimmers swim over to their boat, grab their bottle or cup, drink it down, exchange perhaps a word or a grunt with their crew, then resume swimming. Rostislav fed without stopping, remaining two to three yards out, directly along the port side of the boat. Mike, Derek, and the boat crew stayed in the cabin, while Rostislav's swim crew positioned themselves in the stern. When they had his feed ready, one of them would shimmy down the side of the boat and hang off with a cup in his hand. Rostislav would move in: right-hand stroke, flip on his back, right-hand backstroke, grab the cup with left hand and bring it to his lips as though doing a left-hand backstroke, swallow, drop the cup, finish the left-hand backstroke, flip back over, do a right-hand freestyle stroke, and zip away. He never slowed down, and I don't remember him missing the cup ever. Because he never stopped, it was virtually impossible to time the feed. It was impressive.

Throughout this routine, Rostislav's crew shouted and hooted encouragement in Czech.

Mike Oram spent most of the swim consulting charts and computers, and doing math. At one point, he snoozed for a few minutes on a bunk in the cabin, while Derek took over the tiller. Mostly, though, Mike was paying very close attention, even when it didn't look like he was, fully comfortable and in his element. His mastery was so complete that it led to an interesting exchange with one of Rostislav's crew about five hours into the swim.

"He is doing good?" the crew member asked.

"No, he's slowed and won't make it," Mike responded.

"Sorry?" the crew member asked, confused.

"He's slowed since the first two hours, when he was ahead of world record pace," Mike replied calmly. "He'll finish about twenty minutes behind the record."

"Sorry?"

"He will not break the record."

The crew member stuck his head out of the cabin and conferred with his colleagues in Czech. Then he stuck his head back in and asked once more, just to be clear, "He won't have the record?"

"No—you see?" Mike said, holding up a printout charting Rostislav's swim. He'd plotted it against Petar Stoychev's 2007 world record swim chart. Since Mike had also piloted Petar's swim, he'd been able to print both swims on the same chart and make a running comparison of the two. The crew looked intently at the printout, conferred again in Czech, then went outside and resumed yelling at Rostislav, only louder.

Over the next two hours, Rostislav held his pace and accelerated his feeds, which were rotating among two or three different liquids and gels similar to those I use on my swims. He was rocketing across the Channel a hell of a lot faster on those feeds than I could swim, but I consoled myself with the comforting lie that it was because I was middle-aged and he was in his early twenties.

After having broken the bad news to Rostislav's crew about being off world-record pace, Mike commented wryly, "I wonder if he'll discover a shoulder injury soon." He explained with a grin that many swimmers, either consciously or subconsciously, used the onset of injuries during their swims to justify getting out. "I like to offer them some ibuprofen," he said, "and when they reach for it, I feign surprise and say, 'Oh, I thought your shoulder hurt too much to move. Looks like you can go on and swim some more!'"

His comments reminded me of my Bowen Island swim, and I felt a bit ashamed.

Rostislav wasn't one of those swimmers, though, and he kept swimming intensely. He even picked up the pace in the last twenty minutes. He looked up at France more frequently, clearly focused on invading the blue country. The water off the French coast was very wavy, with three-to-five-foot swells rocking the boat and Rostislav. Up ahead, we could see tourists watching the swim from the cliffs on the French coast.

One member of our boat crew was getting queasy and sick. Despite the rolling waves, I was doing okay, but it wouldn't have taken much to bend me over the railing either. So it was without joy that I shared this conversation with my sick colleague:

"Oy, these waves are killin' me," he said.

"Oh, I'm sorry, that sucks," I replied, trying to think of something pleasant to add.

"It weren't too bad before, but now I've just thrown up over the side."

"Uh-huh."

"I was hanging over the edge, ripping my guts out."

"Ugh."

"And those eggs that Derek made, oy, they came up hard and fast!"

"Uh, great."

"I mean, I sprayed it right down the side of Mike's boat!" he elaborated further, burping and pointing so I could see for myself.

"Excuse me!" I managed, escaping to the other side of the boat. The seasickness pill I'd taken wasn't protection enough from his detailed descriptions.

Rostislav pulled himself cleanly and elegantly through the waves toward the French shore, which had no beach at the spot we were heading toward.

It was littered with boulders and abutted by a sheer cliff stretching about fifty meters into the air. Perched at the cliff top were viewing platforms filled with tourists watching the proceedings. Rostislav clearly had the goal in sight as he sped toward his rocky landing. His final stroke was somewhat anticlimactic as he simply touched the rock and then clambered up on it. Once landed, he turned to look back on the open Channel.

Two hundred meters offshore, Mike's boat, and all of us on it, were rocking and rolling in the surf. Despite looking tired themselves, Rostislav's crew summoned the energy for some wild cheering, while up on the viewing platforms, there was some sprinkled applause and cheering as well.

All in all, Rostislav's time was an astounding seven hours and sixteen minutes. Not a record, but impressive. And he landed within one minute of the prediction Mike had made at the five-hour mark—perhaps even more impressive. Both were masters at their craft.

Rostislav sat on the rocks and stared calmly out across the Channel toward Dover, where we'd started. In the distance, his friend Tomislav was still stroking toward us and the end of his own Channel swim. I watched Rostislav pensively savoring his accomplishment and wondered exactly what he was thinking.

I also wondered what I'd be thinking after my own swim. I'd daydreamed about a victory yell of "*Je suis navige la Manche, viva la France!*" but I didn't know what I'd be thinking. Would I be spent, in pain, yearning for sleep? Exultant and energized? Weeping tears of joy? Or seasick and dreading the four-hour boat ride back to Dover?

Only time would tell.

After Rostislav swam back to the boat and accepted his congratulations, he turned a fetching shade of pale green and began tossing up over the side of the boat. His wife held him in support while the tourists looked away. Spent, he stumbled down to the cabin and asked if he could rest on the built-in sofa. Mike congratulated him again and nodded. The spent swimmer lay down and was asleep in an instant.

Meanwhile, his crew, freed after seven hours of nonstop moral and material support, made themselves comfortable for the rollicking four-hour return cruise. Having spent the journey focused on Rostislav, most of them had to heed the call of nature. As if jointly planned, they marched in unison back to the side of the boat facing the beach and viewing platforms, and in full-monty view of the tourists, hiked down the front of their shorts and watered the French coastline while the spectators watched impassively.

It was a unique, somewhat primitive, way of leaving their mark and saying, "Vive La France," I suppose.

Chapter 8

Breaking Freda's Rules

After observing Rostislav's swim, I was looking forward to some training in Dover. I intended to do a six-hour swim the day after Rostislav's record attempt, as well as a few other swims throughout the following week. I knew there was no chance I could pull off a swim anywhere near as impressive as the one I'd just witnessed, but that wasn't the point. I was simply looking to build on my fitness from the Bowen swim and enjoy one of my favorite places and pastimes. Years of marathon, triathlon, and other training had taught me that the most important and overlooked aspect of training is the joy of it, the simple pleasure of doing something you love just because you love it. And there are few things I enjoy more than swimming in Dover, surrounded by the Channel community.

In case you haven't gathered it, Dover is a special place for the open-water swimming community—arguably the place where the sport was invented. While people had been swimming in open water before Matthew Webb's first Channel swim in 1875, that was certainly a breakthrough moment for the sport. Women's open-water swimming was similarly thrust into the spotlight in Dover by Gertrude Ederle and the other female swimmers in the twenties, each vying to be the first female to cross. Other swimming venues, including the Manhattan International Marathon Swim (around Manhattan Island), the Catalina Channel swim off the coast of California (from Catalina to the mainland), or various other venues in the United Kingdom and Australia, bring together open-water swimmers, but none can offer the combination of history, community, facilities, and conditions that Dover does.

Dover Harbor itself is basically a walled-in, mile-wide, deep, and heavily protected oval pool. The beach is a bit less than a mile wide and curved in a gentle arc, like a seashell. It features an imposing seawall to the north and a relaxed walkway to the south, dotted with ice cream and sailboat rental shops. Swimmer's Beach is in the center, almost directly in front of the two somewhat goofy-looking Channel swimmer statues (of nobody) that the Dover Town Council erected years ago. Looking out toward the Channel from Swimmer's Beach, there's another imposing seawall about a mile away that protects the harbor from nature and man's worst intentions. It was behind this outer seawall, within the confines of Dover Harbor, that the Allied Army retreated during the Dunkirk evacuation early in World War II.

There are two openings in the outer seawall that are visible from Swimmer's Beach, one on the left at about ten o'clock and one on the right at about two o'clock. The ten-o'clock opening is for the Channel ferries regularly going in and out of the dockyards located just north of the harbor. Dozens of Channel crossings by ferry companies such as P&O and Seafrance leave and arrive at the ferry docks every day, often filled with tourists looking for bargains. Sometimes a ferry pulls out of the docks and into Dover Harbor to park for a few minutes. I used to enjoy swimming out to them, but that's now against the rules and the Channel beach crew will give you a dressing-down if you do it. If memory serves, the epithet they used on me was something like "Bloody Yank."

On the right side of the harbor, there's a lighthouse just south of the two-o'clock outer seawall opening, and it fits the setting to a T. It would seem surprising if there were *not* a lighthouse to complete the view of this somewhat rundown but still picturesque Victorian seaside town.

After many years of Channel swimmers splashing around, there are solidly established rules and routines on Swimmer's Beach itself. These are ably administered by a team of volunteers led by a woman named Freda Streeter. Freda is a sweet yet firm grandmother who's spent every weekend between May and September since 1984 on Swimmer's Beach helping, coaching, guiding, and kicking the asses of Channel swimmers training for their day.

Why?

"I love to help people fulfill their dream," she says simply.

Freda is about five-foot-five, with hair that is sandy brown mixed with gray wisps. Her warm face attests to her character, and the folds around her eyes and mouth verify her years, experience, and having raised three children. A retired teacher of troubled youths, mostly boys, she's been involved in swimming for as long as she can remember. When she was sixteen years old, she founded the Beaver Club for teaching swimming to the handicapped. Freda is mother to three—Alison, Karl, and Neil—and grandmother to one: Zak. Alison, a decorated Member of the British Empire, is the most successful English Channel swimmer in history, with forty-three crossings to her credit, forty-one of which were crewed by her mom. Neil is also part of Channel swimming history, as an accomplished pilot. The Streeter family is a Channel swimming legend.

Freda started corralling and caring for Channel swimmers at Swimmer's Beach in 1984, when the previous chaperone emigrated to Australia and left a hole where a coach belonged. She hasn't had a free summer weekend since.

I first met Freda in 2006, when I went to Dover to get ready for my first Channel attempt. One of the other swimmers pointed her out, and I walked over to introduce myself.

"Hi, Freda, I'm Mike," I said.

"Hi, Mike," she answered warmly. "How long are you swimming, then?"

"Forty-five minutes."

"Ahhhhhhhh, go on," she said with a look of disgust. "I'm putting you in for an hour and a half."

"But . . ."

"Here's your swim cap. You're number 5; get going. Now!"

Freda was already looking past me. "Hey, *you lot in front! Get out of the way; I can't see my swimmers!*" she yelled. The alarmed group looked up and scattered immediately in a frenzy of towels, gear bags, and waddling swimmers.

The stories I'd heard about the Channel General ruling Dover Beach with a velvet fist were true. I later asked how she'd describe herself, and the adjective that quickly popped out of Freda's chuckling mouth was "bully." I thought that was a rough bit of self-critique for a woman who'd started helping others when she was just sixteen and who had spent a large part of her life teaching troubled kids.

Two years after our first meeting, I experienced Freda's tougher side personally. In 2008, I was in Dover before my second Channel attempt. On my first Saturday morning, I wanted to swim early, before the crowds showed up, so I got down to the harbor and into the water at 5:00 a.m. By nine o'clock, I had a nice four-hour swim under my belt. I came out of the water feeling refreshed and relaxed, looking forward to catching up with Channel friends and Freda. Freda had a slightly different agenda.

She came over and gently took my hand.

"Freda, do you remember me? I'm Mike Humphreys. I swam in 2006 but came up short halfway across the Channel . . ." I began.

"Yes, dear Mike. You know, I came to the beach this morning and found yer bag, looked out, and saw yer head bobbin' way out in the 'arbor." At this point, she was gripping my hand tightly. "Don't you know long-distance swimmers shouldn't be swimming in the 'arbor without someone 'ere on the beach to watch?" she asked, staring into my eyes intently, her grip tightening further. "What you did—it's not safe," she said firmly. My knuckles were smashed against each other at this point, my fingertips turning bright red.

"Uh, yes, ma'am, well, uh, I was awake early, and, uh, tomorrow, you know, tomorrow I was planning on starting with the group!" I stammered. "How about that?" I finished, venturing an appealing grin.

Freda rewarded me with a soft smile, pulled me down for a kiss on my cheek, and then patted me on the head like a whipped puppy before she walked away. It took ten minutes to get the feeling back in my fingers, so I vowed not to break Freda's rules again.

The next morning, she was waiting to greet me the moment I got to the beach . . .

"Nine a.m., Freda, just like you told me," I said brightly.

"Mike, sit down here and talk to me for a minute."

"I haven't done anything wrong," I said nervously, thinking about my still-sore knucklebones.

"How long are you swimming today?"

"I was thinking about going ten minutes," I said, always a wise-ass.

"You're going three hours."

"Uh, ma'am, I have to taper . . . please?"

She ignored me. "You'll do three hours. And you'll come up to the beach after one hour and feed."

"Uh, ma'am, I have my feeds in here in my swimsuit, I have these gels . . ."

"Those won't work." she said dismissively. "You'll need water, too. Are you using Maxim?" she asked, referring to a popular Channel feeding mix.

"Actually, I'm using Perpetuem, similar to Maxim."

"Mike, do you know what the harbormaster said to me this morning? He said, 'Keep your swimmers in closer, not way out there by the boats like that idiot swimming alone yesterday morning.'"

"He did not! You're making that up!"

"He did, I swear it," she said, "and the police came to see me yesterday and said they were worried because they saw your clothes on the beach but couldn't find you in the water. They thought you'd gotten into trouble."

There's a time to make a stand and a time to concede. This was the latter.

"I'm here on time today . . ." I offered meekly.

"You'll swim no farther out than I tell you," she barked.

"Uh . . . okay."

"You'll come in to the beach at feeding time, whether you feed or not, so we know you're safe."

"Uh . . . okay."

"Put this swim hat on, now."

"Uh . . ."

"Go. Now."

I never broke Freda's rules again.

Chapter 9

Ground Zero for the Channel Community

Freda Streeter had been the heart and soul of Swimmer's Beach since 1984, but by the time of my Dover training in 2009, its arms and legs consisted of a team Freda had put together, including Emma France, Michelle Toptalo, Barrie and Irene Wakeham, and others. A successful Channel swimmer, Emma is an accountant originally from Surrey, who wasn't even comfortable swimming freestyle with her face in the water until a few years before she did her first Channel relay in 2005. Barrie and Irene, both born and bred in Dover and now retired (Barrie had been a professional welder), joined the beach crew in 1999, a few years after their son Lee swam the Channel in eleven hours and forty-five minutes.

I asked Emma about organizing the beach and her Channel swim, looking for insights, as always.

"I didn't like the training," she said, "and I didn't like the swim itself."

"Sorry?"

"Kevin Murphy once said he felt the same, you know," she added.

Kevin Murphy happens to be the most successful male Channel swimmer of all time, having completed a total of thirty-four crossings, three two-ways and twenty-eight single-ways.

"He said he did his swims because they were big challenges. For me, the training was very difficult. On my bad days, I couldn't make it twenty minutes without complaining. Most training sessions, I felt like I'd pass out."

"How did you manage?"

"Freda tricked me," Emma replied simply. "She turned my training swims into something about other people. Freda would send me out from the beach to help other swimmers by saying, 'Just get in for a few minutes with that swimmer, dear; she's afraid of swimming alone.' I'd get in and swim with whoever it was for a bit and then, after I got out, Freda would ask me to get back in and help another swimmer. She's perceptive about people like that. Eventually, I got fit despite myself."

"I was unsuccessful the first time I tried to swim the Channel in 2007. It took me eight hours to get to the first shipping lane; I was sick a lot and going so slowly it would have taken me thirty to forty hours to finish. Then, in 2008, I made it. The first half of my swim was good fun—I couldn't believe I was doing it. But the second half was just hard. I didn't like it."

Along with tricking Emma into getting fit for her swim, Freda asked her to begin helping organize the beach in 2007.

Periodically throughout the year, Emma, Freda, Barrie, and Irene talk regularly about what is and isn't working. In this way, they've evolved a highly orchestrated system of safely managing a population of swimmers that can swell to more than 125 on the busiest days (typically at the very beginning of the season). Among the kinds of things discussed by Freda and her team are controversial moves like my joy of swimming close to the ferries, as I had on previous training swims and been called on the carpet by Freda.

The season on Swimmer's Beach kicks off the first weekend of May and generally ends the last weekend of September. Before the season starts,

Emma creates a set of guidelines based on her team's discussions and distributes them to those planning to train in Dover that year, using a popular online chat room to circulate them as widely as possible. As most aspiring Channel swimmers soon discover, that Channel chat room (accessible only by invitation: swimmers contact the CS&PF through their website, and the CS&PF provides the rules and access) is an invaluable gathering place, overflowing with passion, opinion, advice, and occasionally a snitty comment for newcomers such as, "Don't waste our time by asking anything dumb that you didn't research in the archives first!" and "Wetsuits are the primary cause of the decay of modern society!"

Swimmers that want to train with Freda and crew are instructed to fill out the registration forms Emma, Michelle, or one of the others has distributed and bring them along on the day they begin training. The paperwork is designed to help the beach crew track who is the water when and, more important, when they should get out. Swimmers who don't live in the United Kingdom are typically allowed a bit of leeway on the paperwork, but I've never taken advantage of that. (My knuckles still hurt from Freda's tough-love welcome in 2008.)

Once swimmers have handed in their forms, they're given an identification card that acts as a ticket to a colored swim cap every weekend they show up to train at Swimmer's Beach. The cap provides them with the invaluable help and support of Barrie at the water's edge throughout their day, whether they need feeding, cheering up, or just a little help finding their beach shoes so they don't have to stumble up the pebbly beach barefoot.

To avoid bottlenecks at the water's edge, swimmers training for solo swims go into the harbor at 9:00 a.m., while relay swimmers hold off until 10:00 a.m. Throughout the summer, Freda forcefully suggests how long each swimmer should spend in the water, depending on his experience and objectives. For the most part, she suggests swims of twenty to forty minutes on the first day to allow for acclimation to the bitter-cold springtime water temperatures. After that, she gradually stretches each swimmer's time in the water throughout the rest of the summer.

Feedings on Swimmer's Beach are major productions. Dozens and dozens of swimmers feed regularly, more or less at the same time, forcing the Wakehams and other volunteers, including Louise Kent and Michelle, to run around frantically trying to make sure everyone has what they need. Picture fifty wet, cold people swimming into the beach simultaneously and standing at water's edge, waiting to toss down small paper cups filled with liquid carbohydrate feed. Most chase that with a bit of chocolate or a biscuit before turning around, walking slowly back into the water, and resuming their practice. As soon as each feed is over, the volunteers start getting ready for the next wave.

As the season gathers steam, full-scale Channel swims begin, and the group that shows up to train each weekend gets smaller as people go off and do their swim or relay and "retire" from Swimmer's Beach. In the end, about 150 to 200 attempts are made every year, beginning as early as late June. Many of the swimmers are at personal crossroads in their lives, driven for one reason or another to attempt the challenge. People with agoraphobia proudly conquer the outdoors, the shy become confident, the quiet become rowdy pranksters, and the arrogant become measured (I have some personal experience with this last transition).

At the end of the season, after everyone has made his or her attempt or been forced by weather to wait another year, Freda and her beach crew finish the summer with about 10 percent the number of swimmers they started with. These are the hardcore Channel addicts, the people who come back year after year. They are the people for which swimming the Channel and being part of the Channel community have become a way of life.

The Channel is a way of life, too, for Freda, Emma, Barrie, Irene, and a core group of other helpers, Channel pilots, and crew members. And it has become a way of life for me—and for Miyuki Fujita.

Chapter 10

Miyuki and Ishii

Miyuki Fujita, from Okazaki City in the Aichi Prefecture of Japan, comes from a family of traditional candymakers. In person, Miyuki is a relatively petite bundle of muscle and smile, typically wearing a multihued T-shirt and accompanied by a towel emblazoned with colorful Japanese animation, a camera, gifts for friends, and her coach, Haruyuki Ishii.

A swimming coach for the handicapped, Ishii is the son of a nonferrous metal trader and lives in Edogawa-Ku in Tokyo with his wife of thirty years. About five-foot-eight and stocky, with tousled salt-and-pepper hair, Ishii can usually be found observing or orchestrating Miyuki's latest swimming endeavor dressed in casual coach's attire and waiting for an opportunity to contribute whatever she needs at the moment.

Their partnership in open-water swimming is the stuff of legends, with seven successful forays across the Channel and more than twelve swims total, including a couple of Japanese records.

As my Japanese skills are limited to ordering dinner in Tokyo and polite hellos or thanks, I interviewed Miyuki and Ishii through a translator. To relax them, I started with a softball question and asked them to describe themselves.

Miyuki replied, "Woman who causes a storm."

Ishii countered, "Man who causes disaster."

They seemed relaxed enough, and I could sense their comfort with each other. How did they describe themselves as a team?

"Completely harmless."

I first met Miyuki and Ishii in Dover in the summer of 2008, when I was preparing for my second Channel attempt. They are mainstays on Swimmer's Beach, and anyone who spends time there training will sooner or later enter their orbit. They're quick to introduce themselves, and they love to help other swimmers by lugging feeds, equipment, or whatever else is needed on the waterfront during training sessions.

Miyuki was born in 1966, the oldest daughter of the founder of FUJIYATA, a well-known maker of traditional Japanese confections. One of two sisters, she adopted her father's great love of the sea. She learned to swim in elementary school and developed into a successful athlete, specializing in butterfly and distance freestyle events.

Miyuki married young, in 1984, when she was just eighteen. For a time, her daily work and life left no time for swimming. A few years later, she resumed training, and in 1998 she dipped her toe into open-water swimming. Shortly thereafter, in 1999, while watching a TV show about a group of Japanese celebrities doing a relay swim across the English Channel, piloted by Mike Oram, she had a revelation. She made up her mind to go to England and subsequently swim to France. And she began training in earnest.

She quickly fell in love with open-water swimming, and in 1999 she signed up to participate in a number of races. In 2000, she signed up for a race around Jogashima Island in Miura Province, for which Ishii was the organizer. Ishii was already an accomplished coach by that time and had supported swims not only in Japan but in the Malacca Strait

(Indonesia to Malaysia), Strait of Gibraltar (Spain to Morocco), Tsushima Channel (Japan to Korea), and the East China Sea (Taiwan to Japan). He'd also coached swims in the Yangtze River in China and the Amazon River in Brazil. Miyuki and Ishii teamed up after the race, and years later their partnership has blossomed into one of the most successful swimming duos of all time. With Ishii's assistance, Miyuki has swum to France seven times by herself and once by relay, posting some impressive results:

- August 3, 2002—12 hours, 3 minutes (relay)
- July 14, 2005—17 hours, 3 minutes
- August 2, 2005—13 hours, 41 minutes
- July 18, 2006—13 hours, 34 minutes
- July 10, 2007—13 hours, 59 minutes
- August 10, 2007—13 hours, 54 minutes
- July 23, 2008—14 hours, 2 minutes
- August 3, 2009—17 hours, 18 minutes (part of two-way attempt)

Ishii was instrumental in Miyuki's successful first crossing in July 2005.

"I cannot swim anymore!" she told the boat crew when they were just off the coast of France. "It is cold!"

Ishii happened to be in the galley mixing Miyuki's nutritional supplements when she started to lose faith.

"Mr. *Ishii*! Mr. *Ishii*!" Miyuki shouted. "I want to be on the boat!"

"Miyuki! Go! Swim!" Ishii shouted back, after coming up from belowdecks. "For what did you come to Dover? You promised me to swim, didn't you?"

Crisis averted, Miyuki continued swimming. When she finally landed after seventeen hours, she hugged Ishii and congratulated him on their joint achievement.

Miyuki swam the Channel five more times over the next four years. In 2009 she attempted a double crossing, making it to France but not quite back to England as planned.

"Why a double crossing?" I asked the woman who had been somewhat dismissively referred to as a "housewife" and "someone who works in her husband's sweet-making business" by the Japanese press.

"No Japanese has succeeded in two-way solo swimming across the Channel, and I want to be the first," she said simply. "It's my wish."

For her accomplishments, Miyuki won the Gertrude Ederle award for most meritorious English Channel swim by a woman in 2005. She also holds the record for her other swims with Ishii: four crossings across the Tsugaru Channel. The Tsugaru Channel is a turbulent strait between the islands of Hokkaido and Honshu in northern Japan, where the Pacific and the Sea of Japan crash into each other. Incredibly, three of those swims took place during the same week in late August to early September 2006, and with Ishii's support and encouragement, she maintained her speed and averaged twelve hours for each leg. Imagine completing a twelve-hour swim across a rough, cold Channel—and then turning around and doing it two more times within a week.

I prodded Miyuki and Ishii about their connection to the sport and to each other, among many other subjects. Miyuki reflected and, perhaps focusing on the shared experience that was most memorable, commented about her double-crossing attempt in 2009:

"I always wanted to be the best and do something unusual, so I aimed to complete the two-way crossing, not just one way, as no Japanese person has ever successfully swum the two-way Channel crossing," Miyuki said.

(Note: As of the writing of this book, there have been fifteen English Channel swimmers from Japan.)

"On my first attempt, I had to stop after ten hours due to pain, and I didn't finish even one way. A week later, I had another opportunity to swim the one-way. I swam for seventeen hours thirty-five minutes but had to give up just three kilometers from the French coast."

After her first unsuccessful attempt, Miyuki sought advice from Freda Streeter, who urged her to try again.

"The next year, I began training again for the one-way swim and followed Freda's advice. Since then, I have successfully completed the one-way crossing six times," she told me proudly.

She continued, "I went back to Dover again. I felt ready to attempt the two-way swim. I planned to stay in Dover for thirty-five days and waited nervously for the big day. Neil Streeter, the boat pilot, would choose the day with the best weather conditions for the swim. The other swimmers had gone to swim one after another and everybody kept asking me when I was going to swim, but the days passed and I still had no idea when I would get to swim. I started to feel very frustrated, but I could not do anything but wait and trust Neil to pick a good day. For the two-way swim, we would need two consecutive fine days. It was possible that the weather conditions would not permit me to swim because the weather was constantly changing. I told Neil that if the two-way was not possible, I still intended to swim at least one way before flying back to Japan."

Just before Miyuki was scheduled to leave England to return to Japan, Freda shared the news that the weather was clearing and she'd be able to swim within days. Relieved, Miyuki and her crew prepared for her swim.

"On Monday, I was on the beach with Jenni, an official Channel observer," Miyuki explained, "when Neil called her to say that we should all meet at the marina at 19:00 that evening for my two-way challenge! I was overjoyed. I was going to attempt the two-way swim! Our boat was the *Suva*. Once on board, I applied the Channel grease to my body. When the boat came close to Shakespeare Beach, Ishii, my coach, farted. Everybody on the ship started to laugh, and the atmosphere became very relaxed. Even when I was swimming in the dark, I remembered it and laughed. It was nice to have a funny thought to make me smile while I was swimming, particularly when it became dark."

Miyuki swam on into the night. Despite being accustomed to night swimming, she started feeling sleepy. She was revived by cheering from a relay team passing her on their way back to England after finishing their swim. Hours later, morning came and Miyuki realized she was still far from France. Her average one-way crossing had been in the fourteen-hour range, but she had already been swimming more than seventeen hours. Tired and dejected, she asked to get out, but Ishii convinced her to swim longer, to continue her two-way crossing attempt. Three hours later, on her way back to England (note: according to CS&PF rules, swimmers are allowed ten minutes on the French beach before beginning their return), Miyuki asked Ishii again if she could give up, but instead of allowing her out, he cheerfully encouraged her with the news that the weather was getting better by the hour and would be clear for the rest of her swim. In just eight hours, she could reach her goal of a double crossing and land back in England.

"I was determined to swim for another eight hours," Miyuki said. "I tried very hard, spurred on by the thought that my dream of the two-way Channel crossing was about to come true. My husband, the pilot, my colleagues, everybody would be delighted! What would I do if TV reporters were waiting for me at Narita Airport? What would I do next after my dream had come true? Maybe I could try to swim the one-way ten times! Or perhaps I should try to become the oldest Channel swimmer! Pondering over these random things, I pushed myself to continue swimming. Night came again, and it became cold but I didn't stop. I saw the lights of England as I swam closer and closer.

"I drank another feeding and said to the people on the boat that I could not swim anymore, but they told me to keep trying. I screamed, and my voice echoed in the darkness over the Channel. It was the first time that my body was chilled to my very bones, and even my wrists started to ache. I gave up about five hours from England (about four miles, given the conditions and Miyuki's current speed). I was mentally and physically exhausted. I could not swim the last five hours. Because I was tired, I convinced myself that I could not do it."

As I contemplated her story, Miyuki summed it up. "To be a successful long-distance swimmer, you have to be mentally strong. I had swum thirty hours in the pool and twenty hours, seven minutes in the sea. Now, I have to use this experience to aid my future training for my next Channel swim. On my first swim, I stopped after just ten hours, but now I was able to swim for about twenty-nine hours thirty minutes. I never dreamed I would be able to swim for so long."

Miyuki would be back for another Channel swim, either a single or another attempt at her dream. And I had no doubt her partner and friend, Ishii, would be at her side.

Chapter 11

Swimming Across Bellingham Bay— October 2009

September 2009 was an uneventful swimming month for me. While in Seattle, I worked mainly in the pool, focusing on sets and interval workouts to improve my speed. For many open-water swimmers, pool training is fruitful but dull—a necessary evil—and I'm no exception.

But I'm an extreme commuter, and the pool is often my only option for training. I spend one-third of my time at my second home in Atlanta, taking care of my youngest son, and the rest of my time in Seattle. In Atlanta, training time is hard to come by, and most of the available open-water venues are muddy or too warm for training. Often, the best training I can manage is a few miles at 5:00 a.m. in the fifteen-yard pool at my apartment complex before I wake Connor to get him ready for school. It's great to have that pool—don't get me wrong—but there's no monotony like swimming three or four miles in a fifteen-yard pool five days in a row. It's like training for a running marathon on a treadmill in a closet. The most exciting things within my field of vision are the dead bugs swirling on the pool bottom, or an occasional glimpse of a few neighbors who have come out to watch me impassively as I swim back and forth. To pass the time, I imagine what they're thinking:

"Wow, that guy's been going forever," thinks the young woman with the mountain bike hanging from her deck ceiling.

"That idiot woke me up again!" grumbles the guy on the top floor, smoking lazily.

After one Atlanta stay in early October, I returned to Seattle eager to get back into open water and headed to Bellingham to swim with Dale. I was looking forward to swimming with her again; it had been a couple of months, and I missed her. To make the drive more fun, I was driving the Porsche I'd just gotten. I'd been dreaming of a Porsche since I had gotten the Matchbox version at age nine, so I was as excited as a kid on Christmas morning.

When I reached the Bellingham exit on I-5, I glanced at the outside temperature display in the car, saw "39" blinking, and apprehension grabbed hold. I knew that the water in Bellingham Bay would be below sixty degrees, but had hoped for an air temperature above forty. Air temps below that can make cold water downright uncomfortable and dangerous. A common rule of thumb is that any combined temp (air plus water) of less than 120 degrees comes with a distinct risk of hypothermia. I was looking at a combination of less than a hundred. Great.

Water pulls heat from the body much faster than air does, up to thirty times faster, because water is much denser than ambient air. And it only takes a decrease in core body temperature of about five degrees before you begin to experience hypothermia. As every kid knows, normal body temperature is 98.6 degrees Fahrenheit, and believe it or not, hypothermia sets in at a body temp of about ninety-five. Water just a few degrees below your core body temperature can be deadly, and there are examples of divers dying of hypothermia in eighty-degree water.

Hypothermia sets in when your body can no longer maintain its normal temperature. In an attempt to protect your core (heart, lungs, brain), your body systematically begins to shut down circulation to everything else. In open-water swimming, your body typically reserves warm, circulating blood for the working muscles and the core organs. Everything else gets cold and usually numb (which reminds me: shrinkage sucks—and that's all I'll say about that). Trained open-water swimmers commonly find themselves in water down to about sixty degrees, and many swim comfortably down to fifty. Swimming at those temperatures is heavily dependent on proper training and other ambient conditions. In fifty-five—or sixty-degree water, there's a big difference between sunshine and warm air on your back versus clouds, rain, or frigid air.

I was facing the latter. And truth be told, I was not a natural cold-water swimmer. I'd always been thin, and it was difficult for me to gain and maintain body fat for cold-water insulation. I was comfortable with Channel temperatures (high fifties and low sixties) but had difficulty matching the fifty degrees and down that some other cold-water swimmers could manage. The reasons for that included body shape and size, experience, and probably—to be brutally honest—bravery. I was better built for warm open water, but I didn't enjoy that as much. Cold water was challenging, and I relished the overall experience more than the brutal sun, dehydration, and more prevalent carnivorous wildlife that accompanied the warm-water version of the sport. Plus, there's really no warm water in Seattle.

After getting off of I-5, I rolled through Bellingham and into downtown Fairhaven. Founded in the late 1800s, Fairhaven (now officially part of Bellingham) has a pretty little downtown, with restaurants, shops, and water activities to keep both tourists and locals happily busy. On the west edge of town is a small park dedicated to water-sports enthusiasts such as kayakers and surfboarders. I've occasionally seen sunbathers splash in the water at the height of summer, but due to the generally dicey water temperatures, I usually have the swimming scene all to myself. There's a warning sign in the pavilion that says something like:

"Warning: Cold Water! You could die! The water in Bellingham Bay is regularly in the low 50s. If you're thinking of swimming without a wetsuit, get back in your car and have a latte—idiot!"

No exaggeration there. Over the years that Dale and I trained together in Bellingham Bay, numerous people were overcome by the cold and perished. They *died* in the water I was just about to swim in.

I ignored the sign and started to get ready for my swim. A group of wave surfers was getting ready to go out too, and I hoped that was a sign the water was more welcoming than I feared. I tested the water temperature: only fifty-three degrees. And the thirty-eight-degree air was gusting and blowing. In total effect, it was frosty. I asked myself every cold-water swimmer's favorite question: "What the hell am I doing out here?"

It's a good question. The easy answer is that I needed to be in the water that day to train for the Channel. And that I loved swimming in Bellingham Bay with my Dale puttering alongside in her boat. But on a deeper level, why does a swimmer get into frigid water for long periods of time again and again when the experience is often unpleasant? There are probably as many reasons as there are open-water swimmers. Personally, I'd be afraid to pinpoint what draws me to cold-water marathon swimming for fear of reducing it to some simple cliché like "because it's there." My driving force is more convoluted, and while I admit there's an element of "because it's there," there are many other reasons. For me, Channel swimming is a one-stop shop where I can test myself against an overwhelming challenge. It's where I can share a journey with my many open-water swimming friends. Where I can live out warm memories of camaraderie from my competitive swimming days. Where I can indulge an appreciation for English culture and tradition developed through years of living and traveling in England and its commonwealth. And where I can leave behind the ambiguities of everyday life's agendas, committees, and bewilderments in favor of the cut-and-dried, the black-and-white question: did I achieve it—or did I not?

While I was getting my gear ready, I attracted the attention of a friendly woman about my age who managed to share her life story with me in about four minutes. It's very impressive that we Americans do this so readily. In most countries, it takes years for people to feel comfortable enough to share intimate details. I once worked on a project with an associate in Germany who had worked for his boss for twenty years and still called him "Mr.," but that day at Marina Park, it took four minutes for a complete stranger to share with me that she was divorced, with an adult son, raised on Vancouver Island, maintained citizenship in Canada and Sweden, had been a tour-guide operator but now wanted to be a writer, was caring for an elderly friend who was dying, and used to swim but stopped when she passed her fortieth birthday. Oh, and her name was Robin. To be fair, Robin was very friendly and a pleasant diversion from the cold air battering my skin as I stripped and sprayed on sunblock.

Down at the beach, Dale pulled up in her Zodiac inflatable boat. After saying good-bye to my new friend Robin, I carried my stuff uneasily to the beach. Dale was grinning broadly, and it was great to see her, despite the arctic blasts ripping at me. She was wearing a parka, gloves, heavy boots, and a skullcap. I think she was grinning because she was warm as toast and I was shivering like a politician on trial.

"What are you worried about?" Dale asked. "*I've* got the worst of the weather in the boat."

"That may be true some days," I said, laughing, "but not today. This is so cold my assets are shrinking and I'm not even in the water yet."

I stripped further while Dale belted out her unique laugh. After I'd thrown my gear in her Zodiac, she rowed offshore to wait for me to start my swim.

Since I was stripped to my suit, I was colder on the thirty-eight-degree beach than I would be in the fifty-three-degree water—but that knowledge didn't help much when my subconscious was telling me to get my ass back in the car. I waded in. The water was brutally cold, but at least the bits of me under water were spared the frigid breeze. Standing there was like standing in a hot tub on a snowy winter day. Despite that, I stood a moment to let my lower extremities get accustomed to the water and get my mind around the swim, and then plunged in, bolting away from the beach.

To put it mildly, I was motivated to swim like a bat out of hell just to generate some body heat.

It normally takes me about twenty minutes to get to Buoy 2 in the middle of Bellingham Bay, but I did it that morning in twelve minutes. The ebb tide was helping a bit, pushing me gently toward the buoy, and so was the set work I'd been doing in the pool—but mainly I was trying to get warm. I pulled hard, kicked like hell, and concentrated on good form. Every five strokes, I used a warming trick, blowing warm air out underwater down my chest. It didn't thaw anything out, but it was a mood lifter. I'd have gladly given my kingdom just to pee out a nice ninety-eight-degree puddle to swim through.

Despite the cold, it was brilliantly sunny, and the Bay was clearer than I'd ever seen it. I watched underwater as the beach fell away and was replaced by a seabed with thousands of strands of slimy and sinewy plankton and kelp floating from the surface down to the seafloor. I could see giant starfish surfing across the seabed and thousands of feeder fish swimming about, unwittingly waiting for some predator to snap them up. Given the clarity of the water, I was enjoying exploring the sea's ecosystem from above; it took my focus away from the cold. Despite it being virtually pointless, I also looked around on the seabed nervously for any signs of the last victims claimed by the Bay. A couple of sailors had gone down in bad weather a few hundred yards from where I was swimming, after their sailboat capsized in the spring of 2009. They had never been found. Seeing their remains after four months in seawater might have been enough to help me swim at Olympic speed, but thankfully I didn't see a trace.

As I mentioned, Bellingham Bay and the Puget Sound have a long and fairly regular history of claiming the lives of water enthusiasts. In addition to the sailors that June, another man died of exposure that summer after falling out of his canoe into the Sound, and an experienced sailboarder died the previous year when he got separated from his board and suffered exposure in the Bay. On a sunny day or a moonlit evening, the waters of Bellingham Bay and Puget Sound look inviting—but the water temperature is a master of ceremonies that does what it wants, even to people with lots of experience.

Dale and I passed Buoy 2 and kept going. We weren't doing a long swim, but I started to worry that the wind would be too much to swim back against if we went too far, so we turned around and faced into the ebb tide for the longer swim back. When Bellingham Bay is in an ebb tide, the water is rushing out to sea from Marine Park, so the return toward the beach is tough going. I mostly forgot about the cold because I was working as hard as possible just to inch forward into the maelstrom, throwing my hands forward and yanking them back in a continuous, wallpaper-peeling motion. Pulling against the ebb was like swimming up a salmon run in a hurricane. There was nowhere safe to breathe, and every moment of reflection meant two strokes backward.

We kept at it, me stroking furiously and Dale trying to crab her boat against the wind and tide. Finally, the seafloor began to climb again, and the starfish sprang back into view. We finished a few minutes later.

"You could have gone farther, much farther," Dale said. "That Bowen Island swim did wonders for your confidence and stroke."

Looking back, I decided she was right, so we talked about coming back the following weekend. Getting dressed was an exercise in trying to remove and replace wet with dry, cold with warm, and bare feet with socks and shoes while my hands were shaking like a cornered virgin. Robin had watched us for a few minutes after our start, but had driven off sometime after we became too small to see from the beach. I managed to get myself put back together and gratefully collapsed into my car, turning the seat warmers to "high."

Soon enough, my backside was toasty, and the rest of me was flushed with satisfaction, pleasure, and warmth.

Chapter 12

Qualifying

My confidence was definitely bolstered by the Bowen swim and my subsequent swims in Dover—as well as by Dale's conviction that I could go farther. I wanted to try some longer swims, so to finish off the season, I asked Dale to come down to Seattle. I wanted to get a bit ahead of my 2010 training schedule and put a check mark next to my six-hour qualifying swim, and I was hoping she'd crew for me on Lake Washington for the qualifier. The Channel Swimmers & Pilots Federation requires proof of a six-hour qualifier swim in water sixty degrees or colder as part of its duty of care when it processes Channel swim applications. The qualifier can be completed anytime in the eighteen months preceding a Channel swim, and must be documented by an attending crew.

I first attempted a six-hour swim in 2006. My friend Arne and I planned it together. I would start at the University of Washington canoe rental pier, swim east alongside the Evergreen Point floating bridge for about an hour, then break north at Evergreen Point to swim along the east side of Lake Washington for a couple hours before returning along approximately the same route. What we didn't plan for was the wild winds that strafed the lake that morning. We managed to get about thirty minutes out before Arne's canoe began gyrating in circles, caught in the grip of the thirty-mile-per-hour winds. The water was about fifty-eight degrees and I was skinnier in those days, so I had to keep swimming to stay warm. I watched with deepening concern from water level as Arne's canoe spun more and more wildly until he couldn't control it any longer and the canoe flipped him overboard. I swam over and found Arne floating next to the upside-down canoe, grinning.

"I guess I lost my iPod and my phone down there," he said cheerfully, pointing at Lake Washington's one-thousand-foot depth.

We were eventually rescued by a motorist who had seen Arne capsize from the Evergreen Point Bridge and called the police. Lesson learned. Don't go out alone in a canoe on a windy day, or you might get spit out like a watermelon seed on July 4. We threw in the towel that day, and I swam my qualifier at a later date with Dale.

A couple years later, in anticipation of my 2008 Channel attempt, I was better prepared. I had a motorboat and waited for a better day. I wasn't worried about the boat capsizing that day, but the swim had nonetheless been a hassle to plan because of the erratic water and air temperatures in the Seattle area. In April, lake temperatures hover around forty-six to forty-eight degrees. May's longer days bring that up to anywhere between the low fifties and sixty, depending on whether Seattle's springtime weather menu has included simple rain, dusty mist, drippy drizzle, or angry thunderstorms. All of that lake-cooling rain eventually gives way to Seattle's long summer days, and by the time June rolls around, Lake Washington temperatures are often well above sixty—too warm to meet the qualifier requirements.

In addition to the big-water lakes such as Lake Washington (about thirty miles long and great for distance swimming) and Lake Sammamish (about fifteen miles long and crappy for distance swimming), Seattle offers the Puget Sound. The logistics for Sound swimming are trickier because it's colder and you can't simply swim the coastline—but the Sound is a beautiful swim. It boasts the islands of the San Juan archipelago, abundant wildlife, and views of the Olympic Mountains. You pay for that oneness with nature, though, with colder water. Most of the Sound hovers between fifty-eight and fifty-three degrees year-round. That's cold enough to quickly affect, and even kill, open-water swimmers, though extensive experience and training can result in the ability to regularly manage those temperatures.

All of these temperature issues came into play as I planned my 2008 qualifier swim. I knew I had only about a one-month window—and out of those four weekends, two were reserved for hanging out with my sons. I put the demands on my time aside, and in June of that year, I swam a satisfying and easy loop around Lake Washington with my friend Glenn Ader and stamped "paid" on the qualifier requirement.

To qualify for my 2010 Channel attempt, I wanted to swim the qualifier early, preferably in autumn of 2009. I had penciled in ten swims between six and ten hours in length leading up to Dover, and although that would allow lots of opportunities to qualify, I didn't want to be worrying about the official swim in the last few months before I left for the Channel. I wanted to relax and enjoy those training swims. After Bowen Island, I already felt in shape to start doing some longer swims. Weighing everything carefully, I decided to do my qualifying swim in October 2009.

And that's how Dale, Barb, and I found ourselves standing on the dock at Kirkland Marina the morning of October 10, preparing my friend Brian's boat for a long day on Lake Washington. The air temperature was in the low forties, and the water was in the high fifties. As usual, Dale was dressed as if she were headed out for crab fishing in the Bering Sea, wearing multiple alternating layers of fleece, Gore-Tex, cotton, and wool. *That should keep her warm,* I thought.

There were eagles circling, the sun was brilliant, and Lake Washington was whispering invitations in my ear. I was looking forward to the day. Natural beauty aside, though—it was cold. I was shivering before I got in, at least partly due to my body's Pavlovian response to the signs of an impending swim.

We spent a little time acquainting ourselves with Brian's pristinely maintained speedboat and stowing our gear. There was a small cabin belowdecks, and I ducked inside to check it out. "Hey, guys, look at this," I said, holding up a bedpan-like device. "It looks like this is where you'll be peeing for the next six hours," I said with a grin. Dale laughed loudly, while Barb looked at me balefully. Considering she was about to burn her Saturday overseeing me while I swam, swam, and swam some more, I was probably pushing my luck by mocking the sanitary facilities she'd have to deal with. I tried a make-up kiss, but she just flashed me one of those malevolent smiles we reserve for disappointing soul mates and said, "Just wait, funny man, just you wait."

We pulled out of Kirkland Marina and stopped about five hundred yards out, just past the end of the piers. With all of my gear adjusted and my skin slathered with enough sunblock to ward off a nuclear blast, I dropped off the boat's transom and dove underwater about ten feet. I scared and scattered some feeder fish below the boat and then looked up at the underside of the hull before surfacing. I looked around, grinned at Barb and Dale, and started swimming toward Evergreen Point and the Route 520 floating bridge.

Evergreen Point is the small peninsula sticking out into Lake Washington from the towns of Medina and Kirkland, along the eastside of Lake Washington. Between the late 1800s and the 1930s, the land was mostly controlled by Eastside families and used for private recreation. By the 1950s, a growing population on the Eastside had created the need for a second Lake Washington bridge to augment the I-90 floating bridge three miles south that had opened in 1940. Work commenced, and the Evergreen floating bridge between Evergreen Point and the Montlake neighborhood on the Seattle side of Lake Washington opened in August 1963. With the second bridge in place, the population exploded, and towns such as Kirkland, Bellevue, and Redmond began sprawling outward toward their current footprints. The bridge is the bane and beauty of many Seattle commuters, its miserable rush-hour traffic somewhat mitigated by stunning views that include every bit of Mount Rainier's glory on clear days.

We reached Evergreen Point and waited for a clear and safe, pleasure-boat-free moment for me to swim under the non-floating part of the floating bridge. The passageway under the bridge is punctuated by immense concrete pillars that make me feel tiny every time I swim through—a little like passing through the entry of a government ministry in a George Orwell story.

Next, we made our way along the Medina waterfront, one of my favorite places to swim. There are lots of beautiful homes around Lake Washington, but that's not the reason I like swimming along Medina: swimming past Bill Gates's house means I get to wake up his security detail. When I swim by, they often pop out of the heavy woods that surround the waterfront yard of his compound. The first time I experienced this was probably the most fun. Two or three minutes after I'd come into view of one of Gates's docks on a swim in 2008, five sturdy-looking guys appeared out of nowhere and started carefully tending the vegetation on the property, staring at me intently while they vigorously pantomimed raking and hoeing. Some of them even had real rakes and hoes. I don't fault Gates for having security, of course, but I'd have expected the team to be more subtle than a gang of mercenaries from a Bruce Willis action movie. Perhaps underwater cameras watched from below as well—who knows? One of these days I'm going to swim by and turn around and wave, just to see if I can score a scolding.

This day, we passed the Gates compound without arousing any security "gardeners." No submarines attacked from below, and I wasn't sniped from the trees. My infantile amusement foiled for the day, we headed toward Meydenbauer Bay.

We reached and passed Meydenbauer Bay, now encircled by expensive homes instead of coal and lumber transport ships, in about three and a half hours and continued south along the eastside shoreline. The weather had warmed up, and the day was brilliantly sunny and cheerful. The beautiful weather had brought out the pleasure-boaters, and Barb and Dale were busy waving Jet-Skiers off and watching for drunk boaters rampaging across Lake Washington. The boaters' wakes added a lot of chop to the water that made it a confused surface to swim in, but it didn't come close to reaching the Channel's potential for chop. We passed the mouth of a passage between Mercer Island, an upscale, politically conservative area within the bastion of Seattle liberalism named for Aaron Mercer, and the mainland. The narrowed mouth had a lot of boat and kayak traffic flowing through it and we had already done more than four hours, so I stopped and suggested to Dale and Barb that we turn around and swim in the other direction to avoid the traffic. They readily agreed. I think they were both relieved that the swim would soon be over and were looking forward to visiting a real bathroom back at the Kirkland Marina.

We headed back north toward Gates's private army and finished the swim without incident. My 2010 Channel swim qualifier was already done! It was a comforting milestone to have reached, and I was confident as I headed into winter and indoor training.

It was also the last pain-free swim I would have for months.

Chapter 13

A Swimmer's Story—Sue Pepper

I welcomed November 2009 in Atlanta, my second hometown. I keep an apartment there so that I can spend about half my time with my sons, a routine put in place as a result of a simultaneous divorce and career change in 2001.

My training started to suffer due to a flare-up of osteoarthritis in my right shoulder after my qualifying swim. My confidence had shown its downside: it had led me to overtrain, a mistake I'd made many times before, in both swimming and other sports; I had not yet learned my lesson. I'd kept training hard past the end of the season, and my arthritic shoulder was showing its displeasure. The constant ache and grinding made it difficult to swim much, but I was trying to stick to a regular routine but with shorter distances, fewer miles. Despite the injury, on the morning of November 9, I was impatiently looking forward to my swim workout. All I needed to do was drop my son Connor off at school, and I was free to swim, grinding pain or not.

At the hour we should have been walking hand in hand to school, I found myself stuck staring at a small bunny-like creature jumping from one platform to another and another on a tiny screen. I lost my patience.

"Come on, Connor," I said, "you'll be late for school."

"Okay," he said, not moving, continuing to play a Pokémon game intently on his Nintendo DS. I had had enough of that, so I took the device from his hand and endured the silent treatment for doing so all the way to his school.

"Have a great day!" I said cheerfully, getting a grunt and a mutter in return.

When I got to Dynamo Swim Center, where I'd trained on and off since 1992, I was still preoccupied with my shoulder and Pokémon. I needed a better way to set limits for Connor on video games but was drawing a blank on how exactly to handle it, as I'd done with his older brothers. Not an unusual problem for parents, but it was bugging me to the point where it threatened to interfere with my workout.

I spit in my goggles to prevent them from fogging during my swim and put aside thoughts of cartilage-free bone-grinding and ritual murder of Pokémon in favor of a more inspirational workout topic. Every marathon swimmer I know has his own mental library of things to think about during long swims. Mine was filled with family issues, stories made-up and true, work problems, and lottery ticket daydreams. Probably because I'd received her swim season report via e-mail the night before, on November 9 I was thinking about my friend Sue Pepper. I dropped into the water, sprang off the wall to begin my three-mile warm-up, and reflected on Sue.

Sue Pepper is an aptly named, tightly wound woman in her fifties from Kent, United Kingdom, with a penchant for punctuating sentences with emphatic facial expressions that discourage debate. About five foot four, with sandy brown and gray-tinged hair, she has a firm handshake, an ascetic wit, and a story to tell. In person, she manages the delicate balance of coming across simultaneously friendly and fierce. "Determined" is an apt compromise descriptor. Sue is an accomplished English Channel swimmer with four relays under her belt and a British record in the 1500 meters.

She also has multiple sclerosis.

Sue started dabbling in sports when she was seven years old and picked up her first field hockey stick. The feeling and power of that graceful implement transfixed her, and from then on, she was consumed with any sport that involved sticks or racquets. When she talks about herself as a player, she grins wickedly, and you're glad you haven't met her on the field. She proudly describes a full-speed collision on a field hockey pitch that left a much larger competitor gasping and prone but Sue scratch-free.

"After field hockey, I picked up badminton," Sue recalls. "I was a violent person, and hitting things sort of channeled all of my aggression. I dread to think what sort of person I would have become if I hadn't had that avenue."

In response to my questions about badminton, she said, "I started playing in earnest at age twenty-five, when my engagement broke up. When I got hold of a shot, the player at the other end *knew* that I had gotten hold of it!" Sue offered a grim smile at the memory.

She progressed through years, levels, and competitors in various sports, always excelling and often ascending to the role of official. She loved every moment and wouldn't have changed a thing—but she admits that these passions, the outlets for her aggression, came at the expense of her relationship with her parents, which was threadbare at best. They felt her behavior didn't become a lady or bring honor to the family.

Sue's multiple sclerosis came on somewhat suddenly, like a tornado that suddenly tears your house's foundation out from underneath you. One day in January 1995, she was a successful legal executive litigating a case when she simply slumped to the courtroom floor, unconscious. She'd had mild symptoms for some time—difficulty focusing, fatigue—but none of it had registered as serious. That's not unusual with MS—sufferers often ignore early signs as insignificant.

The disease is an autoimmune condition in which the body's own defense system attacks the central nervous system, damaging the areas of the brain and spinal cord known as "white matter." The disorder destroys a fatty covering around the nerve fibers that insulates them. When this covering is destroyed, the nerves can't effectively conduct messages to the muscles, and those muscles fail. The name *multiple sclerosis* comes from the scars the condition leaves in the white matter.

In Sue's case, MS robbed her of full control of her leg muscles and the amazing hand-eye coordination that had made her so formidable at field and racquet sports. It's worse in her right leg, so her left leg tends to pick up the slack and hold her upright. Sometimes even that fails, and she simply drops to the ground as if she's been switched off. The first time I saw that happen, on Dover Beach in 2006, I offered to help—and got a steely grimace in return. I don't know if she was angry at me, her legs, or fate—probably all three. I was luckier than other bystanders over the years, who have been treated to the loud expletives of a frustrated athlete.

Sue also experiences Uhthoff's phenomenon, bouts of unconsciousness associated with the disease, when her body and brain overheat and can't cool themselves normally.

After her MS diagnosis and English Channel swimming, the tenuous bond with her family disintegrated altogether. Her parents couldn't understand why she didn't retire to the comfort of their home and live out her days "properly" on the pension afforded her by the National Health Service.

"They wanted me to be an academic young lady," Sue explained. "But I was *not* academic, and I was certainly *no* lady! They wanted me to go to the university," she continued. "They wanted me to become, well, everything Mother wasn't. They couldn't understand why I wanted to bash the hell out of something—but I loved my hockey! They still don't approve of my life, and they've given me no support. My mother is dead now, but before she died, they wouldn't come and watch me in any of the swimming things."

We both thought about that for a moment, and finally, I asked her why she thought that was.

"I don't know," she answered wistfully. "But I know they felt a certain embarrassment that I was disabled, even though it wasn't their fault. I know Father felt it was some big blight on the family. It's the kind of thing that some people have to face, but all my Mother was interested in was the good Pepper family name."

What next? Retirement was the first reality. Her lapses in consciousness and difficulty focusing meant she could no longer work. Just like that—her career was over. It got worse. Doctors advised her not to exercise, ever, at all.

"What do you do when you've had your whole life, work, and sport taken from you?" she asks rhetorically, looking down.

After the shock wore off a bit, Sue pondered what to do with the rest of her life. There was every likelihood that she'd live as long as the next person—but how would she occupy herself?

Dismissing out of hand the medical advice against exercise (as I habitually did when my muscles, tendons, and joints were overtrained) and knowing she needed a sport of some sort toward which she could direct her pent-up energy, Sue took inventory of her remaining abilities, assets, and liabilities. She couldn't do anything that relied on running, hand-eye coordination, or fine control of her arms and hands, nor could she do anything likely to cause her to overheat and black out.

That didn't leave much.

Sue doesn't remember how, but eventually the idea of swimming came up. It didn't much interest her because she thought it dull and couldn't swim four strokes without sinking. But . . . her sanity was more pressing than a lack of swimming skills, so she got in touch with the community sports development council in her local county, the Kent Sports Development unit, and explained her situation. They invited her down to train at one of their affiliated sports clubs with a pool.

"I didn't have any choice," she pointed out. "I couldn't run, couldn't leap, couldn't coordinate . . ."

Sue had a new focus, a new outlet.

Within eight months, she was racing in disabled championships and tilting at windmills in her new sport. For example, at the time Sue started swimming competitively, the longest distance disabled swimmers were allowed to swim was 400 meters. "The bloody coaches were blinkered into thinking that was all anyone with MS could do," Sue laughed contemptuously. But still, she wanted more; she wanted to try for 800 or 1500 meters. At an event in 1996, she asked the Great Britain coach why she couldn't try longer distance swimming.

"With your MS, you can't do that," he assured her confidently.

There is no better way to motivate Sue Pepper than to tell her what she can't do. She started working with a private Masters swimming coach, Connie Hogg, who supported her desire to race longer distances. In 2000, after she'd set the British 1500 record in the disabled category, her coach enrolled her in a Catalina Channel relay without her knowledge. (The Catalina Channel is similar in distance and difficulty to the English Channel.) For this particular event, the rules stipulated that at least one person on each relay team had to have MS. Despite her early swimming successes, Sue didn't think she could manage the relay because she didn't know how to swim in the sea.

Her coach put her in touch with Freda Streeter.

When Sue first went to Dover Beach to train, Freda was worried. She didn't know if Sue could swim in the sea, and the sight of Sue actually scared her. The open-sea training, however, was a revelation. The cold water actually helped Sue's MS! No matter her state when she got to Dover, whether her weak leg was failing or she was blacking out, the cold saltwater changed everything. Sue would leave the thick Dover Harbor water with increased strength, flexibility, and mobility—and she'd experience no MS symptoms for days. She could run, jump, leap, do anything. She was *Sue* again.

In 2003, Sue swam in her first English Channel relay: thirteen-plus hours. In 2005, she completed her second, in fifteen-plus hours. And in 2006, she aced her third in thirteen-plus hours again.

In September 2009, Sue swam her final Channel relay. Her team struck out for France at 11:00 p.m. on Monday the twenty-first, but they were prematurely turned around due to deteriorating weather and wind conditions. Sue had been on the verge of getting violently seasick anyway, so the turnaround was a relief of sorts, although her condition drained her confidence. Her coach, Tanya, prescribed rest and recuperation for Sue while she and the rest of the team waited for better conditions. Sue was skeptical and worried about ruining the swim for the rest of her team, but complied and waited with everyone else.

Come 6:00 a.m. on the morning of Tuesday the twenty-ninth, bolstered by a few days of rest, Sue was at Dover Marina with her team to try again. At just after seven thirty, the first swimmer jumped in and they were off, each team member swimming an hour in turn. The wind picked up again and became Force 4 (11-15 knots: windy for a swim), and the boat was tossing around like the proverbial corkscrew. Each time the pilot boat gyrated, Sue's legs were overmatched and she fell on the floor. Her MS had progressed to the point where she needed a wheelchair most days on land, and the gyrating conditions on water didn't help the situation.

Sue swam twice in the relay, and those were the only easy times of the day for her. In the water, free of the need to rely on her legs and cooled by the Channel, Sue was in her element. Getting in was a challenge each time, however, as the pilot didn't trust Sue's safety on the steps at the back of the boat; she was dropped off the side each time. To get back on board after her turn, she grabbed a line and pulled herself arm over arm until her coach and Lance could grab hold and haul her up. Some hours later, the last team member, aided by a giant spotlight on the boat illuminating the French coast, landed after fourteen hours and thirty-one minutes. They'd done it!

Sue had now completed four relays, and given her deteriorating health and the burden they imposed on her relay teams and crews, decided that would have to be enough.

Four Channel swim relays in spite of multiple sclerosis: that was Sue Pepper's experience.

Back at Dynamo, I thought about Sue and her discomforts as I pulled myself back and forth, back and forth, back and forth endlessly across the training pool. My shoulder wasn't getting any better, but the discomfort had dissipated into the background. It seemed only fitting. My son's worrisome Pokémon addiction and my shoulder bones rubbing against each other seemed petty worries compared to the disintegration of the myelin sheaths holding together Sue's central nervous system.

Sue was an inspiration. If she could do it, I could too.

Chapter 14

December Reflection

I typically slide from autumn into winter while still in summer training mode until, sometime between November and mid-January, I'm forced to accept that summer is over. It's too cold and dark in the mornings to swim outside before work, and as I watch my fiftieth birthday loom, my body aches to remind me it needs a winter's break.

After spending most of any given year defining days, weekends, work, and holidays around swimming, it's an odd feeling to go back to a sane life. My goggles and swimsuits spend only a few days a week drying in the bathroom, the smell of chlorine recedes to the background, and I cut back from eight-thousand-calorie days to a more normal diet. One month I'm gleefully churning out twenty-five-mile weeks, and the next month I'm swimming maybe a fourth of that and reacquainting myself with a bicycle. It's a bit like having your kids grow up and move out. One day you're an active dad, and the next you're hoping for a few days of their time at Christmas. It might be more relaxing, but it's not entirely comfortable.

Nature abhors a vacuum, though, and when I take a break from swimming, other things tend to fill the gap. Mainly it is the three Fs: friends, family, and food. I sleep in a bit later than 5:00 a.m. and take languid breaks at lane's end to chat with other swimmers, and my training sessions are unplanned; I formally call them "whatever the hell I feel like."

Once I give in to it, I usually enjoy this time of year a lot. My hiatus in 2009, however, was the best and the worst of times.

It was the best because I was loving the easy training, looking forward to my Channel swim in 2010, and anticipating good times with friends and family who'd volunteered to crew on long training swims. I was planning ten swims of over six hours in length, including at least three eight-hour and three ten-hour swims. Those longer events would have intimidated me in 2006 or 2008, but in late 2009, I couldn't wait to get started.

It was the worst because there was a sense of the finite about it all. After next year, it would be done. I would have swum the Channel. My confidence was absolute. After my swim in September 2010, I'd be overjoyed at having finally made it across, sure, but I was also afraid of waking up the morning after.

Who would I be if I wasn't a guy trying to swim the Channel? Would I go on to other swims? Would I write more books after this; my first? Would I shift gears entirely and ride a bicycle across the United States, or maybe climb Kilimanjaro or Everest? Or would I just sink into my couch and watch reruns of *The Shawshank Redemption*? What would I do?

By the end of 2009, I'd been the "aspiring Channel swimmer" for five years. It was an aspect of my identity that got tiresome sometimes—as when I was being introduced to new people at social events. But in addition to that, perhaps because of the nature of the pursuit or perhaps because I'm an obsessive-compulsive who views the world through such prisms, the Channel had become the key factor in the structure of my life. It affected my diet, social schedule, family time, vacation planning, budgeting, what I thought, when I thought it, and even what I wore. Since the start of my Channel training, I'd had to replace my entire work wardrobe to fit the belly fat and shoulder breadth I'd developed. When you have sculpted, scheduled, and remade so much of your life, personality, and physique, all in pursuit of one goal, what happens after you've reached it? How long can you reflect on the successful attainment of a dream before turning back and facing your life without it, and harder yet, finding a new one?

These were difficult questions.

On the "best of times" side, I felt mentally ready and confident to cross the Channel.

You know you're ready for your Channel swim when you're eager to get up early in the morning and swim in cold seas or lakes; when the prospect of that has you begging off your spouse's favorite reality show to get to bed early because you can't wait for morning to come; when you're standing by the waterside in the morning dusk, wind whipping across your bare, fat belly—and your reaction is to laugh; when you take that first step in and your toes are instantly iced and you think *I'm freezing!* with glee instead of dread. You know you are ready when you're sitting in meetings while someone drones on endlessly through their PowerPoint slides and you think, *I'd give anything to be back in the freezing sea in churning water right now*; when you are constitutionally unable to drive, walk, or fly past any body of water, anywhere, without thinking, *I wish I were swimming in that!*

Finally, you know you are ready when the thought of your Channel swim is frightening only because you know it will ultimately be over and you might no longer be who you've become. You won't continue to define yourself as a Channel swimmer who gets up at the crack of dawn and races for the water. Who will you be? What will you do? And why will you do it?

I was ready and frightened.

It was the best of times and the worst.

Chapter 15

Why and How and Who

Mike Oram once said to me that one sign that a swimmer was ready to swim the Channel was that he or she could design a suitable training program without help. After my Bowen Island swim and a successful training year in 2009, I felt I understood what Mike meant and was comfortable with the regimen I was planning for 2010. It never hurts to ask advice, though, so I decided to seek feedback from successful Channel swimmers. I'd tried that earlier, in one-on-one conversations and by posting questions in the Channel chat room, but those efforts mostly resulted in quick, less-than-useful anecdotes. "I swam until I couldn't" or "Put your head down and get on with it" are colorful responses (and very English) but not particularly helpful. After all, I "put my head down and got on with it" in 2008 and ended up barely conscious, unceremoniously dragged and dumped into the pilot boat.

In an attempt to get a broad sense of the experiences of successful Channel swimmers, I decided to distribute a survey to as many Channel swimmers as I could find and aggregate their responses for a view of what people had *done*, not what they said.

Though I often work with numbers, I'm not a statistician, so the survey results weren't scientifically compiled. Nonetheless, one morning in January when it was too cold to swim, my kids were with my ex-wife, Barb was working, and peace and quiet reigned in my household, I opened a bag of Reese's Peanut Butter Cups and began to work my way through the survey results. The exercise confirmed the soundness of my plan in some ways and drove me to augment it in others. Some of the comments caused me to choke on my Reese's—particularly the one that called Michael Phelps a wimp.

Survey Participants

- United States   41%
- United Kingdom   32%
- Australia   6%
- Ireland   6%
- Italy   3%
- South Africa   3%
- Mexico   6%
- Japan   3%

Twenty-eight Channel swimmers participated in my little survey, and they had completed a total of thirty-five swims. The swimmers broke down like this:

- Female—52%
- Male—48%
- Average Age—39
    o Oldest—57
    o Youngest—16

Relatively speaking, the group had less open-water swimming experience than I expected:

- 18% between 1-2 years of open-water experience at the time of their swim
- 39% 3-5 years
- 43% 5+ years

I started open-water swimming in the early nineties, in preparation for my first triathlon, but that was relatively easy stuff compared to training for the Channel. As of early 2010, I had five years of focused open-water experience.

"How long did it take?" I asked those I surveyed.

Average swim was 13 hours, 15 minutes.

Fastest was 9 hours.

Slowest was 22 hours, 14 minutes.

Wow! Nine hours is impressive and inspired my envy.

But the twenty-two-hour answer inspired outright awe. Fighting a war of attrition against the waters of the Channel, feeding on liquid feed laced with saltwater, shoulders stroking endlessly over 70,000 times—nearly a full day and night? Channel swimming is a sport where it's more difficult to go slowly than to go fast.

"Why did you do it?" I asked.

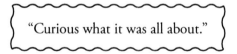

"Curious what it was all about."

- 48% for "the challenge"

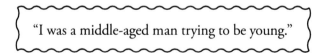

"I was a middle-aged man trying to be young."

- 33% because they were lifelong swimmers and the Channel is swimming's pinnacle

- 6% for the same reason George Mallory gave about climbing Everest: "Because it's there."
- 4% to raise money for charity
- And 9% for other reasons

"When I was a child, I saw a film with a lady called Esther Williams in it about swimming the channel and I told my mum one day I would like to do that, and at the age of forty I did it."

I asked whether they had used Channel grease (a mix of Vaseline and lanolin) or other lubricants. Everyone except one swimmer had done so. Most used these mixes simply for chafing protection, and nobody mentioned any insulating properties, contrary to popular perceptions born of pictures of 1950s' Channel swimmers covered in chunky grease.

I wondered how they fed on their swims. An overwhelming number, 90 percent, used some combination of one of the relatively new sports beverages or feeds introduced over the last twenty years. Only 10 percent relied on real honest-to-God food.

I wanted to know where and how much my fellow swimmers trained for their swims.

Duncan Heenan—14 hrs, 58 minutes, 1988

My Channel obsession started in 1983, when I decided to run in the London Marathon. My daughter, then nine, said glibly that *anyone* could do that . . . . I brooded on her dismissive attitude . . . and later announced that I would do something really hard—swim the English Channel! The family did not take me seriously, and when I started going missing for long training sessions and coming back exhausted late at night, for a while my wife even thought it was a cover for an affair.

My first attempt in 1984 was a real failure . . . so when we tried again on the next available tide, I had not slept for forty-eight hours but still felt I had to make the attempt. At 2:00 a.m., after just three hours in the water, I was badly stung in and around the mouth and face by jellyfish and soon became too ill to continue. Despite the bitter disappointment, I had gained a love of the sport during a year's hard training, and I knew I had not even given it a fair try. So I kept swimming and competing on the BLDSA (*ed. note: the British Long Distance Swimming Association*) circuit, and in 2006, as soon as I could afford another go, I tried again. This time, in eleven hours I got to within five miles of France, but after thirteen hours I was seven miles off, and being pushed back by the tide. I was willing to continue, but the weather was cutting up rough, and the team on the boat persuaded me to abandon the attempt. This left me with the feeling that, with the right luck, I could do it, so in 1988, just before my fortieth birthday, I tried again.

I set off from Cap Griz Nez (*ed. note: Heenan started from France, something the French Coast Guard no longer allows*) at 06:06 on 7 September, with my long-suffering wife in the boat almost as nervous as me. After three hours I was sick, and bouts of this lasted two hours, leaving me unable to eat any solids all day, but I survived on chicken soup, Lucozade, and honey. The actual swim was fairly uneventful and really quite boring, with the added frustration of not being able to see the English coast until we were only four miles off, due to the haze. However, fourteen hours fifty-eight minutes after starting, I climbed on to the rocks at Folkestone Warren, six miles up the coast from Dover, where I was aiming at, due to the tide pushing me westward. I vowed "never again," as I had what I wanted.

The average respondent trained by swimming thirty-four kilometers per week, or just over twenty-one miles. The highest mileage training routine was about forty miles per week, while the most efficient routine was just nine miles per week.

My own routine was about fifteen to twenty miles per week, punctuated by the weeks when I did very long swims, some thirty to thirty-five miles total.

So I felt okay about that aspect of my regimen.

The swimmers who responded to the survey completed about 56 percent of their training in pools and 44 percent in open water, largely due to the exigencies of winter. Almost half the swimmers noted that their winters were 100 percent pool and their summers were 100 percent open water.

My routine was about the same. As soon as it got warm and light enough to swim safely, I abandoned the concrete prison with lane lines painted on the floor called "pool" and embraced Mother Nature. I actually had grown to hate training in a pool.

According to the survey, 72 percent of the respondents' pool time was spent doing intense speed work (vs. simple swimming back and forth), and 62 percent of them did their pool training as part of a swim team of some sort.

While I was doing speed work and swam regularly with a group of friends at my pool, I never swam with a team and didn't intend to. I'd tried that a few years earlier, but my work and parenting responsibilities made the team's rigid training schedule too difficult.

I was comfortable with that difference, but the answers to my next question raised a red flag.

"How much of your open-water training was in saltwater?" I asked.

Two thirds of the swimmers spent between 75 and 100 percent of their time in saltwater.

Since Lake Washington was just a couple of miles from my home and my ocean training was way up in Bellingham Bay, eighty-five miles to the north, more than 65 percent of my training took place in freshwater. I'd have to work on that.

Then I asked, "How much of your open-water training was in cold water (below 65 degrees Fahrenheit/18 degrees Celsius)?"

Eighty-eight percent of the swimmers had done more than 50 percent of their training in cold water (none in wetsuits).

Just like me.

"What was the most difficult thing about swimming the Channel?"

"COLD!"

The responses varied widely. My favorite was from one of the youngest swimmers in the survey, a teenage girl:

> *"After landing on the beach, I had to swim back to the boat because it was too rough to take the little boat in with me. The waves kept slamming me against the pier, and I got real cut up, as well as losing my goggles. I kept thinking 'and Michael Phelps whined when his goggles leaked in a pool . . . what a pansy!'"*

"My swim was supposed to be nine hours long *(ed note: i.e. that was the time the swimmer planned for it to take)*, and that's what I had mentally prepared for. The current changed early, making the swim four hours longer than my pilot said. Getting past the ten-hour mark was the hardest thing for me, and knowing I still had three hours to go was hard, especially when they kept saying I only had one hour left."

Some spoke about the difficulties of swimming through the night in the dark. Some had other troubles.

"On my first channel attempt last September, I had to be taken from the water by the pilot, as one of my crew fell on board the boat and was promptly knocked unconscious. The pilot was ordered to return to shore by the Coast Guard so that he could receive medical treatment. Now, when I got out, I was the only one who was not seasick, and I had to do some first aid as two of my crew had already gotten sick on top of their injured friend. At one stage, all of them took turns getting sick on each other. It's funny now, but not at the time. He was assessed by the paramedics and released into my care. The symptoms of concussion and seasickness are very similar. When we returned to Dover, the swim was declared a no-swim and wiped from the record. I went back the following week, and the weather was unswimmable."

Some apparently had no trouble at all.

"I had little difficulty. I had a near-perfect day in the Channel. Conditions perhaps could not have been better. Very fortunate . . . it was beautiful. I did get physically tired, and my neck was very strained. At one point, I felt my blood sugar was low, and I knew there was an error in my feeding. But I felt it early and asked for a stronger mix, which was done, and I recovered. It helped to know ahead of time about the six-to-seven-hour zone, when the body transitions to burning fat and the symptoms. I was able to swim through that time. At the end of my swim, I felt very strong."

That's what I was hoping for: a perfect day in the English Channel. I sat back and contemplated the survey responses and the empty bag of Reese's Peanut Butter Cups on the desk in front of me. Both had fed me in ways I hoped would help when I had my day in the water. Reflecting on the survey feedback, I still felt good about my training routine. I decided to tweak my ocean-versus-lake swimming ratio, but I felt I was otherwise on the right path.

In the warm silence of the peaceful house, I slipped into a daydream about my Channel swim. I was about two hundred yards from the French beach and basking in the moment of realization that I'd make it. I saw the rocky shore ahead; my pilot boat was bobbing in the rolling surf behind me; my crew was cheering. I looked down and saw wisps of the seabed beneath me, with starfish littering the bottom. I smiled underwater like a Cheshire cat and wept like a father of the bride. Just fifty yards, twenty-five yards, ten yards, I was almost there, so close . . .

Downstairs, I heard the garage door open, and then Barb called out cheerfully, "Mikey, I'm home!" My vision of the French beach dissipated slowly, and I settled back into the here and now, with eight months of hard training ahead before I'd have my chance to see France from the water for real. I smiled to myself and hollered back downstairs, "We need to go to the grocery store, honey. I'm out of Reese's!"

Chapter 16

Lisa Cummins

"How far did you go?" asked my friend Mike Blume one Saturday morning at the Pro Club in Bellevue.

"Not far, 3,500 yards. I'm resting for the next few weeks," I said. "I didn't take it easy enough in November and December, and I need some recuperation before I get serious this year."

"When's that?"

"March 1. You? You doing the spin class today?"

"Yeah, it's a good class and gets my heart rate up in a way our pool workouts don't. But . . . it doesn't do the same thing for me as swimming. I'm a swimmer, and not swimming sort of negates who I am, you know?"

I did know. Mike had pretty much summed up the lingering torture of every sports injury I've ever had. The injuries generally happen because once I get going, I never want to stop—I don't even know how to stop. Obsessions and addictions run in my family, and this approach to sports is surely mine. Swimming was me, and I couldn't stop until I succeeded at swimming the Channel. Judging by my results to date, I'd been going about the whole English Channel thing pretty badly. Winston Churchill once said, "You can always count on Americans to do the right thing once they've exhausted all the alternatives," and that pretty much summed up my training for the Channel. I was hoping to get past the alternatives at last and do the right thing.

Lisa Cummins skipped the crappy alternatives that I had so far wallowed in and went right to the success. A successful Channel swimmer who took a unique approach to her first attempt, Lisa set out to do a double crossing without having done a single one. While deep in training for her first Channel swim, she decided that swimming to France wasn't enough—so she intensified her regimen and doubled her goal. She was the first woman to complete a double without having first done a single, and only one man had beaten her to it. She was also the first Irish person to accomplish a double crossing.

Lisa was twenty-seven and had a PhD in computer science when she swam back and forth across the English Channel. At the time of her swim, she was only the twentieth person in history to have double-crossed. She was born and raised in County Cork, Ireland, a verdant chunk of land that rims the bottom of Ireland, known as the "Rebel County" for the role its strong-willed inhabitants played in both the Irish War of Independence in the early 1920s and the attempted overthrow of the English throne that became the War of the Roses in the late 1400s.

Standing about five foot seven, with a cheerful, toothy smile—particularly after a pint or a swim—Lisa got her start in sports at about seven or eight, when she learned to swim. She was lifeguarding by the time she was ten or eleven and teaching swimming by the time she was fifteen. She swam at least twice per week in high school and rowed competitively for five years.

Lisa's English Channel journey began in earnest while she was on an internship in California. She had been thinking of attempting the Channel when she read Lynne Cox's iconic book *Swimming to Antarctica*. She returned to County Cork in September 2007 and ran a marathon, accomplishing another goal she'd been determined to reach during her twenties. She hated that experience, though, and shelved running in favor of swimming in the open sea.

Lisa built up her distance and fitness in the summer of 2008, working with a coach who had trained eight other successful Channel swimmers; Ned Denison. Her first swim of the year was in March, when the water was only about forty-five degrees Fahrenheit (7 degrees Celsius). Her longest swim that year was eight miles in the open sea, and by October 2008 she was swimming about twenty miles (32 kilometers) per week. At that point, she was still focused on doing a one-way crossing.

The winter of 2008-09, Lisa took a break from training, and the idea of a double crossing began to germinate. She kept it quiet to avoid any negative reaction from other swimmers who might consider the idea foolhardy and try to talk her out of it, but she ramped up her training accordingly. By March 2009, she was regularly swimming seventy-five kilometers per week (approximately 47 miles) and doing twenty-five-kilometer (approximately 15 miles) pool sessions. Feeling ready, she called Lance and Mike Oram and asked them if they would change her booking to a double.

"We often get such requests," Mike Oram told me. "In cases like Lisa, we say 'yes' and then check out the swimmer's background from our various sources. Pilots will often accept a request for a crossing regardless of any history, as it is a sport that is full of unknowns."

After talking to Lisa's training group in Ireland, Mike and Lance agreed to change the booking to a double.

By the time Easter rolled around, word had gotten out, and people were talking about Lisa's impending two-way. She was dismayed that a number of swimmers lived up to her expectations and tried to talk her out of the double crossing, but she was not dissuaded.

"I felt that if I only made it to France and not the return, I'd still be a Channel swimmer, and I'd have learned from the experience," she explained.

In April 2009, Lisa participated in SwimTrek in Malta, a popular swimming vacation/training trip coached by Freda Streeter and regularly attended by Channel swimmers. She spent the next four months in the sea, training six days per week in open water. Her short training days were about four hours in length, while her long days could stretch to fourteen. The water averaged about eleven to twelve degrees Celsius (about 51-54 degrees Fahrenheit).

The average swimmer burns about 800 calories per hour while swimming, so Lisa was burning about 3,000 calories on short days and 11,000 on longer ones. She had set a target of maintaining about twenty extra pounds of body fat throughout her training, so she couldn't afford to undereat. Including the calories she burned during non-swimming hours, she had to consume between 5,500 and 12,500 calories per day to keep her weight where she wanted it. And since she was spending so many hours in the water, she had scant time to consume the necessary nutrition.

The press has regularly had fun illustrating the diets of Olympic swimmers like Michael Phelps, who also consumes 12,000 calories per day during training. But Phelps doesn't need to maintain twenty extra pounds of body fat to stave off death-by-hypothermia—so Lisa faced a bigger challenge. To consume that many calories per day, Channel swimmers eat as much as they can of everything, but often resort to calorie-dense foods like ice cream and sweets to maintain their required daily intake.

Her training complete, body fat layered on, and confidence high, Lisa began her swim on September 19, 2009, at 10:35 a.m. from Samphire Hoe. Samphire Hoe is a fishing, hiking, and wildlife park built on the massive concrete lid where the Chunnel emerges from underneath the

White Cliffs and speeds off to France. The conditions were absolutely calm at the start, and so was Lisa.

The first four hours were easy: easy feeding, easy swimming—happy swimmer.

Then the demons started dancing in Lisa's mind. She regretted signing up for the two-way. There was no way she'd make it back. Thirty-plus hours of swimming? What had she been thinking? She knew then she couldn't do a double crossing. But she also knew that she could do at least fourteen hours, because she'd done that regularly in training. So she focused on that, and she didn't share her doubts with her crew.

About fourteen and a half hours into her swim, at 12:50 p.m., after spending four hours staring at and swimming toward a lighthouse on the French coast, she landed in France.

It had been easy so far.

She walked up on the beach and was surprised to find some French lads partying there. In the water behind her, Lance Oram blared the pilot boat horn to signify her successful one-way swim.

According to CS&PF rules, Lisa was allowed ten minutes on the French beach before beginning her return swim. She spent that time drinking water, sucking a lozenge to sooth her saltwater-battered mouth, and regreasing herself for the second leg of her journey. Nobody else was allowed to touch her.

The way Lisa remembers it, she got only about seven minutes on the beach instead of the ten she was allowed by the rules. For some reason, her crew forced her to restart early. When you've swum twenty-two miles and are about to swim twenty-two miles back home, three extra minutes of rest matters.

When her crew chief, Tanya Harding, head coach at Elton Training and Swimming Club, called, "Time!" she walked back into the water and started swimming home, promising herself she wouldn't get out until she reached England or Lance forced her to get out.

The Channel felt cold.

The lighthouse was now off to her left, sunrise some hours off.

The swim back was tough.

The sun rose on a cloudy day, and she began having serious problems with her left shoulder. At every feed stop, it would seize up, and she was forced to spend five minutes stretching it out. To combat this, the crew lengthened her feed intervals to forty-five minutes from thirty. That didn't help the shoulder much, but it minimized the delays due to the stretching sessions.

She'd hoped for a helpful tide on the way back, but that never materialized.

It seemed to take forever to reach the separation zone and then the English shipping lane. At thirty-one hours into the swim, Lance called down to her that they needed to hit land soon or they were facing an additional eight hours of swimming, fighting tides all the way.

So, after thirty-one straight hours of the toughest kind of open-water swimming, Lance asked Lisa to start sprinting.

In order to summon the requisite strength for that, Lisa wanted to know where she was in the Channel. Many Channel pilots won't answer this question for fear it will discourage the swimmer, but Lance simply replied that they were two miles off the English coast.

At the next feed, he said they were one mile off the coast. At the next one, he said they were 600 meters off the coast.

"Where am I going?" she asked the crew anxiously, unable to see more than a few feet ahead in the darkness and not certain of her progress.

"Shut up and swim," she was told, not unkindly.

At thirty-five hours and twenty minutes after she entered the English Channel at Samphire Hoe, Lisa landed near the Nuclear Power Station at Dungeness, twenty miles down the coast from where she started. She remembers Lance yelling for her to get out of the water.

Lisa crawled out of the Channel on her hands and knees, checked to make sure she had cleared the water, and then collapsed.

After a moment, her shoulder seizing and her entire body and spirit exhausted, Lisa came to the realization that there was no dinghy to carry her back to the boat for her return trip to Dover, as is sometimes the case. Lance felt that it would be safer to have her swim back to the pilot boat. Many feel that keeping swimmers horizontal after so many hours in the water is safer than having them suddenly stand or sit and start recirculating cold blood pooled at their extremities. So, she summoned her formidable will and strength once more, picked herself up, and walked back into the water to swim out to the boat.

Two and a half hours later, Lisa Cummins walked off Lance's boat at Dover Marina and into the record books. She was enveloped and cheered by her family and friends, and back in County Cork, an eager press.

"Mike?"

I came back suddenly from my reflections about Lisa's achievement and found Mike Blume staring at me.

"Sorry, I was thinking about a Channel swimmer I know for a moment there," I said, reflecting that I'd do well to emulate Lisa's resolve. "I'd like to do that spin class with you sometime, but I think it'll have to wait. I need to rest and recuperate my shoulders, and in any case, I can't afford to burn the extra calories."

"Anytime," Mike said amiably, and walked off with a wave.

I stood for a moment and pictured Lisa landing in England after her double crossing and crawling ashore, and then I pictured myself landing in France similarly. As always, it gave me chills.

Chapter 17

Tim's Tale

I met Tim Strange at Swimmer's Beach, but I can't remember exactly when. Maybe that's because Tim exudes such an easy friendliness that to meet him is to feel as if you've known him forever. Walking onto Dover Beach with him is an experience: everyone gives him a wave, and most come to chat. A few minutes after I met Tim, I started thinking about asking him to be on my crew.

Tim swam the Channel on August 16 and 17, 2005, finishing in sixteen hours and thirty-two minutes, becoming the 796th swimmer to cross. Tanya Harding was his crew chief, Kim Morritt assisted, and Lance Oram performed the piloting honors. In addition to Tim's crossing, August 17 was an auspicious day—it was the tenth anniversary of Tim's mother's reprieve: an all-clear from her doctors after a bout with cancer.

To get to know Tim a bit better, I invited him to join me in a Starbucks in London's Trafalgar Square, just under a statue of Lord Byron squinting at the horizon. I was waiting for him and aimlessly watching the tourist hordes snap photos when I spied him walking across a pedestrian zebra toward me, smiling broadly under his Hugh Grant mop of brown hair and wearing the used work shirt of a cemetery worker named Bob.

Tim grew up one of three sons of a nurse and a teacher in a suburb called Bromley, about ten miles southeast of London. It was a comfortable life, as evidenced by his choice to settle down with his wife, Caroline, and raise his own three kids just a few miles from his childhood home. Life in Bromley provided the sort of comfortable foundation that often produces easygoing, confident, well-adjusted people like Tim.

Tim was a swimmer growing up, but not a competitive one. He remembers his parents piling everyone into the family caravan and spending summer after summer at Folkestone, just down the coast from Dover. These seashore sojourns instilled in him a love of being in the sea; becoming a swimmer seemed like the natural order of things. He was just eight years old when he proclaimed to his father that he would swim the Channel someday.

Tim describes himself as "easygoing, flexible, diplomatic when I have to be, determined, stubborn, quite blunt, and not a crowd-follower." My shorter version: he's a friendly nonconformist.

"I haven't done the career thing," he tells me over coffee. "I've pursued different jobs, work that I find enjoyable, and volunteer work." Tim pays his bills through photography and teaching at the Priory School, which is known for its somewhat unorthodox approach to education.

I asked him to describe his Channel experience.

His day started early, he told me, in Portsmouth, about three hours from Dover, where he and his wife Caroline had been on holiday with his family. After a call from his pilot to confirm that his swim was going to happen that day, he nervously loaded up on porridge and bananas and hit the road to Dover. His lack of sleep and the long drive in the wee hours played havoc with his mind as he sped toward the starting point.

It was a very warm day and relatively late in the morning—about ten minutes after nine—when Tim swam off Shakespeare Beach. He wouldn't touch land again until after 1:00 a.m. the following day. The Channel was very flat, with none of the curdling swells and heaving it's known for.

Tim had already participated in three Channel relays with Tanya Harding, the same crew chief that guided Lisa Cummins across the Channel in 2004 and 2006. The scene at those had always been relaxed, with Tanya allowing people to mill about the Harbor parking lot for an hour or so before they were off. For Tim's solo, Tanya was more of a taskmaster, and they were on their way minutes after his arrival. Having organized many Channel swims, Tanya knows that doubt can consume a swimmer's mental state before a swim, and she wanted Tim to get going before too much loitering fatally infected his self-confidence.

"I trusted her implicitly," Tim says of Tanya. "Other than my parents, my brothers, and my wife, I think Tanya knows me probably best emotionally because she's pushed me to my limits. She's seen me get upset, she's seen me cry, she's seen me swear, she's seen me, you know, go halfway down Lake Windermere, the very first time I ever did a long swim, and tell her, 'You can forget the Channel. There's no way I'm doing that.' She laughed at me at the time and said, 'That's funny.'"

With Tim and the crew aboard, Tim's Channel pilot, Lance Oram, navigated his boat, the *Sea Satin,* out around to Shakespeare Beach, something he'd done countless times. When he stopped the boat, Tanya turned to Tim and ordered, "Jump off the boat," for his official start. From the transom, Tim was heartened to see that his parents, Caroline, and his stepdaughter had managed to get there to see him off. Tim dropped nervously off the back of the boat and swam to his family. They had a quick chat, telling Tim they were nervous too, and that it looked choppy despite seeming relatively calm. They promised to meet him on the other side, in France.

Tim was soon on his way, emigrating to France. "Mentally, I was 100 percent ready," he says, but he admits to wondering in awe, "Am I really doing it now?" The cold water cascaded along his body, and he settled in for his long day of swimming.

Tim spent the first couple hours grimacing through a headache brought on by his goggles, which were pinching his head too tightly. Goggles are a special curse for open-water swimmers. No matter how many times you adjust them in training, they never quite fit or feel right on a big swim day. They pinch, chafe, cut your nose, leak, or fog up. The only thing worse than wearing goggles in the Channel is the unthinkable prospect of *not* wearing them. And for Channel swimmers, there's a special goggle hell. While the days of Channel swimmers slathered in chunky Channel grease are gone, most still cover themselves with sunblock and use Channel grease here and there to avoid chafing. The mix of these substances gets all over the swimmers' hands and makes it difficult to adjust the goggles without fouling them and making it impossible to see. To avoid swimming blind for ten to twenty hours, Tim had four spare sets on the boat.

In addition to the goggle-ache, Tim was nauseous. His big breakfast, plus a chocolate bar and cuppa tea on board before jumping in, were hitting him hard. An average-sized person can digest approximately 250 to 300 calories per hour during heavy exertion. During a workout, the blood circulation required to absorb anything more than that amount is mostly busy feeding working muscles instead of helping the intestines digest food. In addition, counterintuitively, the body digests complex carbohydrates more easily than other foods. Too many simple carbs or proteins, and the rate of digestion slows even further, to under 250 to 300 calories per hour. Basically, the food in Tim's stomach had coalesced into an undigested lump. Thankfully, his first liquid feed wasn't scheduled until almost two hours into the swim, so he had a chance to burn off the bomb in his stomach, albeit uncomfortably. He even managed to change his goggles at the feed.

The crew was watching Tim conscientiously, but that didn't stop them from frying up some bacon sandwiches on board the *Sea Satin*. Knowing that his own diet over the next fifteen to twenty hours would consist of gritty, flavorless liquid forced through a mouth swollen grotesquely by saltwater, Tim was feeling a bit grumpy about bacon odor wafting off the boat.

After his first feed, Tim realized with a surreal jolt that he was actually out in the open English Channel—swimming it! He settled down and began to enjoy himself, humming a few songs that he'd heard on the ride to Dover that morning. Olympic swimmer Michael Phelps once said in an interview that he habitually replayed tunes in his head during swimming; Tim was no different.

At about three or four hours into the swim, Tim's shoulder felt strained, so Tanya included some painkillers in one of his cups. The pain abated, and a bit of boredom set in. He tried to focus on his stroke mechanics and maintaining his normal pace of fifty-three to fifty-four strokes per minute, so that his shoulders would hold up for the duration.

Time passed.

At the sixth or seventh hour, Tim started to cross the separation zone between the English and French shipping lanes. He'd been told by Ali Streeter that, since the Channel was relatively shallow in a number of places, you could usually hear the pebbles on the seabed rattling against each other in the movement of the tide and shipping traffic. He listened and stopped for a second to proclaim to his crew with surprise, "I can hear the pebbles on the beach!"

Tanya and the crew misheard him, thinking he'd claimed to hear the waves crashing on shore in France, still more than nine hours away. They wondered if Tim was losing his grasp on reality and began watching him more closely.

Time passed.

Not untypically, the seventh and eighth hours were more difficult. This is the point at which a Channel swimmer has been swimming for a very long time but is still facing something in the neighborhood of half of the swim. That reality hits like a ferry in the forehead. In his eighth hour, realizing the full magnitude of what he'd signed up for, Tim started to hate the English Channel with a passion.

"My, this is tough, isn't it?" he asked Tanya on his next feed, breathing heavily.

"Yeah, of course it is," she replied, looking at him as if he were simpleminded. "It's the *Channel*."

Figuring he needed cheering up, Tanya read him some text messages that had come from his mom, aunt, Freda Streeter, Caroline, and members of his swim club. "Oh, your aunt just texted saying, 'Keep going, keep going,'" Tanya said. At first, Tim figured Tanya was making this one up. Other than his immediate family, he'd been careful not to tell anyone that he'd be in the Channel that day because "If you're a failure, you won't have to tell anyone." Word had spread nonetheless, and Tim's swim was being closely followed.

When Tim told me about the messages of support, I thought, *I should have tried that in 2008, should have asked friends and family to text my crew with messages of support during my swim.* In anticipation of my own Channel swims, I had opted to write a blog—which spread like wildfire on a windblown prairie—but once I was in the water, that did little for my morale. It also turned me into "that guy who tried to swim the Channel twice and didn't make it."

The sun began to set in the eleventh hour of Tim's swim. It was completely gone in an hour, and he was feeling alone in the dark, endlessly swimming. The crew needed to be able to see him, of course, so they called him over to the boat to apply luminescent light sticks to his cap and swimsuit.

Ignoring his pained and cramping muscles, he pushed his backside up in the air so Tanya could pin the light sticks on his ass.

That didn't sound like fun, so I stopped Tim's reflections for a moment and made myself a note to pin light sticks on myself before my swim so I wouldn't be forced to float face down in pain halfway through my swim with my backside in the air, waiting for my crew to poke the backside of my suit with a sharp pin.

"That's when you kind of get depressed," Tim said, looking off into space. "I remember I had cramps pretty much everywhere: all the way down my stomach, down both thighs, into my calves . . . I knew in my head that if I stopped for a feed, went upright and treaded water, or reached out to grab something, it was all just going to seize up."

Tim told Tanya, "I can't feed anymore. I've got to swim because I've got this cramp. It just really hurts. I just want to keep going. All I want to do is get to France."

"You have to feed," Tanya said adamantly.

The feeds just kept coming, Tim explains. "Take a sip, swim a few strokes, take another sip, swim a few more strokes, have a bite of chocolate or something, and then a few more strokes." As the dark intensified, Tim crawled methodically, one stroke at a time, through the French shipping lane. Freda Streeter, who'd coached and cajoled him on Swimmer's Beach, radioed Tanya and asked when she thought Tim would get to the finish. Tanya relayed Freda's call to Tim, and it buoyed his spirits for a few moments. A few moments later, he'd forgotten it and was once again just stroking to France, one hand at a time.

In the gloomy dark, Tim saw lights on the French coast—but his depth perception was off and he thought the lights came from passing ships, that he was still in the French shipping lane. He thought he had farther to go than he actually did, and, time having taken its toll on his easygoing nature, it pissed him off. One set of lights in particular vexed him because he thought they were coming from the Varne Lightship, an automated set of lights set permanently on the Varne sandbank in the middle of the Channel to help ships navigate the waterway. The Varne sandbank is about nine miles off the coast of southeast England. If that's what he was seeing, it meant he was only halfway across the Channel.

"Would you please radio that damn boat and tell it to move?" he barked at his crew, exasperated.

"I'm afraid we can't do that—it's the lighthouse on the French coast," Tanya said. "It's just two or three miles away!" That lifted his spirits for a moment.

Time passed.

The fourteenth hour of Tim's odyssey rolled around. He was tired of his feeds, had lost all sense of time, and didn't know how often he was being called over to the boat. He remembers thinking, *God, please give me anything but Maxim* (Maxim is the liquid feed Tim used on his swim) *at my next feed! Anything, God, just no more Maxim!*

The "flexible" aspect of Tim's nature was absent for the moment.

Time passed.

Tanya relayed a message to Tim. "Lance says to speed up or you're not gonna make it! You need 100 percent effort now."

"Are my mom and dad there? Is Caroline there?" he asked uncertainly, looking toward the beach. He put his head down and swam.

Time passed.

The end was close, and he began to dream about touching bottom, walking in France. He looked again at the lighthouse lights that he'd been watching for hours and hours and thought, *I'm not on target; I'm not on target in the bay!* He kept stroking anyway, as hard as he could, in the direction he'd been pointed.

The French lighthouse on the outer edge of the bay was gone, he realized with surprise. Had he missed it? Was he off course? He looked up and around and saw the lighthouse behind him, and the French cliffs standing silent guard in the dark night just ahead. He was closing in on the beach.

For his mother, the moment was extra special. As I mentioned, Tim's swim was on the tenth anniversary of her reprieve after a bout of cancer. She had realized at that point that she'd live long enough to see her son swim the Channel, and now he was doing it. When she finally spotted him from the shore, she couldn't wait—she ran into the water to meet him yelling, "Come on, come on, Tim!"

"Don't touch him; he has to finish on his own!" Tanya commanded loudly.

After more than sixteen hours, Tim stood and walked ashore, toward the open arms and smiling faces of his family. At that moment, he did the only thing he could think of to mark the moment: he struck a goofy bodybuilder pose he'd done for his mom when he was a kid. His parents had the champagne and flutes ready for the celebration, and his father handed him a full glass.

Tim's story sounded great. I thought, hoped, my own story would be similar when I finally made it.

"When I walked up that beach, I felt I could do anything," he said. "I felt as if I could turn around and swim all the way back to England."

As we finished our coffee and chatted like the friends we'd become, I wondered again if Tim would come along with me on my swim. I wanted him there, though at that point, my 2010 crew was pretty solid so I hadn't asked him. I filed away the thought for the moment, hoping something might happen to allow him to join me.

Chapter 18

Tanya Harding—East-Ender Angel

Since Tanya Harding had successfully coached Sue Pepper, Lisa Cummins, and Tim Strange, I decided it would be worthwhile to try to learn from her methods. I found that the success rate of her swimmers was virtually perfect: 100 percent of her coached solo swimmers had eventually made it across the Channel. I also wanted to get to know her, if for no other reason than that we'd both been around Channel swimming and knew some of the same people. I saw her at the CS&PF annual general meeting and asked if she'd share some stories over a cup of coffee. That started my education on Tanya.

By her own description, Tanya is an East Ender. If you don't know what that means, the East End of London is a storied section of that most storied city, a place of docks, Cockneys, the Kray Brothers crime family, and locals engaging in a bit of street-smarts skullduggery followed by a cuppa tea at mum's house. The area has gentrified of late, and these days you might catch a glimpse of a transient banker in a shiny suit—but for most East Enders, tradition and family are everything, and change is incremental.

About five foot five, cheerful, and solid, Tanya is mother to a twelve-year-old daughter. She sports a regularly unleashed pixie smile and a trusting manner that encourages comfort from relative strangers. At forty-four, she's the head coach at Elton Training and Swimming Club, and she's been around English Channel swimming a long while. She first came to Dover to swim when she was ten years old. Freda Streeter was already helping Channel swimmers and hanging around Swimmer's Beach, so Tanya soon became fast friends with Freda's daughter Alison, who was there swimming and hanging out with her mum. Tanya, Alison, and many other Channel swimming personalities grew up together, orbiting Channel swimming through their teens, twenties, and into their own parenthood years. All that swimming acclimatization worked, and Tanya became an accomplished competitive swimmer.

Tanya's dad was an electrician and her mum a bookkeeper. Her husband is a London fireman, and Tanya works as a public agency health and safety manager in Dover, having departed the East End years ago in body, if not in spirit. The Elton Club is up near London, so being the coach means lots of motorway miles commuting back and forth on the M20 past sheep, Chunnel power lines, and more sheep.

Tanya has swum six English Channel relays herself. Given her experience and resources, it seems likely that she could have accomplished a solo crossing as well, but she claims never to have had any passion in that direction.

"Relays are fine, but I don't *want* it enough to do a solo, see. You have to want it very badly to be out there by yourself," she explains.

Ten years ago, Tanya turned her attention to helping others reach their dreams when she became head coach at Elton. Since then, she's helped twenty relay teams of kids and adults cross the Channel and has served as coach and crew member to some of the most notable Channel swimmers in history:

- Jackie Cobell, who in less than one year went from geriatric bypass surgery to setting a world record for the longest Channel swim in history (28 hours, 45 minutes).

- Lisa Cummins.

- Ros Hardiman, a polio survivor without the use of her legs, who captured worldwide attention in 2008 when her twenty-five-hour, unsuccessful Channel swim went viral on the Internet. She faltered just 700 meters off the coast and then followed up the next year with a twenty-hour successful crossing.

"What did it feel like pulling Ros out of the water?" I asked.

"Tears," Tanya answered simply. "I had a look to make sure Ros was okay, of course, and then I found a quiet corner on the pilot boat and cried for her."

Tanya's record, after working with twenty relay teams and ten solo swimmers? The opposite of my own Channel attempt record: 100 percent success. (Three of her solo swimmers were unsuccessful on their first attempts, but they all crossed successfully on subsequent swims.) At this point in our coffee chat, I was tempted to put down my notebook and beg Tanya to join my own crew.

When I asked her what it takes to ensure that swimmers will succeed, she said the most important factor is that they have complete faith and trust in her. She reserves absolute control and discretion over training, swim planning, timing, and the arrangements on swim day itself. She tells the swimmer when and where to show up, what to do, and what not to do.

"It has to be that way, or their heads get in the way," Tanya insisted. "If they listen, they succeed."

My mind wandered back to my swim at Bowen Island, where my own head got in the way until my crew forced me to finish the swim. I began to appreciate Tanya's methods.

Tanya starts each year at Elton with between sixty and seventy swimmers, some left over from the previous year and some new ones. Every one of them has his or her swimming strokes and goals poked and prodded on a one-on-one basis. Tanya finds out what each swimmer's highest hopes are and then devises a plan to help get him or her there, one by one. They relinquish control to Tanya, and she guides them down an appropriate path.

The Elton Club has a long Channel-swimming history, boasting numerous record swims, including the youngest swimmer ever, at eleven years of age, so there are always swimmers at Elton aspiring to cross the Channel. After a winter of training them at the club, Tanya brings her swimmers to Dover Harbor about a week before the season begins. The water is painfully cold in late April, in the high forties (F), but Tanya likes the fact that they have the beach to themselves and she has the swimmers' full attention. Under those conditions, she can assess each one carefully.

Most of the swimmers are teenagers, and if you've ever tried to get a child to brush his teeth or take a bath, you can imagine trying to coax a group of teenagers to put on skimpy swimsuits on a freezing public beach and plunge into sub-fifty(F)-degree water. Tanya manages it every year.

She starts them off with short swims, a couple of ten—to fifteen-minute sessions to acclimate them to the water and assess their conditioning. If need be, she gets in the water and swims alongside them. She gradually increases the swimmers' time in the water throughout May, June, and July. For the ones planning solo Channel swims, she needs to know how they might do in a variety of circumstances. Can they handle night swims? What happens after they breach five to six hours in the water? How well do they handle the feeds she decides upon? In late July, she enrolls the solo swimmers in the ten-mile Lake Windermere swim sponsored by the British Long Distance Swimming Association (BLDSA).

"How do the first-timers handle everything?" I asked her.

Tanya grinned. "Well, sometimes they complain. But they have a choice: they can tread water or they can swim. They're not getting back on the boat because that boat, my boat, is going on without them. They have a choice on the relays, too, as they are standing on the boat waiting their turn. They can go into the water fully dressed or in their swimsuit—but they're bloody well getting in!"

Sounds harsh, but remember that 100-percent success rate. The swimmers need someone to follow blindly, someone to fear—or their heads get in the way. For that reason, Tanya doesn't let family members come on the swims. Never mind that deep down, Tanya's a softy. Remember, she was the one crying when one of her swimmers, a disabled swimmer named Ros Hardiman that we'll talk more about later, didn't make it to France. Ros was too busy planning her next attempt to bother crying.

I had one last question. "Why do you do this? Why spend every summer of every year, year after year, doing this?"

"It's the beaming faces of those kids when we get them to France," Tanya said with a dreamy smile. "There's nothing like it."

Chapter 19

Training in February

February rolled in and injuries continued to taunt me, particularly my right shoulder. The injury was still relatively mild, but frustrating in that I knew it would take rest and rehab to alleviate it. I was confident that it wouldn't derail my swim in August, but it almost completely disrupted my training: I was swimming only one or two days per week. I cross-trained extensively, spending hours and hours on elliptical machines and stretching. The Channel paperwork that needed to be completed ahead of time kept me busy, too, but that wasn't a satisfactory substitute.

Hearing news of my fellow Channel swimmers excitedly ramping up their training heightened my frustration. I was getting left behind, and it was driving me nuts.

I thought what I was suffering from was probably tendonitis—which starts as a bit of an ache and some swelling, but can become debilitating if you continue to train hard. To complicate matters, there were times when being back in the water made the pain subside. And I had the experience at Bowen Island to look back on, where my shoulder problem was mostly in my mind. My challenge lay in knowing when to train through the pain and when to rest.

I often get injured while training in a pool, and have always thought that might be because pools are so much warmer than open water. Perhaps the cold open water acts like ice on my tired muscles, an anti-inflammatory agent. What's more, the tight confines of the pool tend to restrict my stroke, and pool workouts include more sprints, which can strain tired and overused muscles and tendons. Doing 300 to 400 flip turns on longer pool workouts doesn't do my lower back muscles any favors, either.

I was planning to do my first open-water swim of the year on February 27 with Dale in Bellingham Bay. But despondent from lack of swimming and intrigued by the notion that the frigid Puget Sound waters in early February would ease my aggravated shoulder, I decided to bring forward my "opening day" to the weekend of February 6. The water would be about forty-six degrees Fahrenheit, but I had a sleeveless ("Farmer John") wetsuit that would allow me to stay in long enough to manage a decent workout. Some open-water swimmers can train in those temperatures for hours at a time but I can't; fifty-three degrees Fahrenheit is about my limit for swimming longer than three hours.

I guess that brings us to wetsuits. As you can imagine, given the hundred-plus-year tradition of swimmers not wearing anything more than a standard swimsuit (plus cap and goggles), there's a long-raging debate among Channel swimmers about the use of them. If I had to identify the various factions in the debate, they'd look like this:

- Converts. These swimmers think wearing a wetsuit is no big deal. Most in this group have converted from either pool swimming or triathlons, where wetsuits are used to enhance swimming speed.
- Purists. Most of these swimmers have focused exclusively on open water. They are affronted by the buoyancy and cold protection that wetsuits provide and believe that using them amounts to cheating.
- Pragmatists. This is my category. These swimmers are purists at heart but recognize that a wetsuit in February means you can swim longer without being killed by hypothermia—which is good.

We in the pragmatist group don't speak up much, especially in front of purists, for fear of starting a frothy argument. Why set off a multi-hour harangue about how wetsuits are an affront to the traditions laid down by Matthew Webb in 1875, when he became the first human to swim the English Channel wearing a wool swimsuit (ouch!) and basic swim cap?

The issue is legitimately debatable, based on the genuine advantages wetsuits provide. It's been estimated that they can increase a swimmer's speed in the water by as much as 30 percent. And my own experience is that it's *much* easier to float your legs in a wetsuit than it is to kick for an extended time. In addition, the protection from cold they provide is analogous to a boxer wearing armor in a boxing ring. After all, for many of us, much of the challenge of the sport of open-water swimming is in enduring the elements.

The debate over swimming attire was brought into stark relief during the 2008 Beijing Olympics, where the swimmers' high-tech suits helped them break records at a pace that could only be ascribed to the suits, not simply the swimmers' abilities or dedication to training (as impressive as those were).

The argument *for* wetsuits is that they make it possible for more people to participate in open-water swimming and make the sport viable year-round. Converts feel purists should mind their own business and that technology has changed virtually every sport. Remember back in 1986, when Greg LeMond became the first American to win the Tour de France, thanks to the new aero bars? Why should swimming be any different?

In the open-water community, the debate flares whenever someone swims the Channel in a wetsuit and boasts proudly of being an English Channel swimmer in a news interview. The article inevitably makes the rounds on the Internet, and indignant purists light up the chat rooms. My personal sympathies lie with swimmers who do it the traditional way (one swimmer, one standard swimsuit, one swim cap and goggles). And the simple truth is, the only way to do an official swim, certified by one of the two sanctioning bodies, is without a wetsuit. You can't honestly claim to have made an official Channel swim if you did it in a wetsuit. Period.

That said, I do use a wetsuit in the winter. When faced with the choice of swimming in a pool or cross-training when it's cold, I'd prefer to risk the purists' wrath, don the rubber suit, and enjoy the open water.

*   *   *

February 6 dawned in promising fashion with the sun out and birds chirping. My morning newspaper was dry, which is not the usual state of affairs in Seattle in winter. It was cold, though. Leaving for my swim in Lake Washington, I had some trouble with my garage door—it was frozen shut. Sunshine notwithstanding, I didn't think that boded well for the local water temperature. And I was right.

When I got to Madison Park, the water was calmer than heaven and colder than hell. The water was forty-six degrees F. It would be my coldest swim ever.

I got the usual stares while stripping down. Those are fun, I admit. There's a sense of purpose about training for something like the Channel that feels heightened when there are witnesses. Less fun are the questions as I exit the water. I try not to be antisocial, but it's difficult to discuss the water temperature while shivering violently like a condemned leaf. There's also danger involved. Our bodies proactively manage their own circulation when we swim in extreme temperatures. To retain warm blood at our core, the circulation to muscles that are not being used slows down considerably. As we swim, the blood in our extremities becomes much colder than the blood in our core, near our organs. When we emerge from the cold water, our bodies immediately begin to reorganize our circulation to harmonize with the air temperatures. Cold blood in our hands and feet gets pumped toward our hearts. If that process occurs too quickly, we can suffer cardiac arrest. And die.

I have a vision of me lying beachside in my Speedo some winter's day, having just keeled over from heart failure.

"Geez, what happened to him?" somebody will ask.

"Middle-aged guy trying to be young, I guess," someone will answer. "C'mon, kids, step over him and let's feed the geese!"

On that February day, I put aside the vision and focused on the task at hand, getting into the water. (The entry is always the hardest part, even in summer, when the water is much warmer. It's something about shocking the skin, I guess.) I walked in up to my ankles, calves, knees . . . then took a deep breath, slipped in up to my waist, and exhaled. I stood there a moment catching my breath and shivering brutally, and then dipped down, dove under the water, and came up stroking—my normal approach. The water was brutally cold, and I commenced an argument with myself that went something like this:

"Get out!"

"Swim faster, get warm!"

"Get out!"

"Swim!"

And so on. The voices in my head continued that way for about five minutes, until I started getting blessedly numb. The only place that stayed rudely cold was under my arms—probably due to the concentration of blood vessels going through the area and their position facing into the flowing cold water. I glanced up and saw that Mt Rainier, about ninety miles south, was winking majestically through the clouds. That distracted my attention and gave me something to swim toward on my southbound laps of Madison Park Beach. No such luck on the northbound laps, so my thoughts tended to alternate as follows:

F---ing cold!

Wow, that's beautiful.

Holy s---, it's cold!

I'd like to climb that sometime.

And thus it continued, for about thirty minutes. When I started losing articulation of my hands (a sign of impending hypothermia), I swam ashore and walked out quickly, vibrating violently while I tried to warm up. I managed to quell my hands long enough to get dressed and began my drive home, heat on full blast, heated seats set to "bake."

Believe it or not, I actually enjoyed the swim, even the cold. It was exhilarating to be out and in the water, as always. The only lingering frustration was my right shoulder, which didn't feel much better despite the active icing afforded by Lake Washington. I arrived home at odds with myself—elated over the swim but concerned about the injury. I began to worry in earnest about the Channel swim itself.

My right shoulder had the power to spoil my swim—spoil my year.

My crew from my 2010 Channel Attempt cheerful before the challenge
ahead—from left, Brent Hobbs, Evan Humphreys, Ros Hardiman, Dale
McKinnon, Mike Humphreys (the author)

The author contemplates his 4th failed attempt at swimming the Channel
on Mike Oram's *The Gallivant* in August 2012

Brent Hobbs prepares to start the clock at the beginning of the author's swim around Bowen Island

A line of sandals and Crocs awaits swimmers' departure from the water at Swimmer's Beach in Dover; to protect their feet from the rough surface of the stones lining the water's edge.

Dale McKinnon, held in place by Brent Hobbs, leans overboard in rough seas to pass a feed to the author on his 2010 Channel attempt.

Freda Streeter chats with Irene and Barry Wakeham from their vantage point at the top of Swimmer's Beach in Dover

Dale McKinnon parks her hand-made Dory rowboat
after a training session with the author in Bellingham Bay

Channel swimmer Jeffrey Hulett hikes @ Leadville, revisiting the scene
where he successfully completed the grueling Leadville 100,
a 100 mile ultra-marathon running race

Ros Hardiman, one year after her epic 25 hour attempt that ended mere yards from success and French soil, finally successfully finishes swimming the Channel. Disabled due to polio, Ros is seen pulling herself courageously and painfully up onto the rocky French beach to comply with the CS&PF rule that Channel swimmers must clear the water under their own power.

Sue Pepper sits on Swimmer's Beach in Dover preparing for a training session in cold Dover Harbor, seen to the right of Sue in the photo.

The author, Mike Humphreys, seen leaving the water in Dover Harbor after a training swim in 2010. Barry Wakeham is seen to the left of the photo—fulfilling his volunteer role of helping swimmers feed during training, get in and out of the water on the pebbly beach.

Another shot of the author leaving Dover Harbor after a long training swim. Approximately one third of the breadth of Dover Harbor can be seen behind him in the photo.

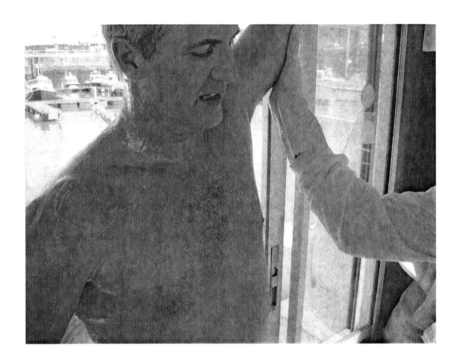

The author shows his distaste at the excessive Channel grease being applied by his crew and friend, Brent Hobbs, before his 2010 Channel attempt. Brent is an adherent of the old school that the more lanolin on Channel swimmers, the better. Most swimmers have abandoned the practice of years ago of heavily greasing up to ward off hypothermia and simply use channel grease to avoid chafing skin in the salty Channel waters.

The author is fed through a bottle on a line thrown into the Channel
by Brent Hobbs and Dale McKinnon

Cliff Golding, crew on the author's 2012 Channel attempt,
rests and recuperates after his second successful Channel swim in 2003.
Like the author, Cliff made multiple unsuccessful attempts
at swimming the Channel.

Bryan Wilkinson, crew on every one of the author's channel attempts,
chats with Dale McKinnon before the boat leaves the harbor
on the author 2010 channel attempt

A good shot of Shakespeare Beach, where many channel swims begin, and where 3 of the author's four attempts began—just south of Dover Harbor.

Freda Streeter and the author share a hug on Swimmer's Beach in Dover.

Multi-time English Channel swimmer, Miyuki Fujita, and the author; also on
Swimmer's Beach in Dover

Dover Harbor as seen from the World War II bunkers up on the White Cliffs of Dover to the south of the Harbor. From this angle, it's easy to see the breadth and depth of Dover Harbor which make it a unique open water training location.

Chapter 20

Fires of Obsession

On February 8, I took two aspirin out of a bottle and stared down at them. Two little white pills in the palm of my nervous and sweaty hand. They were coated in a shiny substance to make them slide down more easily, and each had a small cut across the middle to allow for breaking and consuming half-doses. I stared at them as they sat impassively next to the lifeline cutting across my palm.

For most people, there's nothing all that notable about aspirin. The drug has been used since the 1800s in its current form and is an effective analgesic used to combat pain and inflammation. It's even used widely to counter the risk of heart attacks and stroke.

For me, an aspirin is something else. It's dangerous.

It was in 2002 that I last popped a couple of aspirin. I'd been using them for years in an anti-inflammatory regimen to help me get through training and overuse injuries—a not-uncommon practice I learned from my running and triathlete buddies.

One evening in 2002, I went out for a couple beers and some pub food with friends on a deck overlooking Kirkland's slice of Lake Washington waterfront. It was a relaxed Thursday, one of those evenings where work problems recede into the background while you decompress, secure in the knowledge that the weekend is around the corner.

Later that night, I woke up feeling awful and rushed to the bathroom in time to vomit blood all over the tile before passing out for some hours. Pub owners may disagree, but fish in a pub is generally a risky proposition so I figured the food was the culprit. I slept most of the next day and, feeling better, went about my normal routine.

That Monday, I woke at 5:00 a.m., dressed, drove to the fitness center, and started my workout. I planned to change into my running clothes at the fitness center and then do a three-mile run on the neighborhood streets before doing some weights indoors. The weather was sunny and warm. I got out of the club parking lot and onto the street before I noticed anything was wrong.

I couldn't run, I couldn't breathe. Here I was a marathoner with dozens of long-distance races under my belt, and yet I couldn't summon the energy to run more than a hundred feet without panting like I'd sprinted up Pike's Peak. After a few steps, I doubled over and gasped aggressively until I'd recovered. I turned, went back inside the fitness center, and changed back into my street clothes, worried and frightened.

The next day, I visited my family doctor and told him what had happened. He asked me some questions and then looked at me with an expression of incredulity.

"The last guy like you who came to see me almost died," he said.

"Sorry?" I answered, stunned.

"The aspirin," he continued. "I think you've been bleeding internally from the aspirin eating away at your stomach. You can't run because you're so anemic from blood loss that there are no red cells to carry oxygen to your muscles."

The look on his face said what he didn't: "You idiot, you've been killing yourself with aspirin so you can feed your obsession to run farther and faster."

He put me on iron pills immediately to combat the anemia, ordered an esophageal scope test, and forbade me from traveling for a month. He also drily advised me to lay off the aspirin.

The scope was, er, unpleasant, and confirmed a round hole in my esophagus where there should have been pink and shiny, unbroken tissue. I was bleeding out like an hourglass with a pinhole.

In the years since that incident in 2002, I'd mostly used rest and ice to address overuse injuries. I'd also used ibuprofen, but mindful of past lessons learned, I'd not used it as regularly as I'd used aspirin earlier. The years had been filled with the common aches and pains that endurance athletes get, and I was no exception to the norm. My shoulders, in particular, had become grouchy after five years of intense open-water training. The right one was especially irritable right now. I couldn't train as needed.

The ice and ibuprofen had never worked as well as the aspirin. Knowing that, I was weighing the aspirin in my hand carefully, weighing the risks and rewards, weighing my need to be in the water. Without regularly increasing my mileage, my chances of getting across the Channel were nil. I rationalized that it was only a few months until August and my swim, and then I'd rest my shoulders and recover.

I remembered that night in 2002.

I considered the aspirin, perched delicately between the laughter and longevity lines in my palm and weighed the eight years my stomach had to heal, versus a couple aspirin once in a while between now and August.

When does passion become obsession? When does who you are become dependent on what challenges you pursue? When do you lose yourself in pursuit?

When is enough enough?

When I was a boy, my father would take my brother and me to his favorite bowling alley most Saturday mornings. My dad was the best bowler you've never heard of. Maybe that doesn't mean much to you, considering that bowling isn't exactly a World Cup sport. But at the local alleys, my dad was a player. He'd regularly bowl thirty-two games or more on Saturday mornings and was astounding to watch. He never kept score, and he'd get irritated if anyone else did. He didn't need attention—he just wanted to get better. Passersby stopped and stared frequently, astounded as he simply banged out strike after strike after strike, nonstop. And the only things he'd mark on the score sheet were the strikes. Nothing else mattered.

I remember watching him bang out twenty strikes in a row regularly. Twelve strikes is a perfect game.

But for my dad, it was never enough. He wanted every shot to be a strike and saw no reason why that wasn't possible; he saw nothing that precluded him from bowling thirty-two perfect games straight. Anything less was just irritating. He got irritated at the gawkers because to him they were just drawing his attention to the few throws that weren't strikes.

On those Saturdays, he'd keep practicing until his bowling hand was bloody. He'd wipe it off, patch the broken and tattered skin on his thumb with some sort of liquid plastic, bowl a few more games, and scowl at anything that wasn't a strike.

I guess I learned something from him.

I'd failed at the Channel twice. As of February 2010, I'd been training for more than five years to navigate that bit of water between Dover and Cap Griz Nez. It had cost family time, dollars, immeasurable mental energy, friends' goodwill, and everything I had. I was introduced at parties as "our friend who keeps trying to swim the Channel." I was that guy.

I didn't want to be that guy. I needed a pain-free shoulder to train.

I swung my hand to my mouth, popped the aspirin in, and chased them down with a splash of water. They tasted bitter, gritty, and poisonous.

In due course, my shoulder quieted down and felt better. The doubts? I simply pushed them away.

And I trained.

Chapter 21

Injuries and Inspiration—Ros Hardiman

In late February, despite the aspirin, ibuprofen, rehabilitation exercises, stretches, nightly icing, and a severely restricted swimming schedule, my shoulder continued to bother me. There was a sharp pain when I lifted my arm above my head, punctuated by a dull and ever-present ache that suffused the muscle.

I was frustrated, discouraged, and bored of cross-training. In addition to restricting my swimming, my shoulder was keeping me from my favorite cross-train sport: cycling. Riding my racing bike forced my weight onto my hands, arms, and shoulders, and that was painful and risky for my shoulders. I couldn't return to running, as my marathon days had left their own legacy of injuries, so I was reduced to using exercise machines in my fitness club. And I was tired of hours on an elliptical trainer, which contributed to my fitness but made me feel as if I were training for the Channel by watching the Tour de France on TV.

Also frustrating were the changes to my body. It wasn't about how I looked. I was okay with the twenty pounds of insulating body fat I'd put on over the years. I could have lived without Barb's barbs about "Buddha belly," but I'd get her back for that someday—I was a patient partner. What bothered me was the persistent feeling that I wasn't a swimmer anymore.

I felt weak in my upper body with the right shoulder at continual risk. And I missed all of the signs of being a swimmer. I missed the smell of chlorine, the swimsuit hanging in the bathroom, the mountain of wet towels, and the camaraderie with swimming buddies. Without swimming, I lost track of who I was. It was difficult not to sink at least a bit into a shallow pool of despair and despondency.

It's in my nature to do something, anything, when there's a problem; I'm not good at waiting. So I scheduled an acupuncture appointment—I'd never tried it—and a cortisone shot. If the acupuncture didn't do the trick, I figured, the cortisone would. I wasn't sure that any of it would get me through six months of training, but I was trying to take things one day at a time.

I was contemplating all of this when I connected with a personal hero: Ros Hardiman.

The thing you'd first notice about Ros if you met her in person is completely beside the point. The wheelchair that has sustained her since her battle with polio more than forty years ago, at age six, has little to do with the Ros I know or the inspiration she offers. That her legs fail more than support her is just a tangent to her story, just a leaf on her tree.

Ros's story is not about polio; it's about tenacity.

It's not about the discrimination she's seen. It's not about the time the police lectured her for swimming while disabled, or the time the National Gallery in London wouldn't let her in because they had policies against wheelchairs. It's not about the neighbor who flips her off and steals her handicapped parking spot, forcing her to sleep in her car overnight because there's no other parking spot on ground smooth enough to allow her to roll her wheelchair to her house.

Ros's story is about her expansive smile, her strong handshake, and her energy. It's about how she leans forward onto the edge of her wheelchair because she's so pleased to see you. It's about her enthusiasm and the encyclopedic knowledge she retains on so many topics that, when you think about it, it is no surprise that she's a museum curator by profession.

It's about her first attempt at the Channel.

Ros's first Channel attempt was in October 2008. After dropping off the back of Lance Oram's boat at 5:00 p.m. and swimming to shore, Ros turned around, waved at the boat, and crawled into the water to get started. Dragging herself into the water was difficult but necessary in order to comply with Rule 10(c) of the CS&PF, which states, "*The swimmer must walk into the sea from the shore of departure.*" The rule meant that she was always destined to be horizontal for at least a few more minutes than the average Channel swimmer. It also meant she'd be swimming the Channel with open cuts and scrapes from the rocky starting beach, and that she could look forward to dragging herself out when she reached the other side.

Ros spent twenty-five hours in the water and managed to get within seven hundred meters of France before her crew chief, Tanya Harding, had to pull her out. Tanya later said it was one of the most difficult things she'd ever done, that she and Lance, moved by Ros's determination, wanted to give her every chance to finish the swim. Tanya waited until the last moment possible to make the call, and then jumped in fully dressed to fish her out. When they pulled Ros out, she was still stroking, with a glassy look in her eyes, head down, no longer able to turn her head to breathe.

She'd been a ball of pain since the twenty-hour mark, but Ros wouldn't stop.

The fact that she'd injured her shoulder along the way was obvious. A bruise had blossomed early and spread slowly, like a sunrise, until her entire right side was black and blue. But she didn't stop.

The saltwater had sloughed the skin off her tongue. She didn't stop.

Without the use of her legs, she couldn't tread water for her feeds, so she was forced to use her hands to keep herself afloat while she ate and drank. But she didn't stop.

She daydreamed about Lance's boat hitting her so she'd have an excuse to quit, but she didn't stop.

It took utter incoherence to stop her. If she'd been conscious, she could have counted the French beachgoers in the water, perhaps even remembered the color of their suits or admired the Frisbees they were tossing back and forth. But she wasn't lucid enough for those details to register. She wasn't lucid enough even to breathe.

Knowing she'd gotten that close must have been tough to swallow. Ros's biggest regret? That she wasn't awake when the four hardy crewmen manhandled her out of the water. She regretted sleeping through the fun part.

During her twenty-five-hour ordeal, her friends and many others in the worldwide Channel swimming community were watching and waiting anxiously, following her swim closely through regular online updates. The news that she'd been pulled out hit them hard, as if they'd been pulled out themselves. I remember sitting back in my desk chair, deflated, and just staring at the e-mail starting with the word "Unfortunately . . ." on my screen.

My shoulder pain seemed petty compared to what Ros was capable of doing, had done.

She went back to Dover and the English Channel in 2009, no surprise to any of her friends or crew. That year's swim was different. The start was easier, and the first two hours were like swimming through satin, the diffuse sunlight spilling over her and the boat. She was nauseous, but that didn't stop her from enjoying herself. If nothing else, her 2008 attempt had left her much more confident. She swam through the night and felt very alone, as if the darkness would go on forever. Stroking evenly and steadily, she was so focused that she missed the sunrise over France; the sky just started getting lighter and lighter. And then the jellyfish struck.

"I swam through thousands of jellyfish near France," she told me. "They were stinging me across my face, my body, and under my swim costume. It was very painful, but I consoled myself by mentally reciting every fact I knew about them. Genus, species, diet, etcetera. It kept me busy."

At 7:00 a.m., Lance told her she had about a mile and a half to go, and then finally, at 8:15 on September 26, after twenty hours and seventeen minutes of swimming, Ros Hardiman landed in France, the 1,088th swimmer in history to cross the Channel.

As was required, she crawled out of the water onto the rocky French beach. She pulled herself up onto a rock, sat down, and exhaled. She'd rehearsed what she'd say to the French on arrival, but there was nobody there. Lance hadn't yet arrived in the inflatable raft to retrieve her, so she simply sat on the rock, watching the surf, feeling unreal. She'd done it.

As we chatted about her swims, I felt shame. I didn't know if my shoulder pain was just another mental phantom, as in my Bowen Island swim, and it didn't matter. Talking to Ros got me thinking about how to accept swimming the Channel injured, after a less-than-ideal season of training. She got me thinking about doing whatever it took. Ros was unconscious when they pulled her out in 2008—and in 2009, she went twenty hours before landing. She had two bad legs and a bad shoulder; I had only one arthritic shoulder.

Ros simply did what she did, was what she was, without complaint. I had a lot to learn from her. I asked her if she'd crew for my Channel attempt in 2010, and to my joy, she said, "Yes, I'd be honored."

Chapter 22

Opening Day in Bellingham Bay

As March dawned in the Great Pacific Northwest, locals began emerging from indoors, looking hopefully at the sky for signs of respite after the long, wet winter. We typically have a false spring in February, a few days of sunshine followed by yet more incessant rain—and 2010 was no different. When March came around, despite knowing that the truly dry days of spring and summer don't arrive until July, everyone was out and about; everyone was hopeful.

I was ready to get back out in the open water. My favorite playgrounds, Lake Washington and Bellingham Bay, were still frigid, the water temperatures in the mid to upper forties (F). And my right shoulder was still highly irritated and interfering with my training—but none of that mattered. I was eager to get out and about, particularly in Bellingham Bay. I calmed my anxiety about my injuries with the hope that the cold water would quell any inflammation in my shoulder and allow me to swim without doing more damage or causing more pain. In other words, I employed rationalizations to justify swimming outdoors at the tail end of winter.

Dale and I planned an opening-day swim in Bellingham Bay for March 8, a Monday. It was the only day that week we could manage, as I was returning from a quick business trip to Amsterdam that had consumed my weekend. I took the day off, and that morning I drove north toward Bellingham, where Dale lived.

The eighty-seven-mile drive up I-5 toward Bellingham and my swims with Dale were typically times for reflection. I'd drive across Lake Washington on the Rte. 520 floating bridge, leaving behind Seattle's potent combination of Subarus, Sierra Clubs, and serial killers for the less-intense environs north.

I'd think about life and the swim I was about to do. Often the weather during those rides was miserable with rain, wind (or both), and thick cloud cover peanut-buttered across the sky. Cloudy days generally make me reflective. Sometimes, when the weather conditions were rude enough, I'd watch the eighty-seven miles click down on the odometer like a condemned man watching the second hand tick off his last minute. It was the anticipation that was nerve-racking, not the swim itself. The swim was never as uncomfortable as anticipating the moment when I actually stepped into the brutally cold water.

On my opening day in 2010, I passed the drive time by thinking about the Channel swimmers that I knew in the Pacific Northwest. There was Scott Lautman in Seattle, who had gotten me started on my Channel quest years earlier with advice and guidance. Scott was a local legend, with an incredible ability to swim in waters down to the thirty-degree F range. There was Michele Macy in Oregon, with whom I'd chatted about our sport and swum an eleven-mile stretch through downtown Portland. There were also David Livengood, Tim Cespedes, and others. The Northwest was a great place for Channel swimmers to develop. While sprinkled across the country, US Channel swimmers tend to constellate in regions and cities with an abundance of cold water: San Francisco, New York, the Pacific Northwest, and even Southern California, where you might not expect to find the cold water that exists there. It makes me wonder whether we choose our destinies or whether the hand of fate does that for us.

Nervousness aside, I was eagerly anticipating the swim. It had been too long since I'd stood wind-whipped in Fairhaven's Marina Park parking lot and stared meditatively at Bellingham Bay while waiting for Dale to putter up to the beach in her little Zodiac boat. Too long since, after changing into my suit, I handed her my gear in an orange REI dry bag that matched her own and took a few quick steps into the cold Bay to stroke for Lummi Island, Eliza Island, Dot Island, or Chuckanut Bay, about five miles south. Or even just out to Buoy 2, floating silently and tauntingly offshore about one mile from the Marine Park beach.

Aside from getting my fix of time with Dale, I also badly wanted some reassurance that my Channel swim wasn't completely blown due to my lingering shoulder problem.

I arrived at Marina Park, stripped down, and chatted with Duncan Howatt, one of Dale's friends. Duncan was an accomplished rower who'd won his class in the Head of the Charles, the world's largest rowing regatta, for a few years running before focusing on surf skiing and giving guys thirty years younger some competition out on the water. Duncan was, coincidentally, a car nut, and we chatted about my car and his own modified Porsche while I got ready. Just as we got around to talking about the swim I was planning, Dale arrived and walked up the beach and over the grass into the parking lot.

"Hey! Ready?" she asked, getting right to the point.

"Almost," I replied. "Duncan and I were talking cars."

"Oh, that could take awhile," she responded with a wry look.

We gathered up the gear and walked down the beach. The air was forty degrees. I leaned down to drop my temperature-reading watch into the water and saw the digital numbers blink downward past the ninety degrees-plus it showed while sitting strapped to my forearm, down to eighty, seventy, sixty, fifty, and finally settle. Forty-seven degrees. Oh boy, I thought, and took a deep breath. I stood back up, and Dale looked at me expectantly.

"Forty-seven," I said.

"What do you want to do?" she asked.

"Put my clothes back on," I answered, looking across the windy, gray water, "but what I'm *going to do* is swim."

Thus committed, I stepped into the water and went through my normal shock-and-awe routine. A few people had gathered to watch what we were doing, and I heard a long, loud horn blare as one of the Burlington Northern trains closed in on the tracks that ran alongside Marina Park. Despite the dreary, overcast skies, the water was clear, so I was able to enjoy the downward view of the flowing grasses that line the Marina Park waterfront, the remains of crabs gone to the big crab pot in the sky, and, as we got a bit farther offshore, colorful starfish at home on the seabed.

The cold receded. There's a point in very cold swims when the initial shock wears off but the attrition war against hypothermia has not yet begun in earnest. It's the moment when even the coldest swims offer an oasis of calm and clear thought, of joy and pleasure. For me, that's usually the "I'm doing it!" moment. For open-water swimmers, no matter how strong or acclimated, hypothermia will eventually win—but mental and physical training, plus body fat and experience, can stave it off for many hours. In the English Channel, Kevin Murphy held the record for the longest time in the water, when he stayed in fifty hours during a three-way attempt. The length of the safety period varies by swimmer and conditions, and is affected by the swimmer's determination. The comfort period is almost always shorter than the safety period. When comfort abandons you and the cold starts to affect your faculties, you become incapable of articulating your fingers, your speech and even your thoughts become slurred—then it's time to get out.

About a half hour into our swim, Dale and I reached Buoy 2, a large upside-down bell-shaped thing that sways back and forth in the water like one of those clown punching bags your mom and dad bought you when you were eight. I stopped and looked back at Marina Park. I felt okay but my hands were cold, and I thought perhaps I was about to experience "the claw," when you can no longer move your fingers from the cold. Swimming back would take a bit more than an hour, making this a good start for the season and a good effort in forty-seven-degree water.

"Okay, let's go back," I called out to Dale. She nodded and turned around, while I abruptly started swimming toward Marina Park. As I swam, I focused on my injured shoulder for a moment. It was numb and felt okay, although the muscles were tight and there was something rubbing in there. I put that aside and looked up at Marina Park in the near distance.

Too soon, Dale and I pulled up to the beachfront. The water depth shrank to seven feet, six feet, five, four, three, and then I stood. I walked to Dale's boat. As I picked my gear bag up from the bow of her Zodiac, I felt something in my right shoulder twinge and retract painfully.

"Nice swim. Meet at the Bread Company for a snack?" Dale suggested.

"Sounds great," I replied, wincing inwardly from the shoulder pain.

"How soon?" she asked.

"Give me twenty minutes to dress and warm up a bit," I responded, distracted.

Dale kicked her tired Nissan outboard into life and puttered off. I watched her go, distracted from the cold by the pain. Sitting just behind the sand line on Marina Park beach were a couple of large logs that had washed up years before. I walked over, dropped my gear bag on the ground, and plopped down roughly on one of the logs. I gently rubbed my right shoulder with my still-frigid right hand while looking across the water at Buoy 2, and pondered my fate.

Chapter 23

Damaged

The human shoulder is an inherently unstable joint. In fact, it's the most unstable joint in the body. It's called a *ball-in-socket* structure, with the *ball* of the upper arm, the humerus, sitting in the *socket* created by the two joints in the shoulder—the glenohumerus and acromioclavicular joints. The bones making up both the ball and the socket are held together by a mass of muscles, tendons, and ligaments known as the rotator cuff. The muscles do the work and heavy lifting, while the tendons attach the muscles to the bone and the ligaments attach the bones to other bones. The ligaments are supposed to provide stability, but nature did a questionable job of planning stability into the human shoulder.

Ball in socket is the term you hear people use, but it is actually a misnomer. A better image would be a golf ball sitting on a tee. And that's part of the problem for swimmers.

In and among the interconnected soft tissues of the rotator cuff are two *bursa sacks,* which cushion and protect the cuff from the bony bits of the ball and socket and from overuse by nutcases trying to swim the English Channel (or play tennis at a high level, or regularly pitch baseballs or shoot basketballs, for that matter). *Sack* is another misnomer, as the bursa sacks are actually each just a couple bits of slippery tissue in between the big, strong functioning parts of the shoulder.

As I've mentioned, the average English Channel swim (if, in fact, there is such a thing) is about fourteen hours long, the swimmer churning about sixty strokes per minute. Fourteen hours times sixty minutes per hour times sixty strokes per minute equals about fifty thousand strokes between England and France.

That's fifty thousand times that the bursa sac has to lubricate the movement for the swimmer. And thousands more if your swim extends longer than fourteen hours, which is common.

Bursa sacs are filled with a viscous fluid, but they are only a few millimeters long and negligibly thick. Asking them to lubricate the most inherently unstable joint in the body while that joint tries to maintain stability against a series of extremely powerful muscles pulling and pushing, pulling and pushing in opposition to rough water that's yanking and shoving, yanking and shoving . . . well, that's asking a lot.

In my case, it was asking too much. And that made March and April difficult.

My right shoulder was cantankerous and bitchy, and I was exploring options, diagnoses, prognoses, and pain relief in as many forms as I could find. The injury bothered me during most daily activities, from e-mailing at work to shopping to swimming. The pain lingered in the top of my right shoulder mostly, pinching and aching. It also ran down the inside of the meat of my shoulder muscles whenever I raised my hands high or did anything remotely substantial with my right arm. I was compensating, and rapidly becoming left-handed as a result.

The injury was one of those things in life you can't control, but it was nonetheless driving me to despair. It wasn't just the Channel but the sense of finality: that at middle age I'd reached the sell-by date on one of my key body parts. I feared it wasn't ever going to get better. I'm not normally one to dwell on birthdays, but the injury brought the limits of time into stark relief.

I made an appointment to see my sports doctor, Dr. Tim Locknane, in Bothell, Washington. Tim's specialty was health care related to physical activities, and he was the best I knew.

*   *   *

"Hi, Mike," said Dan, Tim's office manager, when I arrived. Being a middle-aged marathon swimmer definitely keeps you on a first-name basis with your doctor and his staff.

"What are we seeing you for today?" Dan asked as he pulled out a thick file and opened it. "Let's see . . . Here for your hip?"

"No, that was a couple years ago. It's better now."

"Lower back bothering you?" he asked, referring to a chronic problem.

"No, been stretching that. It's better, too."

He flipped a page. "Right knee?"

"Nope, not running at the moment."

He flipped another page. "Left knee?"

"Uh-uh, I changed my bike pedals."

"Right forearm? Right elbow?" he asked, still looking at the file.

"Nah, changed my stroke."

"Shoulder?" he asked finally.

"Bingo."

He squinted at the file and looked up tentatively. "Which one?"

Once we'd established which limb was giving me trouble *this* time, Dan led me into one of the examining rooms Tim had built when he left a larger medical practice to hang out his own shingle. Tim's an occasional triathlete himself, and I'm continually trying to cajole him into Puget Sound without a wetsuit.

Tim joined me a few moments later, and I explained the situation. He looked thoughtful and said something along the lines of . . .

"Humerus, scapula, clavicle, sternum . . . articular cartilage reducing friction, *osteoarthritis* caused by repetitive motions wearing away . . . flexion, extension, rotation in the glenohumoral joint, humerus, glenoid . . . I mean, it's only a ball and socket! And there's intricate ligament structure, the biceps tendon with a linkage to the biceps muscle . . . possibly rotator-cuff tear, or the synovial fluid is . . . acromioclavicular joint formed between clavicle and scapula, acromion, sternoclavicular joint, scapulothoracic articulation . . . muscle and tendon mechanism permitting the scapula to slide without obstruction along the upper back as the arm is raised or extended during the movements of the shoulder."

My first thought was, *Holy shit, I have arthritis?* My second was, *I wish I'd gone to medical school.*

Rotator-cuff tears among swimmers are common. The cuff tears a bit and then gets inflamed and painful as it's flexed again and again. And osteoarthritis happens to all of us as we get older; nobody lives to a ripe old age without some osteoarthritis in his or her joints. The cartilage gets worn over time, and sooner or later we lose mobility, flexibility, and range of motion. For some of us, it happens sooner—and I was discovering that I was one of those. Lifestyle plays a big part in accelerating osteoarthritis, as do genetics and hobbies. All three factors seemed to be working against me.

At Tim's recommendation, I booked an MRI (Magnetic Resonance Imagery test) for later that week, and it confirmed his diagnosis. As I looked at the indecipherable pictures with him, he explained that I had "osteoarthritic processes" in my right shoulder and an inoperable rotator-cuff tear, probably a result of some trauma to my shoulder years ago. In other words, my cartilage was worn away in a couple spots, and there was some bone-on-bone contact. And there was a hole in my rotator cuff that surgery couldn't repair because it had happened so long ago that the bone had pulled away from the spot where they'd want to reattach the tissue.

Neither would ever heal, Tim said quietly with a sympathetic look.

Tim and I talked about options, and after some long hours spent afterward in reflection, I decided to proceed with training for the Channel. If it wasn't ever going to get better, then it wasn't ever going to get easier to make the swim—actually, quite the opposite. And I still wanted to swim the Channel. I wasn't done.

Tim recommended some mitigation strategies, primarily physical therapy, and I followed his instructions to the letter. I found a physical therapist with a couple decades of experience through a triathlon group, Sara Chisholm, and she became a great source of relief and advice. Sara was even-tempered and of medium height, with brown sandy hair and an easy smile. When we first met, she listened and nodded empathically while I explained the injury. She'd seen patients with similar complaints many times and could explain the issues holistically in a way that felt encouraging. She pulled out her encyclopedic knowledge of stretches, rehab exercises, and don't-do's and walked me through her prescribed course. And then we set about my new regimen in earnest, with biweekly physical therapy sessions and daily stretching and rehab exercises. Most of my evenings at home were spent rolling and working on the floor in front of the TV, with increasingly heavy hand weights providing resistance.

I also started acupuncture. While I'd felt the benefits of the physical therapy right from the start, the effects of the acupuncture were subtler. Jewel Smith, the acupuncturist referred to me by friends, was gentle and experienced, and I did feel better after her sessions. But acupuncture is a non-mechanical process that doesn't produce a black-and-white improvement immediately; at least it didn't for me. It requires time and faith. Despite the ambiguity of the result, though, I felt it was worth it.

Almost anything was worth trying at that point.

Once I'd made my decision to shoulder onward *(sorry)*, I yearned for empathy from my peers: like-minded swimmers. So one morning I signed into the English Channel Swimming chat room and asked about other swimmers' injuries. I was inundated with responses. I got myself a heaping handful of Reese's Peanut Butter Cups and settled in to sift through them.

Ned Denison, an American living in Ireland who sells IT services for EMC Corporation and swam the Channel in 2005, had problems for years, but restricted his swimming to the period between March and November and was able to bring his soreness to an end. I guess the winter provided much-needed rest. He later swam another well-known marathon swim, the Catalina Channel between Catalina Island and California, at a very fast pace.

Steve Beckett, who had two relays and an unsuccessful solo crossing in 2005 under his belt and worked as a partner in private equity in Grosse Pointe, Michigan, suffered from shoulder issues through thirty years of swimming (out of his fifty years on earth) until he decided to try something unorthodox—he ditched his doctors. "Stay away from doctors; they want to either medicate or operate," he said. Steve started consulting physical therapists, learned rehab exercises, and hired a coach to improve his stroke efficiency. Things improved.

Alix Robertson, a property broker for mansions in London's tonier neighborhoods, broke her shoulder in April 2010, but came back from the injury to swim the Strait of Gibraltar in September of that same year. That was encouraging. There was nothing broken in my shoulder—just a little bone-on-bone dancing.

Shannon Swartz, a Pilates studio owner and multiple Channel relay veteran, never had an injury. She attributed that to Pilates (no surprise, but possibly justified), as well as kettlebell exercises and Gyrotonic. I was doing yoga regularly and had tried Pilates, so I could see how those helped. But I wasn't sure what Gyrotonic was. It sounded awful, like something your mom made you drink when you were nine years old and constipated. I thanked Shannon and resolved to double down on the yoga and Pilates.

Nick Caine, an American at Trinity University and the record holder for the youngest American male to swim the Channel, had subsequently had three shoulder surgeries. The first was arthroscopic, during which the doctor rebuilt his cartilage with metal sutures. The recovery took six months, and Nick didn't regain full ability. His second surgery was focused on making clearance for the tendons and ligaments to flex inside the joint. Again, he didn't regain full strength. Nick's third and last surgery was to take care of two of the sutures that were loose and floating in the joint. As of the time he wrote to me, Nick was slowly feeling better and looking forward to swimming on the team at Trinity . . . . I did wonder whether the doctor had rushed too quickly into the surgeries, but I had to admire Nick for withstanding three surgeries before he was out of his teens based on sheer dedication to the sport. That in itself was inspiring.

Alan Smith, a fire service worker and retired diver from the British Navy living in Waterford City, had lots of shoulder issues, including subscapular pain (there was one of Dr. Locknane's fancy words again), but he was able to mitigate his problems with painfully deep tissue massage, laser treatments, and cutting back on his swimming in favor of cross-training. In fact, he cut all the way back to two or three swims per week . . . . That was another reassuring story. Three times per week was about my average.

Phil Garn, a federal agent from Coronado, California, married with no kids, had never had a shoulder injury despite swimming regularly for forty-five of his fifty-one years. Those four-and-a-half decades included a Catalina Channel swim and an English Channel swim in 2009. He used weight training and stretch cords regularly, and those seemed to keep him swim-ready, despite his extremely asymmetrical stroke—the result of a badly broken right arm he'd sustained in a wrestling match when he was fourteen.

Another swimmer, Cathie Slevin, felt her left shoulder "go" while in the midst of swimming across Lake Zurich in 2008. She finished the race with the aid of ibuprofen, but afterward she was unable to move the shoulder. Her doctor diagnosed rotator cuff problems. Physiotherapy and steroid injections didn't alleviate the problems, so in February 2009, she underwent arthroscopy to clean up her damaged tendons. Despite that, the pain kept increasing until, in October 2009, she felt she had no choice but to undergo another surgery to further clean up the unruly joint. Afterward, she learned that her joint was arthritic and would never recover (not unlike my own). Her problems kept her out of open water until March 2010, at which point she resumed training and swam the Channel in fifteen hours in July 2010.

Hey . . . another arthritic. The encouraging stories were piling up! I unwrapped my eighth Reese's of the morning and let it melt slowly, deliciously, on my tongue. Shoulders be damned, putting on body fat for a Channel swim could be fun. I looked back at my screen.

Colin Hill, the marathon swimming technical manager for the 2012 London Olympic Games committee, picked up a scapular injury by, well, picking up his kids. He'd been ramping up the mileage to prepare for his Channel swim, and adding his kids' weight to his own was the straw that broke the swimmer's back. His story turned out okay, though. After extensive rehab and a bit of simple grit at the moment of truth, he crossed in a mere ten hours and thirty minutes.

That was a lot of calming stories in a row; I felt much better. The ninth Reese's went down smoothly, while the tenth and last of the morning waited on my desk in anticipation of its demise. I leaned back in my office chair and exhaled slowly. The smell of peanut butter filled my office, and I was surrounded by shiny gold wrappers.

The simple act of connecting with friends in the Channel community bolstered my resolve, and I decided to press on as cheerfully as I could, taking it one day at a time.

I had a lot to look forward to: swimming the Channel, of course, but more immediately, spending more time with Dale in Bellingham, training.

Chapter 24

Cold and Uncertain

Nature throws spring at the Puget Sound like an artist throws red paint at a white canvas. The splotches of beautiful weather don't always score direct hits, but those that do burst vibrantly. The weekend of May 8 and 9 was beautiful beyond measure, suffused with light, warmth, and buoyancy. Seemingly, everyone in Seattle was outdoors. Family duties ate that weekend for me, though, so Monday, May 10, was to be my day for swimming across Bellingham Bay.

Monday's weather bore little resemblance to its predecessors, alas. Mother Nature kicked the day out of the nest without fanfare or color. The sky was politician-gray, and a biting wind tore at me as I surveyed the Bay from Marine Park. Despite the crappy weather, Dale was waiting cheerfully in her boat, ready to go.

Dale and I typically target either Lummi Island or Eliza Island, choosing one or the other based on the prevailing tides. Named for a local Indian tribe, Lummi Island is the most northeastern of the San Juan Island archipelago that dots the Puget Sound. By water (the only way I know), it's about six miles from Marine Park. The island is home to businesses, nature preserves, farmers' markets, expensive homes, and about a thousand citizens. Eliza Island sits a similar distance from Marine Park but slightly south of Lummi. It's the smaller of the two land chunks, with only about twenty permanent residents and no access by car.

My arthritic shoulder bothered me as we left the beach, but it felt better once I was underway—not surprising since the water was a mere fifty-two degrees Fahrenheit, cold enough to soothe the inflammation. The weather cleared after our start, and we experimented with a new feeding system Dale had devised, chatting amiably during my breaks and feeds. There were starfish and seals beneath us, seagulls and eagles above us, and sailboats tacking around us. We'd decided to target Eliza, but the wind whipped up again and it got rough. Dale's boat was bouncing around and I worried about tweaking my shoulder in the confused waters, so we pulled out a bit before we'd have landed on Eliza.

The following weekend, I was 2,500 miles away, in Annapolis for Lynne Smith's wedding, so my Saturday swim was in the Atlantic rather than my beloved Pacific. Only hours before she was scheduled to be pretty in white, Lynne took the lead as I swam off of Sandy Point in the Chesapeake Bay with a group of like-minded open-water swimmers Lynne had invited to her nuptials. At sixty-three degrees, the water was warmer than that of Bellingham, but chilly enough to make the swim enjoyable. At Sandy Point, we stripped to our suits in view of a hundred new open-water aspirants taking a class on swimming in the Bay. Their sea of black Neoprene wetsuits contrasted with our own little mass of flesh and Lycra, making us the subject of curious scrutiny. Probably some horror, too.

Chesapeake Bay was very calm, and we set out on a peaceful swim to the west end of the Chesapeake Bay Bridge. The bridge itself is one of those concrete monoliths that look as if they'll be standing for centuries. I thought of Dale's ex-husband as we swam past it; she'd once bemusedly told me he'd cracked their sailboat into one of the bridge's concrete pillars while trying to exhibit his sailing skills to onlookers on the span above.

On the flight back from Annapolis, my shoulder was grungy and irritated. I worried unremittingly that the reignited pain indicated that the injury was getting more severe and spent a fitful few days until May 19, which I'd taken off of work for another swim with Dale in Bellingham.

That day, we lit off for Lummi Island at 9:00 a.m. Dale's double-checking of the tides, wind, and weather told us we had a short, maybe two-hour window before the wind whipped her small boat in circles and aborted the swim. I was swimming with one arm, just pulling my right hand through the water without a catch to avoid pressuring my shoulder, and two hours wouldn't be enough time to get to Lummi in those conditions. We figured we'd do our best and leave the rest to fate. The water was thankfully, wonderfully cold, and my shoulder loved it; the inflammation subsided, and I moved like a much-younger Mike.

The weather was sunny, pleasant, and cheerful when we took off. Bellingham Bay is a maelstrom of waters struggling for dominance beneath the surface. It kept me entertained with upwellings, alternately blasting me with forty-degree water from the depths of the Bay and fifty-four-degree floodwaters from local rivers.

I've swum past Buoy 2 so many times that I suspect it will be one of the last things I think of on my deathbed. I'll hear its bell toll and then follow a light home. The water that day was too cold to daydream about long sleeps, though, so I swam quickly past the buoy and aimed for Lummi. Portage Island, another Bellingham Bay island, was just to my right, and as I crawled along I watched its rocky shore with interest. A national park set aside as a nature preserve, Portage is unapproachable, but it makes for a pretty view from sea level.

Dale was puttering along when she realized she'd forgotten to fill her boat's tank with fuel. The boat stopped and started and stopped again until I yelled back, "Hey, what's up?"

"I've got just a quarter tank here," she said. "Only enough to get us home, not over to Lummi. I'll have to row until we get there."

With that, she pulled out the oars, began to row, and hollered at me, "This is great; I was cold before, but I'm warmed up nicely now! And it's not nearly as boring when I'm rowing."

"You think it's cold up there? You should try it down here in the water!" I yelled back.

I swam for a couple of hours, making my way across the ebb tide toward Inati Bay on Lummi Island. When we finally made it past Portage, the ebb tide was no longer blocked by the island, and it started coming at my right side harder, pushing me resolutely south. My bad shoulder had no patience for sprinting, so I used my left arm and kicked for all I was worth, to no avail. I was pointed at Inati Bay and swimming the exact speed as the tide—going nowhere. It was hard work, but I remained hopeful. Dale watched me silently, with a slight smile.

I popped up. "Am I getting anywhere?"

"No."

"No?"

"No," she repeated, emphatically. "You're not gonna make Inati in this tide. Try for that beach farther south a bit," she added, pointing. "There might be a countercurrent by the beach that you can ride up to Inati, if you're lucky."

The beach was a lonely patch of sand surrounded by a clamshell of short cliffs about forty feet high, and it looked fine to me. The goal was reaching Lummi, and there were no penalty points for landing somewhere other than Inati Bay—so in I went to Clamshell Beach. Minutes later, I stood on the mix of sand, broken crab shells, round slimy rocks, and decaying kelp, enjoying the feel of being on land. I took an extra moment to warm up the water in Bellingham Bay in my own personal way and reflected on the swim.

We'd made it in a bit less time than the last time I had swum this route, when my shoulder was healthy. The weather had held out, and I was content with the state of my fitness. The wind was beginning to pick up, the sun was still shining, the water felt very comfortable, and all was well.

After a moment or two, Dale set about readying her nine-foot Zodiac for our ride back. Her small Nissan outboard is augmented by a well-used set of oars clipped in. I'm usually flopped into the front of the craft like a harpooned seal, and Dale perches herself on a simple wooden plank stretched across the boat. While we were tootling back to Marina Park, she asked if I felt confident about my Channel swim relative to my shoulder injury.

"Let's do one more swim on Memorial Day, and if that goes well, we'll know I can swim around the injury, and we'll recommit to the Channel, okay?" I said in response. "I'd like to do ten or twelve miles that day," I added hopefully.

I still felt a little uncertain about my shoulder, but better than I had, since proving that I could work around it on the swims I'd done in May. The Memorial Day swim would serve as a final test. I also had a couple training swims scheduled during the week. The first was a quick swim from Waverly Park to downtown Kirkland, my hometown.

Waverly is a favorite swim. It's a small neighborhood park with few swimmers. There's an eagle's nest somewhere in the vicinity, and the eagles are often flying above, surfing wind currents and surveying Lake Washington for food. The swim goes past some homes that are waterfront-nice without being as showy as some others on Lake Washington. And when the weather is clear, you're treated to a stunning view of Mount Rainier in the distance, behind downtown Kirkland.

I had a nice swim and was enjoying the pleasant buzz I always feel upon emerging, when a Parks and Recreation worker called out, "Hey, were you swimming out there? It's cold, isn't it?"

"Not bad, fifty-nine degrees—a great way to start your day!"

"Wow," he said, looking me over. "You must have been some swimmer in your day!"

The pleasant buzz dissipated. "Hey, it's *still* my day!"

He looked at me dubiously, waved, and walked away. I walked over to my car, and looked at my reflection in the window. Hmmm.

The second swim was a quick morning one at Madison Park. I'd planned it for Thursday or Friday, the 27 or 28, but it rained heavily both days. Rain is tricky for open-water swimming, or at least it is for me. It doesn't affect the swimming much, but it makes the start miserable and getting warm afterward difficult. Walking to the waterfront in a driving rain makes it feel twenty degrees colder than walking down in the clear. Rain or no rain, I couldn't delay the swim past Saturday because I needed a day of rest before my Memorial Day swim—so I crossed my fingers and decided to swim rain or shine.

It was pouring, and the rain had cooled the lake back down to fifty-two degrees. At its lowest depths, Lake Washington stays a frigid forty-six degrees all year-round. The summer sun warms up the upper level (called the thermocline), but that temperature fluctuates in the early season.

It was a cold swim. Shoulder comfortable; everything else not so much.

On May 31, Memorial Day, Dale and I met back up at Bellingham Bay. Our best option for the long swim we'd planned was to head out to do a round-trip to Lummi or Eliza. The tides indicated our best chance was to start at 4:00 a.m. The eighty-seven-mile drive meant I'd be up at 1:00 a.m. Barb wasn't enthused that I'd be waking her up when I showered.

"Why do you need a shower if you're just going to get in the Bay and swim?" she asked. It was a reasonable question, I'll grant.

"It wakes me up."

"It'll wake *me* up."

"I love you?" I offered with a smile.

"Lucky me."

Garth Brooks pumped me up on my drive north to Whatcom County. The weather was cold again, and a torrential storm ripped at my little car, rocking it back and forth. The only thing less appealing than swimming in Puget Sound at that moment was being the girlfriend on the backseat of the sport bike that tore past me at 85 mph. It amazes me what some girls will do for love—such as waking up to a loud shower at 1:00 a.m. on a holiday.

Since it was my last swim of the month, Dale and I decided to make it a little adventurous. After we reached Lummi or Eliza, I'd continue south and get out in Chuckanut Bay, which has a seal estuary in it and lots of small islands dotting the water. The wildlife there is always entertaining, and it's a wonderful place to swim.

We met up at Chuckanut Bay, where I left my car and drove with Dale fifteen minutes north to put in at Marine Park. There had been a footrace the day before, and the park grounds were still closed to the public and littered with paper cups and other runners' refuse. Dale left me at the gate, and I walked the length of the spooky-dark grounds, wondering whether I'd get attacked or arrested. I sat on a picnic table and waited for Dale to bring her boat around to the waterfront from the marina.

I looked out at Bellingham Bay and breathed deeply. Adding to the darkness was thick fog and cloudy conditions, denying me even a peek at the moon. I couldn't see anything, really, but I could hear the water rippling evenly and vigorously. I thought about what I was doing in a closed park in the pitch-black on a rainy morning. It felt like fate. It was where I belonged.

We finally got off about four thirty. The water was chilly but felt manageable, and we reached Lummi in two and a half hours. Instead of actually landing and standing on Lummi, I wanted to turn south and head immediately for Chuckanut. Dale had been in the boat for three hours and she needed to answer the call of nature, so she left me floating alone in the Bay for a few minutes. I should have been uncomfortable floating out at sea alone, but there wasn't much wind at that point; the water was calm, and so was I. I reflected again on why I was there. I daydreamed about my high school swim team, my college years, my years of cycling, running, triathlon, and then swimming. The English Channel was where I was headed, I knew that, and oh, I wanted it.

Dale returned and we turned toward Chuckanut and began passage home. As if to test my resolve, the wind blew harder and the water got choppier until I was forced to abandon my one-arm stroke and pull with both. After about an hour, I worried I was doing damage to my shoulder, so I popped up.

"Are we making quick enough progress against this crap?" I asked.

"How's your shoulder?"

"It's okay, but I'm worried that one of these rogue waves is going to tear off my arm."

"Swim to Portage? Eliza?" she asked.

"Eliza seems wise," I said, and she nodded.

Wise didn't mean easy. The wind had whipped up even more, and the chop was about three feet. Every breath included a sip of the Bay, and my disabled shoulder got angrier and angrier. It took another forty-five minutes, but we finally made it into the calm of Eliza Bay and grounded on the beach. I walked past the sign that said, "Private Beach, No Trespassing," sat on a felled tree, and exhaled deeply.

After a few minutes, we piled back into Dale's boat and made for the mainland. We were being tossed around like martinis, and I felt nauseous, having swallowed a bellyful of Bay water. The ride got rougher and rougher until the small boat was regularly crested by waves. Even Dale, with thirty years of boating under her belt, was grimacing and cursing. The water was going right into the neck of her jacket, and she was soggy down to her underwear.

We'd been shadowed by seals as we approached Eliza, a favorite feeding ground, but I hadn't been able to see them myself. As we rode east, though, five or six of them popped out of the water and peered at us. It was a rough hour, but we made it back to the mainland in one piece. The swim had been only a bit over four hours due to the deteriorating conditions, but it was a great adventure.

I decided to recommit to the Channel, shoulder be damned. I told Dale, drove home, and booked my ticket.

We were going to France, and I hoped it wasn't going to be by ferry.

Chapter 25

Doldrums

June started out fine but ended badly. I wanted to spend the month building my fitness and enjoying my training, enjoying the simple pleasure of swimming, but as the month wore on, the stars seemed aligned against that.

The month burst onto Seattle like a water balloon tossed into a wedding party. The sun occasionally peeked through, but Seattle's relentless rain spurted, streamed, gushed, and trickled in. The endless rain gave new meaning to the phrase "watching the grass grow," as everything green seemed to be spreading by inches per hour. There was more moss on my driveway than on a thatched cottage in medieval England. I was living through rain that lived up to the Seattle stereotypes perpetuated in movies and books.

Rain or not, I was swimming. On June 5, I did my first outdoor swim of the month at Madison Beach on Lake Washington. There were two crowds milling about when I arrived. The first was a group of swimmers in the parking lot—a welcome sight. The second was an insurrection of ducks and geese at the waterfront. The geese pecked at the dirt and sand for bugs, while the ducks tended the patch of water lapping against the beach. I walked toward my starting point through the foul melee, and birds parted like the Red Sea to accommodate me. I wondered momentarily why the ducks were watching me so warily, when it struck me that there were a lot of baby ducklings out there. I managed to avoid both the geese and the homicidally protective mother ducks and stepped into Lake Washington.

The water was fifty-nine degrees Fahrenheit—not bad at all.

Lake Washington and the adjoining sky were uncannily calm and clear; this allowed the always-inspiring full view of Mount Rainier sixty miles south that only reveals itself on clear days. I left the protection of the beach and, warming up gradually, sliced through the water south along the waterfront, past condominiums, docks, and tech—and coffee-mogul mansions. After about ten minutes, I stopped, treaded water, and surveyed the scene. I thought I'd heard a boat approaching and didn't want to be surprised by a bow slicing across my head. I'd been scared silly during an earlier swim off Madison Beach when a seaplane landed without warning about fifty feet from where I was swimming. The thought of an encore wasn't appealing.

There weren't any boats, seaplanes, Jet Skis, or even skiffs carrying the University of Washington rowing team around, though, and it was achingly stunning. It was as if Lake Washington were posing for an Andrew Wyeth painting. I wallowed in a moment's float to appreciate the day, as well as my shoulder's obedience.

Something splashed out of the water to my left, and then came another flash from a different direction. I scanned the lake surface and saw that I was surrounded by stickleback fish breaching the water in tiny four—or five-inch arcs. They looked like miniature sharks as they tried to catch breakfast flies. Stickleback get their name from the sharp, skeletal stickles protruding through their skin, their defense mechanism against predators. They're a well-studied species due to their rapidly evolving biology. To swimmers in Lake Washington, they're better known for the painful cuts their skeletons carve into our unsuspecting feet when they die and wash up onto the waterfront.

With all the fish breaching, I looked around nervously for eagles. I was wearing my silver swim cap and didn't want my head confused for a fish by something with wings and talons. After I'd satisfied myself about the wildlife, I had an uneventful and comfortable two-hour swim. My shoulder was amiable, and I was even able to stroke with both arms. When I pulled back into Madison Beach, I waved at the other swimmers and made idle chat about the conditions.

"You swam without a wetsuit?" somebody inevitably asked me.

The question always gives me a little ego boost. All in all, it was a pleasant start to the month.

On June 8, I swam with a new partner, Alan Florsheim. My shoulder was much more painful that day, and that slowed me down and broadened the distance between us. Making it even trickier was that he enjoyed the twin advantages of wetsuit and a better stroke than mine. I knew then that my Channel swim would be slower than average: sixteen, maybe even twenty hours. I'd been telling friends I expected that, but had secretly hoped I was being conservative, as is my nature.

Twenty hours in the English Channel, I thought to myself. *That'll be a long day.* Imagine swimming through breakfast, lunch, dinner, an evening's television, bedtime, and on into the night until you finish, a few hours before you would normally wake up again.

It rained on the day before my next swim, and Lake Washington was chilled by the downpour to the low fifties Fahrenheit. Above the water it was cloudy and windy, and the water itself was rougher than a diva's divorce. I was getting slapped around continuously, and my shoulder was tweaked and bad-tempered. I muddled through, swimming monotonously, but didn't finish the swim I'd planned and walked out of the lake dejected, starting a downward spiral that would last the rest of June.

An older woman wearing yoga pants and a Gore-Tex jacket, and sporting a nest of blue hair, accompanied by what I guessed was her granddaughter in a stroller, waved and approached as I left the water. The little girl sucked noisily on a pacifier and stared wide-eyed at me. "I just got back from Alaska, and the weather is colder here than it was there," the woman said emphatically, as if somehow I was to blame. She quickly turned the stroller and marched away without another word.

"Great, thanks," I muttered, thinking, *I'm not Zeus, lady, I don't control the weather.*

The goose crap carpeting the waterfront was in keeping with my mood. I tried stepping around as much of it as possible but ended up squishing right through it in my haste to get to my car and warm up. About thirty minutes after my swim, my nasal cavities gushed out residual lake water they'd apparently been storing. *Perfect,* I thought, and shuddered. I wondered how much goose shit was in it.

Dismayed by my lackluster swim, I headed back to Madison two days later to try again. My shoulder was still bitchy, so I decided to keep my swim to about two hours. I was in the parking lot getting ready when I met another swimmer, named Brendan Halffman, who'd tried to swim the Channel twice. He'd been blown out by weather both times and had never even gotten in the water. While I absorbed that possibility for myself, he and I chatted about swimming together. He was in a wetsuit, though, and my shoulder was once again in a foul mood, so I figured he'd be much faster. When we got in and he motored away, I saw I'd been right. I felt sorry for him about the Channel. The experience of going to Dover twice and getting blown out due to weather both times must have been maddening.

The month dragged on. I was frustrated, worried, tense about my progress. My shoulder hurt constantly, and despite managing a couple of eight-mile swims, my training was uninspiring and undistinguished. There was a voice in my head repeating endlessly, "You're not ready, you're not ready, you're not ready." It was difficult to focus on anything else.

June 26 rolled into town, and I had a chance to regain my good temper and sense of humor. I was looking forward to a swim with Dale in Bellingham.

Then I got an e-mail from her: "Hey, Mike, I can't do our swim this weekend. I have an eye infection."

So much for cheering up.

I needed to swim anyway, so with some effort, I hauled myself to Lake Washington and stormed the water with gusto, trying to banish the demons. I aimed myself at a point along the waterfront about four miles away and started swimming. At first, it was a struggle, but then I started skimming along and felt better. My shoulder was cooperative, and I attracted a school of fish about ten feet underwater that swam along with me for almost an hour. I watched with wonder, tried to count them, tried to determine if they were stickleback or some other species. My heart slowed, and I relaxed as I moved in unison with the fish. I started to think more optimistically as I reached my turnaround. *I can do this, I can swim the Channel*, I thought. I swam the four miles back to my car, all the while talking myself off the ledge I'd been on.

Staying positive should have been easy: unlike many people in the world, I was healthy and financially stable, and had a happy and well-fed family. On top of all that, I was fortunate enough to be within striking distance of achieving an extraordinary goal I'd nurtured for a long time. I walked out of the water after my four-hour swim, tired but relaxed, cramping but comfortable, starving but sustained.

Later, relaxing at home on our comfortable sofa, decompressing further, I finally felt good. I smiled to myself and leaned forward to pick up Lynne Cox's book *Swimming to Antarctica* from my coffee table.

Just then, Lynne Smith called. She couldn't crew in the Channel for me as planned. She was heartbroken and apologetic, but her aging parents needed her at home. Silently panicking, I reassured her that everything was fine, that I'd find a replacement, not to worry.

"Who was that?" Barb asked.

"Lynne," I said, deflated. "She can't crew for me."

We talked for a few minutes about Lynne and her parents. Barb and I had both lost parents recently and could empathize. Then Barb turned the conversation in a more practical direction. "Who's going to save you if you pass out and sink again, like in 2008?" she asked, worried.

I didn't know.

Chapter 26

Cliff and Brent

Losing Lynne was a blow. All of my Channel-swim visualizations had included her cheerfully watching over me, as in 2008. When I had succumbed to hypothermia and passed out, she'd saved me—and that had made her an indelible part of my Channel experience. With no time to lament, I turned my focus to solutions.

I reconsidered the problem from various sides. I needed someone who understood the Channel, had swum it, and could be my companion swimmer.

The CS&PF rules allow a companion swimmer to join in a few times during the crossing, but only after the first three hours and only for one hour at a time. Each one-hour session must be followed by at least two hours of solo swimming. While in the water, the companion swimmer must stay alongside or behind the Channel swimmer—never in front, so as to avoid providing pacing assistance. The companion is also allowed, even encouraged, to swim along for the last couple hundred yards, in case the swimmer has a problem standing and walking onshore in France after so many hours prone in cold water.

At first blush, the two people that came to mind were Cliff Golding and Brent Hobbs.

I needed time to think further, and my prework swim in Lake Washington the next morning afforded just that. The swim started fine, but my goggles repeatedly fogged and I couldn't see where the hell I was going or, more importantly, if there were anyone coming at me in a boat or Jet Ski. Finally, I swam toward land and stood just offshore near someone's waterfront property to clear them.

"Hello?" I heard from my right. I turned and saw someone coming out of the back of the waterfront house.

"Good morning!" I replied, grinning. "Beautiful day, huh?"

"Can I help you?" he asked, looking at me suspiciously.

"Er, no thanks, I'm just clearing my goggles."

"Uh-huh," he said, sitting down with his coffee and watching me steadily. I finished rinsing and felt the man staring at me suspiciously until I'd left his immediate area. I guess he viewed a chubby, middle-aged guy in a racing suit, standing hip deep in Lake Washington, as a threat.

I swam away from Mr. Homeland Security and, to pass the time, for the rest of the swim considered my open crew position. I started with Cliff Golding.

Cliff is a retired British Army corporal, a warrior-poet type who's been involved in Channel swimming since 1991, both as a swimmer and crew member. He is a steady and reassuring presence on Swimmer's Beach, and many swimmers have asked him to join their teams. Cliff fits the profile of a fit and fashionable professor of physical training, with comfortable clothing, long light-colored hair, an easygoing demeanor, and an air of experience.

A lifelong runner in his mid-fifties, Cliff became interested in swimming the Channel while on his way to Zimbabwe with the army in 1982. He was already an accomplished runner, with a sub-three-hour marathon, extra fit from carrying his army gear around the world over several years in the service. As the long flight to Zimbabwe left English airspace, it banked languidly over the Channel, and for a brief moment, Cliff could see both England and France. He had been aware that people swam the Channel, but for the first time, the challenge captured his imagination; it became a goal. *It's not that far*, he thought. *I could do that!* The plane leveled out and pointed itself south to Africa. Cliff put swimming the Channel on the back burner and let it simmer.

The 1980s became the 1990s, and the Channel began to call him, so he started reaching out to learn how to go about swimming it. A phone call to the Channel Swimming Association led him to Freda Streeter. I thought back to the time I sat down with Cliff in Dover, when he described his Channel career to me.

"I looked up Freda in the CSA handbook, and there was something about her daughter Alison in there," Cliff said over a massive dish of apple pie and vanilla ice cream at Chaplin's in Dover. Chaplin's is a popular post-training hangout, where Cliff and I were having lunch with another Channel swimmer, Thomas Kofler. Thomas, about five foot nine and with a broad forehead framed by dark hair and punctuated by bushy eyebrows, has a serious look that belies his casual and approachable demeanor. He's the head of internal audit at Banco Popolare in Italy. Thomas swam the Channel in October 2009 in just over fifteen hours, piloted by Freda's son Neil.

"Alison had swum the Channel fourteen times, I believe," said Cliff, "and I thought that Freda must bloody-well know what she's doing. I first met them at Freda's local pool in Surrey. I swam with Alison, and then they took me back to their house for breakfast. Freda said she would work me the following year, and then asked what I weighed. I knew exactly: twelve stone two pounds (170 pounds) at five foot eleven. She told me to put on another stone (fourteen pounds) by the following May."

Cliff started training at Swimmer's Beach in Dover and made his first attempt at the Channel in 1992, unsuccessfully. He tried again in 1993, '94, and '95—still no dice. Friends and family were sympathetic and understanding, but he felt like a fraud. He didn't want sympathy or understanding. He knew he was failing for the wrong reasons; he knew that he was giving up.

In 1997, Cliff started another Channel attempt with the same doubts and weaknesses that had plagued and defeated him earlier. These included a painful left shoulder, a painful *right* shoulder, and a nagging resignation that he need only swim farther than he had in the past in order to save face. As Cliff crested the seven—and eight-hour marks and swam past the farthest point he'd ever gotten before, he began hoping for an excuse to get out. His shoulder was bothering him; his *other* shoulder was bothering him. He watched the boat and hoped it would break down. That would be an unarguable reason to stop. This train of thought lasted until he passed the eleven-hour mark.

Then something changed.

Cliff realized that his shoulders had stopped complaining and everything else had receded into the background. His doubts were silenced, and he knew—he believed for the first time—that he could do it. So he did.

On July 17, having been piloted proficiently by Mike Oram and his boat the *Aegean Blue*, Cliff emerged from the water in France thirteen hours and seventeen minutes after he'd walked unaided off the beach in England. He was a Channel swimmer at last.

"I finally understood the secret," he said.

I leaned forward and listened carefully, afraid I'd miss it in the pandemonium of Chaplin's.

"You need to admit you're scared. I have a theory that women are better Channel swimmers because they are naturally more comfortable falling apart and subsequently picking themselves up. I've seen them stand on the back of the boat in distress, crying and weeping, and then clean themselves up and get back to work. The average male swimmer doesn't do that. He won't admit the doubt and fear, won't cry that publicly, doesn't get over it and on with it."

Cliff's struggles with unsuccessful swims were similar to what I had felt (but had not yet accepted) about my own experiences. His ultimate defeat of fear filled me with admiration and convinced me that he'd be a sympathetic and helpful crewman. I hoped he'd also become a lifelong friend. A simple web search brings up perhaps Cliff's most impressive credit (at least to me): he's named in more blogs and articles about Channel swimmers than almost anyone save Freda Streeter.

I finished my swim in Lake Washington and toweled off. I dug my smartphone out of my car and e-mailed Cliff to ask if he'd be interested and willing to help me cross the Channel.

I had an eight-hour swim from Fairhaven to Guemis Island and back scheduled with Dale that weekend, but it didn't go as planned; the wind spoiled it. Conditions seemed relatively calm onshore, and we managed to get out of Marine Park at 7:30 a.m., only to find a twenty-knot wind waiting in the Bay. We swam for a couple hours, but we were getting battered and beaten. The weather had also whipped up the colder, deeper water in the Bay, and the frigid blasts that normally only tickled my feet and ankles when I was treading water were surging over me from head to toe. At fifty degrees Fahrenheit, the water was colder than I could manage for eight hours. We called it a day dejectedly, and I drove the long miles home from Bellingham worrying about how I was going to get in enough major training swims before my departure for Dover.

My work and family schedule permitted only a few more viable weekends. As I pulled into my driveway, I'd settled on squeezing in a four-hour swim on July 5 in Lake Washington to make up for the lousy swim in Bellingham. That meant I'd need to be in the water at 4:00 a.m. to avoid drunken holiday boaters and finish in time for family obligations afterward.

I slid into the water that morning and found that despite the early hour, the water was boiling with traffic. I counted about twenty boats, three floatplanes, two Jet Skis, and a couple of kayaks sharing the lake—but no other swimmers. One of the boats was driven by a young kid standing on the fantail and surf-driving it like a Jet Ski at full throttle through a no-wake zone. *Safe and intelligent,* I thought. I put my head down and swam along the coast to avoid the boaters' melee. For diversion, I turned my mind back to my crew problem, this time contemplating my friend Brent Hobbs.

Brent, who had been critical to my Bowen Island swim, is of average height and stocky build, typically dressing in casual clothes that I suspect his wife helps choose. He's habitually smiling: your first thought upon meeting him might be, *Hey, this guy looks friendly!*

Brent was raised on Vancouver Island, British Columbia, just a few miles from the Georgia Strait and the open Pacific Ocean. Needless to say, it is an area rife with swimming opportunities; a temperate environment boasting a rich swimming culture that has produced a number of Olympians.

Brent began swimming at a young age and was nationally ranked by the time he was in his late teens. His chosen events were the 1,500-meter freestyle, 400 freestyle, 400 individual medley, and 200 butterfly—the toughest events in competitive swimming. After high school, Brent knocked around college for a year and toyed with triathlons, where many open-water swimmers get their start. After a year of that, at nineteen, he set off to travel the world—or at least as much as his budget would allow. Fortuitously, his frugal meanderings led him to Brighton, England, where the waterfront is the centerpiece of the town.

In 1987, Brent stood on the long, curving Victorian Brighton Beach, with its piers, garishly colored carnival attractions, short and wide whitewashed apartment buildings, and pebbled sand. He stared at the English Channel's lapping waves, transfixed.

Eight years later, he'd moved to the city of Vancouver, met Joanne (the future mother of his two sons), and was working as a nurse. He started open-water training in earnest and made like-minded friends, something that's not difficult for the outgoing British Columbian. Shane Collins, the first person from British Columbia to swim the English Channel, eventually entered the picture, and Brent began learning about how to swim the Channel: the training, a pilot's name, all the details.

Brent's journey back to England, to Dover, had begun.

Some years later, on July 28, 2008, at the age of forty, Brent Hobbs, the healthcare director for patient transport in British Columbia, became the 972nd swimmer to cross the English Channel. He made it in a fast ten hours and forty-three minutes, ably supported by Channel pilot Andy King, on his boat the *Louise Jane*. Realizing a dream of some twenty years was nice—but raising money for the Kelowna General Hospital Foundation and YMCA Strong Kids was even more meaningful.

Brent would be a fantastic addition to the crew, I thought.

Back in Lake Washington, I swam on. Thirsty, I spied a waterfront park and swam to shore to get some water from the fountain to go with the gel feeds I was carrying in my suit. A yoga class was underway in the park, and I walked in and among a dozen limber women in colorful, loose pants on yoga mats. The instructor looked up as she called for the prayer pose, and when she noticed me, her mouth gaped open in surprise.

"Good morning!" I said cheerfully. "Beautiful day for a swim, huh?"

The class sat up and stared at me en masse. Suddenly self-conscious, I tried to walk quickly to the water fountain but felt about as inconspicuous as a giraffe in a purple skirt, so I sucked in my swimmer's belly, waved at the group, and tanked up on water as fast as I could.

Conditions were once again stormy. The clouds overhead resembled white socks that had been washed with cheap black towels. I swam thoughtfully, thinking on and off about Cliff versus Brent. Unfortunately, I only had space for one of them.

As I looked up to breathe, I saw a bald eagle sitting on a tree by the waterfront, ironically near a carved wooden sculpture of itself. The live version gracefully soared off its perch and circled me for a few minutes, then flew away. A few moments later, I stopped for a look around the lake and saw that I'd now attracted two circling eagles. They wheeled above my head, almost perfectly aligned on opposite sides of the circle. Somewhat inanely, I waved at them. They broke formation and flew away, gracefully, disappearing into the gray sky like butter melting into bisque.

It had been a good swim, and my shoulders had been cheerful. I got out of the water and dried myself absentmindedly while still weighing Cliff versus Brent. I dressed at my car and checked my smartphone for messages. Cliff had responded sometime between the yoga class and the eagles. "It would be an honor to be on your boat," he replied.

There was no light, no air, between Cliff and Brent. Both were ideal companion swimmers and great friends that would do anything to help me cross to France, of that I was sure. I thought about what was critical, about why I'd failed in 2008 and 2006. Both failures were my fault, I was convinced, the result of personal shortcomings. I'd quit. I decided that the decision should ultimately come down to who knew me best, who had swum with me more often and knew how to motivate me. That was Brent. The Bowen Island swim was a milestone, and he'd been there, seen my swimming, heard my whining, and motivated me with bananas and fried chicken.

I broke the news to Cliff right there and then, and he cheerfully agreed to stand down in favor of Brent. I thought that someday, after I had one successful Channel swim under my belt, Cliff and I could do a crossing together—and I told him that. His response was, "Anytime."

I e-mailed Brent.

Joanne kindly agreed to put off their planned vacation and gave him an all-clear to join my team instead.

Brent was on his way back to Dover—this time with me.

Chapter 27

Agony and Respite

With my crew situation settled, I was free to concentrate on training during my remaining weeks at home. I was fitful, concerned, trying to make certain I had enough time to practice dealing with the elements that would come into play in the Channel: cold water, rough water, long swims, feeding, and dealing with uncertainty. The last one was what I should have been spending most of my time on.

On July 10, I was in Bellingham for a ten-mile swim with Dale. We started at Marine Park and went south along the natural seawall to Dot Island, a small blob in the middle of Chuckanut Bay.

I was standing at the ready to put in when a shaggy-haired dude walked toward me, after leading a couple of dogs out of a Volkswagen camper van.

"Are you swimming out there today?" he asked, pointing at the bay. "Won't you get hypothermic?"

"Yeah, my friend and I are going down to Dot Island. It's cold but not too bad if you're used to it."

"Wow, right on!"

"Did you stay overnight in that?" I asked, pointing at his van. (Seems we each had something to learn about alternative lifestyle choices.)

"Yeah, I live in it," he said. "I travel up and down the west coast all year and try to be in Bellingham for the summer. I don't have much use for money," he added, superfluously. "What's that stuff? It looks like you're loading on the deodorant."

"It's Body Glide, helps with body chafing in the saltwater," I answered as he looked at me curiously. On the other side of Marine Park, a 5k running race was lining up to start, and some of the runners were staring and pointing. I quickly swabbed on the Glide and put it away in my car.

It was a two-and-a-half-hour route south by water, and the steady breathing of my freestyle meant I spent it alternately staring down into the water, over at the rocky wall, back down into the water, ad infinitum. Occasionally a train would pass, and I could break the monotony by counting its cars. (The last one had thirty-five.)

The swim offered a wildlife bonanza: a colony of seals watched me silently from their island preserve just north of Dot Island, while swarms of jellyfish squished silently around me in the water. I lost a bunch of my skin on the swim, a result of not applying enough Body Glide before I started. I guess I'd been self-conscious and a little hasty in front of an audience.

We finished the swim in about five hours and agreed it had been a nice day. Skin chafing is a delayed pleasure, though, and by the time I got home, I was grimacing regularly at the pain on my neck, underarms, and inner thighs. I trundled up to the shower, hoping some warm water would help matters. Instead, both my shoulders started showing signs of further ill temper, and I winced loudly in pain.

"What's the matter?" Barb said, coming upstairs.

"I lost half my skin in Bellingham Bay," I snapped, "and my damn shoulders are killing me."

"Enjoy your swim?" she asked with a bemused smile.

"Yeah, sometimes it's really an awesome hobby," I muttered.

Later in July, I bowed to modern pharmacology and had cortisone shots in my shoulders. Cortisone is a palliative steroid that suppresses the immune system, thus relieving inflammation and pain for injuries. There is risk in continually using it long-term, but the risks associated with nonsteroidal anti-inflammatories such as aspirin and ibuprofen is arguably worse. One shoulder or the other hurt every day, and I never knew which one to use to open doors, carry my laptop, or brush my teeth. I needed lasting relief.

It was so rewarding to be in peak, elite physical condition.

There's a scene in seemingly every *Star Trek* movie where Captain Kirk hollers down to the engine room that they need peak power immediately or they'll die. The engineer, Mr. Scott, does some magic, and all of a sudden the gauges on the bridge show full power and the starship *Enterprise* streaks away at the speed of light, safe and comfortable.

That's what I felt like a couple days after taking the shots, when the cortisone had been absorbed into my arthritic shoulders. Oh my, it felt good.

By the following Saturday, July 24· I was pain-free at least temporarily, and ready for a long swim. I checked my e-mail before I drove to Bellingham and saw that a fellow Channel swimmer, Chloe McChardel, had swum a two-way and decided to turn around for a third leg. Holy crap.

My swim started with an approximately eight-mile sojourn south from Marine Park to an empty oil tanker, the appropriately named *English Courage*, anchored near Samish Island. Dale and I bobbed around it for a bit before deciding to go back over to Dot Island and finish the swim from there. I got out at Dot for a look around.

"Ouch," I said.

"What happened?" Dale asked.

"I scraped myself on your boat."

"Your ass is hanging out of your suit," Dale guffawed.

"What the . . ." She was right. My suit had torn across the back, and the people at Marine Park were going to get a show when we finished. I got back in the water and started swimming north.

"Why are you shivering?" Dale called loudly.

"I don't know," I replied. "I guess getting out wasn't such a great idea."

"It certainly wasn't for your ass," she countered with another guffaw.

I swam back at a hard pace, probably too hard, but I was enjoying my respite from shoulder pain. By the end of the swim, hours later, I was spent. We pulled into the beach, and I unloaded my gear from Dale's little boat. The beach was packed, and I tried to position my bare backside away from the masses, but that's difficult when you're unloading a boat in the water.

Once I had all my gear, I turned and walked through the crowd toward my car. I was groaning mildly, moving slowly, and attracting more attention than a pregnant nun. I looked so bedraggled that an elderly man using a walker voluntarily walked around me to save me from having to divert. I changed, packed up, and drove to McDonalds, where I put away two double quarter-pounders, a large milkshake, and a larger order of fries. I was still hungry, but I declined dessert. Barb had promised to have dinner waiting when I got home, and I wanted to preserve my appetite.

As I left the restaurant, I checked my e-mail. Jackie Cobell, a sixtyish woman who'd had gastric bypass surgery just nine months prior, had set a world record in the Channel with the longest swim in history—over twenty-eight hours.

I wanted to finish July off with a swim across Elliott Bay, from Alki to Bainbridge Island. If you've ever seen a picture of the beautiful Seattle skyline, you've probably seen Elliott Bay lapping up against the waterfront, keeping all the cruise ships afloat. Alki Beach is a classic beachfront neighborhood on the south side of Elliott Bay, about one mile from downtown Seattle, and Bainbridge Island is five or six miles west of the Seattle waterfront.

My friend Tim Duerr was ready and able—with a new boat, a new truck, and a hankering to play with both on the same occasion.

We put in at Alki and swam northwest to Bainbridge. The water was bracing and teeming with big, juicy, nasty-looking jellyfish with long white, spiky tentacles; they seemed much bigger than other jellies I'd shared the sea with. I was perpetually panicked and sprinted most of the way to avoid them, as if I could somehow swim fast enough to plane above the water. I wasn't sure why they were out in force; it didn't look like a particularly plankton-rich day in the water.

About halfway across the bay, they increased in number and started coming closer, until I was in a constant state of panicky attention. I sort of wished one would go ahead and sting me; the suspense was killing me. About thirty minutes before I finished, I breathed to the left for one stroke, and one of the greasy beasts was right in the pocket of my armpit; I actually stroked him back with the water flow from my hand. On my next stroke, my hand ran into a mass of floating plastic bags, and I almost jumped out of the water like Wile E. Coyote. After that, I somehow managed to accept my fate and stopped worrying.

Elliott Bay is a busy shipping port, plus it has ferries and pleasure boats, so I'd called the Coast Guard earlier that week to let them know about the swim. They didn't seem to care. I guess there aren't any rules for open-water swimmers in the bay. That may be because there aren't very many open-water swimmers in the bay.

As we got closer to Bainbridge, the sailboat brigade was out in force. We passed a couple of ferries going in and out of the Bainbridge docks, but we weren't close enough to wave, as I'd hoped we would be. The water was a bit choppy, but the only really rough stuff was the wake from the Washington State ferries. We squirted into the inland waters at Bainbridge about two hours after we started. I climbed onto Tim's boat, and in spite of those fifteen pounds of body fat I was so proud of, the post-swim shivering started. Tim's a Brit, so he contributed a colorful English expression: I was shaking like a cornered virgin.

Here's what the month had brought: two painful shoulders, a few good swims, a pharmacological respite, a few better swims, and news of two inspirational Channel crossings.

July had been relatively good to me.

Chapter 28

Jeffrey Hulett and Perseverance

August arrived in Seattle, warm and humid. It was to be my last month of preparations, and I was incessantly preoccupied with the Channel. Every activity, every meal, every night's sleep, everything I did was focused on my swim. It was difficult to live normally.

I relentlessly reviewed my planning and questioned everything constantly and repeatedly. There was one issue that had begun to worry me after my discussion with Mike Oram, and it continued to gnaw at me. I'd booked my Channel pilot because I'd used him for my previous swims, but my research suggested that Mike would give me the best chance at getting across. Plus, I'd begun to think of him as a friend. My calls to Mike were reliably met with a booming, "Hallo, *Mike*!" followed by a cheerful, "And what can I do for you today, *young man*? Have you married that girl *yet*?"

I wanted to swim the Channel with Mike.

Jeffrey Hulett would understand.

I'd met Jeffrey at Bill and Audrey Hamblin's B&B in the summer of 2008. He was in Dover for a Channel swim and had brought his teenage son, Taylor. They were an amiable pair, and we quickly became friends, chatting over English breakfasts, touring the sights, waiting together for swims in the Channel.

The Huletts are from Denver, Colorado, where Jeffrey was the general manager of the Brighton Recreation Center, a community-owned fitness complex in the Denver suburb of Brighton. Jeffrey and Taylor both look every bit as clean-cut and wholesome as the State of Colorado's public relations department would want.

Behind the relaxed demeanor, though, Jeffrey had a useful characteristic for Channel swimming.

"I like to suffer," he'd answered when I asked, "Why swim the Channel?"

Jeffrey swam his first race when he was just about five years old. His early memories are of being the smallest and youngest kid in swimming and of being scared of the bigger kids. But he stuck with it and raced all through school, although he was never a star. When he finished school, he moved on to other sports and swore he'd never swim another lap.

Jeffrey became an experienced runner, triathlete, cross-country skier, and road-and-trail bicyclist. The threads tying those together are pain and persistence—and both came into play when he competed in the Race Across the Sky.

The Leadville Trail Run, aka the Race Across the Sky, is an infamous, grueling, one-hundred-mile running race held on the trails and dirt roads surrounding Leadville, Colorado. It's run at elevations between nine and thirteen thousand feet, and it's not uncommon for fewer than half of the participants to finish.

"I had no business running Leadville," Jeffrey says. "I'm not a good runner, and I don't even have any athletic ability. But I think people generally underestimate themselves. I'm just willing to try harder."

Jeffrey experimented by running part of the Leadville race with a friend in 2002. He signed up for the full deal in 2003 and was forced to pull out after fifty miles. In 2004, he managed to go another twenty-five miles before pulling out, calling it a day at the seventy-five-mile mark. In 2005, he went the distance. He described it to me:

"In 2003, I blew up . . . more importantly, I was defeated mentally and had decided to drop out. It was a decision that bothers me to this day.

"In 2004, as I headed up Hope Pass, I lost all energy. I was on the steepest part of the course, and I could barely put one foot in front of the other. Over the course of the next fifteen miles, the hard downhill running off Hope Pass was taking its revenge, and I got timed-out at the seventy-five-mile aid station.

"In 2005, my feet blistered severely. I had so many blisters that I thought my feet would fall apart—I needed duct tape to hold them together. I managed to finish in thirty hours, but the trauma induced transient global amnesia and I couldn't remember the race, anything that happened. It took me three days for any of it to come back."

How long did he need to rest and recover after that?

"I was signed up for a triathlon three weeks later, so I did it," he said easily.

Jeffrey's 2008 Channel swim was a story of perseverance combined with Mike Oram's drive and support. I was at Victoria House when I heard he'd finished successfully, so I hastened down to Dover Harbor with Bill and Audrey to meet him. Jeffrey emerged from Mike's boat, weatherbeaten and bruised, clutching a blanket tightly, barely walking, shuffling slowly and painfully.

"Hey! Jeffrey! Congratulations!"

He looked at me with a painful grimace and said quietly, "Thanks. But I wouldn't have finished if not for Mike.

"It all went wrong, everything. My feeds went badly, and I got sick again and again and again; I threw up for hours. I was ready to get out at the midpoint. I rolled over onto my back and just floated. My stomach was distended and disfigured, and my left shoulder was killing me," continued the Leadville veteran.

"I decided to keep going, and then Mike stepped in, took over, changed my feeds, and got me going. I began to feel better and swam for a few hours. At that point, Mike and the crew waved a whiteboard at me with, 'France: 4 miles that way,' written on it. I was surprised! I was actually getting there, so I put my head and everything I had into it for a couple more hours. Finally, Mike told Taylor he could get in to finish the swim with me if he was careful to stay ten yards behind me. I finished in ten and a half hours."

I was absorbing his story when we both heard a noise and turned. Mike was stepping off the *Gallivant*, grinning while scratching his belly and pulling up his loose-fitting shorts. Jeffrey shuffled painfully over to him while Taylor watched, looking both proud and worried at his father's appearance.

"I never would have made it without you," Jeffrey told him, looking Mike in the eye. Mike grinned with satisfaction and pulled on his shorts again. (They were loose enough to threaten the display of his alter-ego at any moment.) If possible, Mike looked prouder and more pleased than either Jeffrey or Taylor. It was obvious that, to Mike, Jeffrey's success was Mike's success.

I thought of that moment over and over in August, as I fell into obsession over every detail, every preparation for my Channel swim. My pilot was experienced and friendly, but I wished I'd booked with Mike.

There wasn't much I could do about changing pilots, so I focused my energies elsewhere. In an effort to develop my confidence and build on the Elliott Bay swim, I decided to swim between Madison Beach and the I-90 floating bridge and back in early August.

The I-90 bridge is the second-longest floating bridge on earth, a fact that goes unnoticed in Seattle because the *first*-longest floating bridge is just miles away: the Evergreen Point Bridge. The original I-90 bridge was built in the late 1930s and completed in 1940. It served Seattle for years but sank in a 1990 storm, after local transportation engineers decided it would be wise to leave the watertight pontoons open to the elements overnight. The pontoons filled with water and took the original bridge crashing down to the lakebed.

The replacement span opened in 1993 and stands to this day. It originates on the west side of Lake Washington, spanning Seattle to Mercer Island. It's about one-and-a-half-miles long, and I've swum its length with friends many times, typically at 5:00 a.m. when boat traffic is light. Technically, there's a rule requiring swimmers to stay within fifty feet of shore if unaccompanied by a boat, but we swim in a group and there's no boat traffic that early, so it's relatively safe.

On the first day of August, my plan was to swim the four-mile shoreline between Madison Beach and the I-90 bridge. I'd done the swim many times, usually alone, and it was a favorite. I knew every inlet, shoreline tree, house, and waterfront park along the way.

I arrived at Madison early to avoid the crowds and grab a parking spot that wouldn't require me to walk across Main Street wearing nothing but a racing suit. I slipped into the water before the lifeguards arrived to enforce the rule against leaving for an open-water swim from a community beach. (It's a sensible rule that discourages kids from swimming off into the lake, but it's painful to follow because the rest of the waterfront is either private or slippery and sharp rocks make it difficult to enter or exit.)

The first half of my swim was into a head current, due to the strong winds gusting up Lake Washington. Head currents can be irritating, and since I had to stop at a county park about ninety minutes into the swim for some water, I didn't mind the resulting break. As I emerged from the grassy water, looking like a horror-movie character, I was peppered with questions by onlookers.

"Does the lake give you diarrhea?" one asked. "It makes me sick something fierce."

"Uh, no," I answered. "Perhaps you're swimming on the beaches with all the geese? Their crap contaminates the water."

"How far are you going?" asked another. "I'm waiting for some friends to do a two-mile, but it looks like they may not show."

"I'm headed to I-90," I said.

"Where did you start?"

"Madison."

"Geez, how far is that?"

"Uh, about seven and a half miles, round-trip," I answered, sheepishly. I don't like answering questions like that from other swimmers. It can erect an unnecessary barrier between "extreme" athleticism and the everyday kind.

"Wow, I thought two miles was a stretch," he said. "You must be a hell of a swimmer; I don't think I could ever do that."

"Sure you could—with the right training, anyone can," I said with a smile. "Do I look like a 'hell of a swimmer'?" I added, pointing at my fat belly.

He looked at me doubtfully, grinned, and walked away.

I took a sip of water from the fountain, sighed at having eliminated a potential swimming buddy, and reentered Lake Washington. I finished my swim in good form, albeit with an aching left shoulder, throbbing right forearm tendons, and lower back muscles squealing loudly. The swim required frequent sighting, raising my head to look for boat traffic, and as a result, my lower back muscles were toasted by the time I finished.

On August 6, I heard from Jeffrey Hulett that his attempt at swimming the Catalina Channel had failed. After less than three hours, he'd been forced from the water due to hypothermia. He was annoyed, of course, and we talked about doing Catalina together in a future summer, sharing costs and urging each other on.

As August continued to blossom, so did my training injuries. I tried every trick I knew to ease them: regular massages, chiropractic adjustments, electrostimulation, swim-stroke analysis, and obsessive stretching. On most days, I'd do more than one of these—for example, chiropractic in the morning, massage before coming home from work, and then stretching for a half hour on the family-room floor while Barb and I watched TV and chatted. I also visited my sports doctor for a couple of cortisone shots.

I was battered and bruised, but I still didn't think I'd breached the pain levels Jeffrey had endured. As my body parts ached and creaked more and more, I thought of him often and what he'd overcome, how Mike Oram had pulled him through. I worried about what would happen to me.

And then, all of a sudden, it was time to leave for Dover—and France!

Chapter 29

Arrival

Dover.

I arrived in Dover on August 20 and settled in. Bill and Audrey at Victoria House were, as always, hospitable and openhearted.

As I caught up with them, I was struck again by the extent to which these two have become a Channel institution—as well as the sort of couple so completely intertwined that people naturally refer to them as one entity, as in, "Bill and Audrey are here," "Bill and Audrey did that."

They met at a cycling race in 1952, just after Bill was released from the British Royal Air Force. The two were unknowingly sealing their fates when they both decided to attend the race in the sparsely populated town of Stapleford Tawney, Essex, and came upon each other. When asked about this meeting, Audrey proudly pulls out a faded and dog-eared photo to illustrate. Despite the fact that Bill was the one racing that day, it's Audrey in the black-and-white snapshot, pedaling intensely while focusing on the road ahead, her short hair blowing to the side as she gasps through a crooked smile.

Audrey was raised in the bluster of London, while Bill grew up in the quieter environs of Essex. They married in 1955 and bought their first house in the London commuter town of Hoddeson shortly thereafter. The children came along at regular intervals: Lee in 1957, Debbie in 1960,

Judy in 1962, and Lindsey in 1969. Eventually, the flow of grandchildren began, and didn't let up until they numbered eight. They lived in Hoddeson until 1978, when they moved to the seaside town of Deal. Audrey ran a bridal shop, while Bill managed a factory. Years passed, and 1986 brought a move to Dover. The rest is English Channel-swimming lore.

Though they didn't realize it, the bed-and-breakfast the couple bought in Dover came with a prebooking for a group swimming a Channel relay. Bill was still unpacking and Audrey working at her bridal shop when there was a knock at the Victoria House door, and in poured a large group with all sorts of kit and caboodle, beaming in anticipation of clear swimming weather. After a moment's discussion with the group's leader, Bill produced a wad of keys to every room in Victoria House, handed them over, and said, "Here, I wasn't expecting you lot—so you go ahead and sort out your rooms."

The relay went off without a hitch, and the group enjoyed the first and last dinner ever served by Bill and Audrey. Upon leaving, the swim leader asked if the couple would mind being referred to other Channel swimmers. They didn't—and every summer since has involved busy rooms, lots of English breakfasts, and more than two hundred Channel swimmers, many of whom they consider family. If you have the chance, by all means stop by, go down the steep stairs to their dining room, and check out the many swim charts, letters, and pictures of their swimming family adorned across their traditional patterned wallpaper.

I unpacked and eventually collapsed into bed for a restful evening before an eagerly anticipated tomorrow.

I woke early on August 21 and jumped out of bed. Three quick steps, and I was across the Balcony Room. I took a moment to fiddle with the recalcitrant latch on the floor-to-ceiling double windows and then pulled them fully open to let the Channel air and the view flood in. I was home—and was eagerly anticipating stepping onto Swimmer's Beach later that morning. First, though, I had a Victoria House breakfast ahead of me. Bill and Audrey take breakfast seriously, so there's generally about a pound of bacon, a quart of porridge, sautéed tomatoes, and maybe a half dozen eggs to be consumed and washed down with orange juice and coffee while listening to proud tales of their grandchildren.

An hour after I sat down for breakfast, I pushed myself back from the table with difficulty and waddled off to collapse in my room and digest for forty-five minutes before walking to Swimmer's Beach.

It's trite yet true to write that I was as excited as a kid on Christmas morning about my first swim in Dover Harbor. I planned an easy six-hour jaunt (about twelve miles), to be followed on Sunday by a one—to two-hour (two—to four-mile) swim. The idea was to stay fresh for my Channel attempt without losing my edge—a delicate balance.

As I walked to Swimmer's Beach, Dover's colorful were out and about, enjoying a sunny Saturday morning. It was windy but not dramatically so—a pretty day punctuated by breezes singing the Channel's song. I nodded to an older gentleman walking the waterfront in a jacket and tie. Up ahead, I spied a group of bare-chested teenage boys in shorts, plotting mischief and watching an older girl saunter by. Her low-rider jeans were slipping south, while her G-string was stretching north, leaving the middle terrain open for the boys' enthusiastic admiration. Rushing past me was a woman about my age in a cocktail dress and three-inch heels, hastening her young son to his Nan's house.

I took this all in cheerfully while walking quickly to Swimmer's Beach, thinking about the weeks ahead and behind. I reflected on a chat I'd had with my friend Ricky Klint, who'd stopped by to wish me luck before I left Seattle.

"Well, damn, you can really see the Channel fat now!" Ricky exclaimed, looking me up and down.

"Thanks." I crossed my arms defensively.

"It's all over your face," Ricky pressed on, leaning forward and peering intently.

"Uh, I've been working hard to pack it on," I told him, pointing at my belly and lifting my shirt.

Ricky is a tall, strapping Dane, with biceps straining his shirtsleeves and shoulders like a Roman statue. At the sight of my overflowing gut, he recoiled in horror, perhaps fearing that it was contagious.

"Could have lived without seeing that, Ricky?" Barb piped in helpfully from across the room.

I chuckled at the memory and stepped off the boardwalk onto Swimmer's Beach. I was back in the company of Channel swimmers. Among the first I saw were Ishii and Miyuki. Given their limited English, our chats can be slow and halting as we cooperate to find words. Miyuki flashed me a dazzling smile.

"Mike, bigger!" she said, inflating her cheeks like a puffer fish and pointing to my muffin top.

Okay, not quite so much grasping for words as usual.

"Ten kilos!" I agreed.

Ishii was staring as well, and nodding enthusiastically in accord.

"When are you swimming, Miyuki-san?" I asked.

"Miyuki go twice, this tide and next tide, Mike-san," Ishii answered.

Hmm. I suddenly felt like a lazy slug for planning a simple single crossing.

Swims in Dover Harbor are a back-and-forth affair. You start in the middle and go left or right, north or south, as your preference dictates, and then swim back the other way. And the other way. And the other way again.

I'd arrived at the beach a bit late for the start time as dictated by Freda Streeter and her beach crew, which is at 9:00 a.m. After I'd chatted with Miyuki and Ishii, Freda greeted me.

I hadn't seen her since I'd interviewed her the prior January, but she quickly cut short the small talk. "How long are you in for today?" she asked.

"Uh, six hours—okay?" I asked hopefully.

"Good boy. Let's get you a swim cap and get you greased," she said, nodding at Barrie Wakeham.

I was chatting up Cliff Golding while he good-naturedly layered sunblock on my shoulders, and off to the side, Barrie got ready to grease me up.

"Mike, when are you getting in the *water?*" Freda asked in a singsong voice from her tent at the top of the beach.

"I'm hurrying," I said, "but Cliff's over here talking!" Cliff smiled at this. The sunblock was done. I started throwing my stuff hurriedly into my knapsack.

"When are you *getting in the water?*" Freda asked again, impatiently, the singsong lilt now gone.

"Barrie's got to grease me up," I insisted. I think he'd only gotten one arm done when Freda piped up again.

"When *are you getting in the water?*"

"Okay, okay, I'm going, I'm going, geez, you'd think there was a fire or something," I muttered.

"*What?*" Freda asked pointedly.

"Nothing, nothing . . . . See, I'm going. I'm going, okay?"

Freda finally looked satisfied as Barrie followed me down the beach, still applying grease.

To be fair, when you're volunteering to support and watch swimmers every weekend, five months out of every year, it's reasonable to ask the ones doing six—to eight-hour swims to get their asses in the water quickly so they'll finish early enough to leave free time at day's end. Freda and her team don't go home until they know every swimmer is safely out of the water.

My six-hour swim went smoothly, though I did lose a bit of skin to chafing. The Channel has very high salinity, and that, combined with my extra rolls of body fat, was literally rubbing me the wrong way. The skin under both arms was raw, as were the insides of my legs. I walked out of the water after my swim like a cowboy who'd seen too many John Wayne movies. I sounded like a cowboy, too. I'd forgotten that because the water was so salty, I needed to alter my normal breathing style to keep my mouth closed. All of that saltwater squishing around my mouth had inflated my tongue like a Botox experiment gone awry. Some of the skin in there was sloughing off too—how nice. It was uncomfortable to talk or eat for some time.

When I went back the next morning for my two-hour swim, the weather had kicked up. It was raining heavily, and the skies were grayer than floodwaters in a coal mine. Along with the other swimmers, I got undressed under a sparsely covered shelter on the boardwalk. There were a lot of people crammed under that overhang, waiting for loved ones, reading, knitting, eating, and so on. In addition to the swimmers like myself, in town a couple of weeks in advance of their Channel attempts, the swimmers who were scheduled to go that weekend were assembled, looking glum. The twenty-four-knot wind out in the open Channel had scotched their attempts, so they were making the best of the day in Dover Harbor instead.

I managed a good swim back and forth. Once I settled in, I enjoyed the dramatic weather and was swimming into the beach when the skies really opened up and began to pour on us. The rain was coming down biblically hard, but I decided to stay out longer and enjoy the spectacle. It would have been a waste of time trying to get dressed in the driving rain anyway. Worst case, I figured, it'd be a great story to endlessly bore my grandchildren with someday.

I did stick to my plan of having lunch at Chaplin's with Sue Pepper and catching up. We chatted over a traditional British roast dinner and chitchatted with other Channel swimmers who were similarly attracted to the hearty fare. Among them was Bryan Bachman from Minnesota, accompanied by his wife, Jessica. Also being piloted by Chris Osmond, Bryan had been totally blown out by the weather and was on the verge of packing it in for the year. He'd extended his stay a couple days to give the weather one last chance to break, but had been disappointed.

The swimmers gossiped about some of the season's attempts. I heard there was a swimmer that week vying to be the oldest Brit to swim the Channel, and Liz Fry, a strong swimmer who'd made successful and fast crossings in previous years, was a favorite topic. Liz was in Dover to attempt a two-way crossing, but as the weather was not cooperating, her crew was making plans to go home. Liz was a consultant by trade and the organizer of the Swim Across the Sound in New York that had raised hundreds of thousands of dollars for cancer research. She'd booked her crossing with

Mike Oram and was very experienced. I felt confident she'd make the double sooner or later.

I finished my lunch, said my good-byes, and wobbled back to Victoria House, fighting a combination of too much lunch and the saltwater chafing on my legs, which now felt worse. I wanted a shower, and the last thing I wanted to think about was food, but I stopped at the grocery store along the way nonetheless. It had taken a long time to pack on the body fat, and I didn't want to burn it off that close to my actual swim.

I got home an hour later, made my way up to the Balcony Room, grabbed the TV remote and my laptop, and crumpled onto the bed. I tried to snack on some of my grocery store purchases, but the roast lunch plus eight hours of saltwater swimming over two days had completely toasted my tongue and taste buds, so I gave up quickly. I clicked the remote, and a BBC program started blaring cheerfully out of the ancient TV while I typed an e-mail to Barb, asking her to buy and bring me a larger swimsuit when she came over a few days later. I didn't want my fat rear end to cause any more chafing during my Channel swim.

Barb answered quickly and readily agreed, without even making fun of my misshapen, middle-aged, tired, and battered body.

Is that love or what?

Chapter 30

Calm Before the Storm
and Storms Before the Calm

The following week was difficult in the Channel. Aggressive storms continually passed through, devastating the swimming conditions. The gale-force winds were so loud they kept me awake all night—it was as if Victoria House was trying to evict its tenants.

Monday was a turning point for those unfortunates scheduled on the tide before mine. The sky was overlaid with a layer of thick gray moisture, as if it were raining above the clouds, and wind gusts were predicted to reach fifty miles per hour. At thirty miles per hour and above, the only thing that can comfortably navigate the Channel is a large freighter, so the forecast was fatal news. It was clear that nobody would have a chance to swim. Swimmers and crews started packing gear and memories and heading home empty-handed. At Victoria House, Liz Fry was resignedly talking to her crew about arrangements, her double-crossing chances shot for the season. She reluctantly booked a slot for 2011, which would delay her plans to resume her running career in favor of another year's training in cold water.

The other team entrenched at Victoria House was a group from Mexico that had thrown caution to the wind and extended their stay through the end of September, in hopes they'd be able to swim sometime in those three weeks—a long shot at best. Meanwhile, the long-range weather and wind projections for my own tide were iffy. I began to prepare myself for the possibility of spending my vacation watching 3£ DVDs and staring at the horizon, hoping for a break.

With the wind howling, at least my daily swims in Dover Harbor weren't dull.

On Tuesday, a dramatic south wind threw water over the seawall like a toddler in a bathtub. I did the south-harbor-wall to north-wall swim (about a mile) in about ten minutes. On the way out, the wind assist was so strong that I felt like an Olympic sprinter. Coming back south was another story: I was Daffy Duck towing Wile E. Coyote in a rowboat, and it took three times as long. The force of the waves was all-consuming. Every time I looked up to see where I was going, I'd get slapped with a handful of water balloons-worth of salty sea. To make matters worse, Barb hadn't yet arrived with my larger swimsuit, so I was forced to wear a regular Speedo, the kind that many civilized people associate with Guido the Love Machine. It was better than chafing the skin off my legs, but coming out of the water in that and walking up the beach felt distinctly awkward.

After each day's heavy-duty swim, I faced my daily struggle to find and consume enough calories to maintain my body weight. On Tuesday, I started with a full meal and a pint at the Eight Bells Pub, and then stopped by the sandwich shop next door for a foot-long takeaway. On Wednesday I tried to supersize myself at McDonald's, but was nearly thwarted by the British love of rules.

"I'll have two double quarter-pounders," I ordered.

"Sorry, mate, can't help you."

"Beg your pardon?"

"Illegal. Against the rules. Straight from the 'ead office, that is."

"Beg your pardon?"

"Can't guarantee you'll actually get two 'alf pound burgers, y'see. So it's against the law."

"Uh, beg your pardon?" I said, laughing "I just want a couple burgers."

"Bloody Americans," he muttered. "All right, I'll make an exception, but don't come back 'ere again."

"Did you just tell me not to come back because I ordered an illegal hamburger?" I asked incredulously, unaware at the time that the law prescribed a strict standard on food establishments in their advertising. It was an evolution of law enacted many decades earlier after pub patrons got up in arms about getting less than the pint they'd ordered.

Later that day, Dale McKinnon arrived with her partner, Berns, and the rest of my crew arrived the next day. Finally, on Friday, Barb showed up with Brent Hobbs (and my new fat-boy swimsuit) in tow.

In addition to Brent and Dale, rounding out my boat crew were Ros Hardiman and my oldest son, Evan.

Evan's younger brother, Tyler, crewed for me on my failed attempt in 2008, so now it was Evan's turn. He was to serve as my official photographer and make sure that nobody on the crew was stretching the truth about how far I had yet to swim when I asked. (I was still wary after those "moving goalposts" on my Bowen Island swim.) I also asked him to pass along any texts that friends sent me during the swim.

After Brent arrived, he and I swam together and reacquainted ourselves with each other's strokes. Just so you know, Brent's stroke is to mine as a gazelle is to an armadillo. Seemed like every time I looked up, he was rolling over on his back or counting clouds while waiting for me to catch up.

After everyone arrived, I arranged to meet with my pilot, Chris Osmond, and talk about my swim. Chris is a retired real estate attorney who turned to Channel piloting later in life. About five foot nine, with tufts of gray hair sprouting off his head in various directions, he looks like a somewhat nutty professor. Chris told me I was in second position on his list for the tide, behind a swimmer who was attempting a double without having achieved a single crossing, England to France—a bold move that has only rarely paid off (see Chapter 16, Lisa Cummins). We chatted for about an hour; he congratulated me on my weight gain and agreed to connect by phone as the week and waiting wore on.

As the last couple of days before my own swim wound down, the weather projections cleared a bit, and it looked like there might be swimmable windows for me. I planned to spend the time before my odyssey across that patch of sea reflecting on my life, motivations, and the love and charity of my friends and family.

It was that kind of occasion; I was in that kind of mood. I was introspective, impatient, intimidated—and I was scared.

Chapter 31

The Beginning

On Wednesday, September 8, 2010, my crew and I were on a high when we left Dover Harbor for my Channel swim. Our preswim planning had been positive and collaborative, and everyone knew his or her part. The crew seemed confident. Looking out across the bow of the *Seafarer II* as we motored out of the harbor, it seemed that the Channel itself matched our mood—calm, comfortable, and friendly.

Let's start at the beginning . . .

Remember that each Channel boat pilot books four swimmers on each neap tide. I was in second position on Chris's tide list that week, and the weather and wind had been terrible for a couple of weeks prior to the swim.

My tide started Monday, August 30. The swimmer before me in the queue was the German woman attempting a double crossing despite having never completed a single. I didn't have a chance to meet her, unfortunately, so I'll just call her the German without meaning any disrespect. (The Germans get enough grief over David Hasselhoff.) Double crossings require a long and favorable weather window; fewer than twenty have been successful. As it happens, the German's window started at about noon Tuesday, while swimmers doing solos had been out before dawn. That meant she'd likely finish at about noon on Wednesday, give or take a few hours, and my pilot planned to be ready to take me out Thursday morning at about four o'clock.

I was comfortable with that because it meant that I was more likely to finish in daylight. Swimming through sunset and into the night can feel like running the last half of a marathon blindfolded and led by a leash. And although night swimming doesn't bother me, it does affect both the temperature and the mood. It can also be dangerous, particularly when conditions are rough. If you're tired, hypothermic, or not fully aware, the crew looks away for a moment, and an errant wave comes along, there is a risk that you could be lost.

Tuesday morning, Brent and I swam an easy hour in Dover Harbor. The water felt fresh, and our swim was languid and lazy. I savored the time, absorbing and appreciating the milky, minty-green water and the views of Dover Castle and the cliffs; I was enjoying every stroke. I felt strong and relished my last Channel-training swim. And because the tide had started with clear weather, there was a sense of occasion on the beach, the swimmers chattering like parents planning an elementary school bake sale.

"I'm swimming tomorrow morning."

"What time?"

"Early—3:00 a.m."

"David, how's it going? When are you swimming?"

"Tomorrow!" he answered.

"That's great! You ready?"

"I heard there's a woman out attempting a double today," I heard another swimmer say.

"Yes, she's with my pilot," I chimed in, "and I'm after her, probably on Thursday."

"It looks like I might go tomorrow afternoon."

"Why afternoon?" I asked.

"My pilot's taking a swimmer who's supposed to be fast before dawn, and he thinks he'll be able to do that and return for me in the afternoon."

"Wow, that's fast," I said. "Miyuki-san, when are you swimming?"

"Friday!" Miyuki answered, with a smile stretching to Mt Fuji, where she trains.

We chattered on that way for some time, discussing upcoming swims and swimmers, appraising boats and pilots, and nervously anticipating our moment in the open Channel. It was a last get-together with friends before graduation, complete with lots of photos and exchanges of contact details.

Brent and I wrapped up our swim at 1:00 p.m. and headed to the beach to send the German off and wish her well. My pilot had her swimming out of Samphire Hoe, about five miles south of Dover Harbor. The parking lot at Samphire Hoe is about a mile from the starting beach, and we had to run to reach it in time for her departure. I haven't run regularly in a couple of years, and what with my Channel body fat, it was clear that it would be a couple more before I could run anything like my previous pace. With fresh shin splints and elevated heart rates, we made it in time to wave off the German double-crosser and applaud. As we stood on the flat concrete Chunnel lid watching the German settle into her stroke, Alison Streeter, the most accomplished Channel swimmer in history and now a pilot, pulled up in her boat with another swimmer. We watched and applauded that swimmer as well and walked slowly back to our car.

231

As we watched, the second swimmer immediately gained on the German, which surprised me. I'd have expected a double swimmer to bang out a bit more speed on her first leg than a solo swimmer. I began to think through what would happen if the German were unsuccessful.

Which she was, unfortunately. My pilot called Tuesday evening at seven thirty and told me the news: "Mike, we're back early, and I'm thinking of taking you tomorrow afternoon," he said.

"She didn't make her double?"

"I'm afraid not."

"Oh, that stinks."

"Yes, well, you have to expect these things in the Channel," Chris said impassively. "So it looks like there's a window starting tomorrow at noon."

"Oh, I'm not sure I can take that. My crew and I expected to go Thursday, and I'm not sure I can even find them tonight. Also, why leave in the afternoon? Doesn't it look better in the morning?"

"I'm knackered, to be candid. And I don't think there's much between the morning and the afternoon weather-wise."

"Oh. Well, I'm not sure I can track them down. Let me call around and see if I can find everyone."

"Okay. I called you literally the moment after we returned to the marina, and I'd like to double-check everything for the swim tomorrow anyway. Let me know as soon as possible, please; I have seven swimmers in the queue behind you." With that, Chris rang off.

I hung up the phone, bothered. The weather was out of Chris's control, and experienced English Channel swimmers understand that the uncertainty of conditions is inherent to the pursuit. But Chris seemed too detached for my comfort. I'd hoped for more of a sense of sharing between us, considering our long history.

I managed to find everyone except Brent. (We later discovered that he'd been, er, bonding with other Channel swimmers at the White Horse Pub.) While we waited for him, Dale, Barb, Evan, and I had a spirited discussion about the swim. With her expertise in weather forged over decades of sailing, Dale was bothered about the winds projected for late Wednesday. Barb was apprehensive about me swimming at night, thinking back to when I succumbed to hypothermia in 2008. True to his temperament, my son Evan was sanguine and felt fate's plan had been revealed as a Wednesday swim, so we should take it. I was concerned about the wind and other issues, but I tended to agree with Evan.

In any case, the math related to forgoing Wednesday didn't look favorable. If I didn't take the swim, Chris would take someone else at noon. They'd return sometime early Thursday, and we'd simply end up in the same situation one day later. Or two days later. At that point, Saturday and Sunday looked questionable on multiple weather projection services, so I wasn't confident about waiting and hoping.

We decided to take the swim. We managed to secure the water, food, and other supplies we needed with a late-night run to the local market, then spread everything out in Victoria House's kitchen. It looked as if we'd provisioned a major expedition. Once we'd gotten it all sorted and inventoried, we settled in for some intense fretting, punctuated by occasional sleep.

But the fretting never came. I fell asleep thinking about the walkway that needed repaving in our yard at home and whether I could convince Barb to get rid of that vine-covered trellis in our garden that I hate. I slept deeply, and the night passed.

Wednesday at 11:00 a.m., we assembled and made our way to Dover Marina to get the *Seafarer II* ready for takeoff. We loaded our gear, two or three shopping carts worth, onto the boat and stood around chatting somewhat lazily while we waited for noon. We discovered that Ros's wheelchair didn't fit on the boat, so we got her settled without it and returned her chair to Sue Pepper's car. Sue had driven Ros down to the Marina and stayed to wave us off.

While we waited, we got started with the nasty part of getting ready.

"Stand here," Barb said, "and let me put the sunblock on you."

"Okay," I agreed. "Hey, that's too much!"

"No, it's not. Quit fidgeting."

"I don't need it in my hair!"

"Stand still," she commanded. "Whoops, missed that belly fat, need more there."

"Hey!" I protested.

"You're squirming like a child," Ros piped up.

"I hate this stuff."

"My turn," Brent chimed in, pulling on dishwashing gloves and reaching deeply into a tub of Channel grease. A mixture of lanolin and Vaseline, the purpose of the stuff is primarily to cut down on chafing, although some swimmers believe it also wards off cold. I don't count myself in the latter camp and wanted to wear just enough of the stuff to keep the saltwater from ripping my skin—no more. Brent had other ideas. He coated my neck and began working his way down my back with the enthusiasm of a supermodel's tattoo artist.

"Lift your arms," Brent ordered.

Looking down dubiously, I asked Ros, "Did you wear this much on your Channel swim?"

"No, definitely not," she answered with a grin that didn't hide her revulsion.

"Trust me, Mike, I'm your spiritual advisor here," Brent insisted.

"Uh-huh," I managed. "Hey, Barb, Dale, come give me a good-luck hug!"

"No, thanks!" Dale said. Barb didn't even bother to respond.

Brent finished, and for the next twenty minutes, everyone avoided physical contact with me. I felt like fungus in a locker room. If you'd walked past the *Seafarer II* at that moment, you'd have seen a gray, overweight forty-seven-year-old, his belly bursting over his swimsuit, covered in a viscous material that looked like winch lubricant for an oil freighter. About seven boats away, some German tourists were having a wine and cheese picnic on the stern of their sailboat and pointing at me. Nice.

In due course, we pulled out of Dover Marina and arrived at Shakespeare Beach for my start.

Barb, Sue, my friend Bryan Wilkinson, and others had come to watch me take off from Shakespeare's pebbled beach. As the rules dictated, I swam to shore off the back of the boat and stood clear of the water, both feet solidly on English soil. I reflected for a moment on the French shore, twenty-two miles distant, and then waded in.

It felt a bit chilly, and for a moment, I considered swimming over to the *Seafarer II*, maybe climbing back onboard and telling my crew I wasn't in the mood.

Instead, I settled into my swim.

My feeds started about twenty minutes later and continued at fifteen-minute intervals. Many swimmers feed less often, at thirty-minute intervals, but this rhythm worked best for me. I had started my regimen of shorter, faster feeds after being the observer on the Channel world record attempt with Mike Oram in 2009. In that case, the swimmer had fed every eight to ten minutes. My own small feeds took only about five, maybe ten seconds. Those at the top of the hour were more substantial and gave me a chance to touch base with the crew on my status.

"How are you doing?" Dale and Brent asked simultaneously during one feed.

"Great," I said. "How are you guys doing?"

"Very well, thanks for asking," Brent replied, laughing.

"Is Evan okay?" I asked on a subsequent feed, worried he was getting seasick.

"Evan's fine. He's right over here."

"Okay, I'm gonna swim some more."

I felt good and was mostly focused on whipping up mental exercises to whittle away the time. There was a bit of a Channel chop, but I was comfortable since Dale and I had often trained in confused and rough waters in Bellingham.

After three hours, I could see Brent getting ready to join me in the water for an hour. He cannonballed off the transom in an attempt to inject some levity, but the effect was mostly lost in the chop. I reckon he'd lost some weight since his own Channel swim in 2008, so his girth didn't do the job it might have that summer. He swam over quickly and took his place beside me.

It was nice knowing he was swimming with me, although I couldn't see him. He swam slightly behind me, according to Channel rules, so we could only interact during feeds.

"Nice out here, huh?" I said.

"It's going very well, Mike. You're making great time, and we're already almost at the English shipping channel."

"Great! Let's go see some ships!"

The Channel was getting rougher and starting to show some attitude, but it wasn't getting to me yet.

All good things come to an end, and Brent was back on the boat before too long. A few minutes after he left the water, the Channel decided to show off a little. The wind whipped up, and the boat started undulating. So did I. Soon, the water was rolling into two—to four-foot spikes, lifted farther toward the sky by a difficult-to-measure swell. Each stroke I took was confounded by breakers and coalitions of water pulling my legs one way, head and shoulders another, and my hands any which way the water pleased.

Right then, my real swim began—and my day started to end.

Chapter 32

Fate's Hand

Things were getting dicey and unpleasant.

As I swam along, I tried to retreat into my mind's recesses and think about things other than my swim—bigger things, such as family and the meaning of life. I started playing my life back as if it were a digital filmstrip; scenes from various times came to mind only to be replaced by others. The important moments, the times that had helped define me, such as swimming the Channel, I played over and again to divert my attention.

Because the Channel was now just tossing me around like a rag doll.

I thought about my mom and a time when I was two, maybe three years old. I was coming down the back stairs to the kitchen of my parents' house. It was my birthday, and my mom was at the kitchen sink. She turned to me and called, "Happy birthday, Sunshine!" as she reached for me. I remembered her a few years later, when I was in first grade, and she had a beehive hairdo taller than an actual beehive. I thought about her now, sitting at home waiting for news of her son's swim.

I thought about my swim in 2006, my first attempt at the Channel. Barb had been violently sick off the side of the boat for hours and hours, and I was equally indisposed in the water. I reflected on 2008, when I was pulled from the water limp and hypothermic in the inland waters off France.

Then I was back in the present, in the Channel in 2010, focused on feeding off the boat. Our feeding routine called for Dale, properly harnessed, to lean over the side and hand me my feed in a biodegradable cup. In the early hours, Brent had simply held on to the harness. Now that the boat was rocking so much, he was forced to hold her by the soles of her feet and dangle her over the side of the boat like a pocket watch on a chain. Dale's head and her hand with my feed were alternately one foot above the water and then about four feet up, as the *Seafarer II* swayed violently.

Dale's pretty tough for a sixty-five-year-old, but even she seemed nonplussed by the pitching.

"Give me the cup back when you're done," she said on one of the rough feeds.

"What?" I shouted.

"Give me the cup back! We're going to run low on cups!"

It's tough to throw a paper cup to a boat in a fifteen—to twenty-knot wind when the boat is rocking like a freshly branded bull. So, I'm afraid I was unsuccessful at that maneuver.

Feed over, I was back in the torrents of the Channel and started thinking about my dad. It was 1972, we were living in Vienna, and I was nine. My dad and I were out doing Saturday morning errands in his 1956 VW Beetle. In a flash, it was 1988, and my dad was congratulating me on my college degree. Then it was 1998, and Dad was having his first stroke, complaining about going to the hospital. Flash: it was three years later, and he was handing me a pamphlet describing stroke aftereffects. "This is happening to me," he said apologetically. It was 2006, and we were sitting at a table with a folder in which he'd outlined his affairs. "Take care of Mom?" he asked, struggling with dementia. It was 2009, and we were scattering my dad's ashes.

I was back in the Channel doing what I could against the endless waves. It was time for a feed. Brent and Dale did their upside-down and vertical acrobatics with the harness, the hanging, and the feed cup, while the official observer and the rest of the crew watched anxiously.

"What's happened to the weather out here?" I shouted up at the boat.

"It's whipped up a bit," Brent replied unnecessarily. "Looks like it might be this way for a few more hours."

"Okay, let's swim toward some ships!" I answered gamely.

I thought I could handle a few more hours. It was rough, relentless, and rapacious—yes—but I'd trained for a long day. In the context of a lifetime, it was just one page of the script.

I found a rhythm and swam on, retreating again to the bigger picture in my head.

I was fourteen and holding my sister's hand at camp. Our older brother had run away, and she was inconsolable. Then it was 1979 and I was sixteen, with hair to my shoulders, leaning on my first car. Don was back, safe. Flash ahead thirty years to 2009; we were all together for the holidays, reminiscing over the drama.

I swam, I fed, I swam, and I fought. I focused on other things.

I saw Barb wishing me luck that morning from Shakespeare Beach.

I swam, fed, drifted mentally.

It was 1986, and Christine and I married. It was 1988, 1990, and 2000, and I was in three different delivery rooms—watching each of my sons being born. It was 2001, and Christine I were separating.

It was September 2010, and I was my father's son and my sons' father, swimming the Channel, pulling as hard as I could against the unending tides.

I swam, I fed, I fought, and the Channel fought back. I grew more and more tired but continued on and on, swimming, feeding, swimming, daydreaming. The Channel's tantrum began to wear me down.

I was back in January 2003 and meeting Barb for the first time at a café on Alki Beach in Seattle. She wore a green sweater and ordered a latte and a cinnamon bun that she didn't finish. It was December 2006, and I was asking for her hand.

I swam, fed, and tried to keep my stroke in some semblance of proper form: face down, elbows high, hips high, moving forward. The Channel worked nonstop against me.

"I'm getting in the water with you in fifteen minutes," Brent yelled down.

"Okay," was all I could manage. I'd trained regularly in rough water, but not like these conditions. During my swims with Dale in Bellingham, the swells had sometimes reached three feet, but we'd usually abort if it got any rougher—save it for another day in order to prevent injury and stay safe.

I shouldn't have done that, I thought. *I don't have the game for this.*

I fought the Channel, and the Channel fought back. And then I lost the plot. I could no longer focus on anything other than being done with the rough. The mental exercises weren't working anymore.

It was time for Brent to swim again, and he joined me in the water.

"Mike, you're doing great," Brent said, "but you've got to swim closer to the boat."

We were bobbing about twenty feet off the starboard side. "What's happened out here?" I asked.

"The wind's whipped up over the Varne sandbank, and it's creating this swell and rough."

"I don't have this," I said, and after another moment, "I can't go on in this."

"It's a mental game, Mike. This is going to go on for a while, but you can do it."

"No, I can't. I don't have this."

At that moment, all I could think of was that I wasn't prepared, perhaps not sufficiently trained, perhaps simply not talented enough, to swim in those seas for sixteen to eighteen hours.

"I'm done."

"No, no, you're not," Brent said. "Ros, help us out here." He knew that Ros had gone twenty hours and twenty-five hours on her own swims.

"I'm not Ros; I can't do this today," I said. We were still bobbing about twenty feet from the boat. I began swimming slowly over to the transom platform. Slowly was all I had left.

"Mike, you're going to regret this forever," Dale said.

"No, I'm not, Dale. I don't have the game for this, not in these conditions; I don't want it."

The official observer, Laura, spoke up. "Mike, give me another thirty minutes."

"I don't have it."

I climbed onto the boat and called it. I'd lost the script, the plot I'd planned for my swim and story, and I'd quit. I slumped down for a dejected ride back to Dover.

George Mallory supposedly answered the question, "Why climb Mt. Everest?" with, "Because it's there"—but his actual words have been in dispute for years. Some insist that he said, "Because we're mountaineers, and it's there." I like to think the latter version is the accurate one, because it explains it. They climb because they're mountaineers. What else would a mountaineer do?

I wanted to swim the Channel because I thought I was a Channel swimmer. I wasn't, at least not then. Was I going to be? For the time being, I was a father and a son, a brother, fiancé, and friend. I was also an open-water swimmer and a writer. That would have to be enough for now.

Would I go back?

My mother has a story she's told numerous times, but I'd never really absorbed it. She told me the story again before I left for Dover. It's been more than sixty-five years since the events it describes, so Mom doesn't remember all of the details, but the story goes something like this:

It was a warm day, and Mom and her sisters, Anne and Pat, were at Pine Lake with my grandmother Anna. My mom was four or five, her sisters a bit older. They were on a day trip with their parents. My grandmother Anna was a strong lady who raised four strong women and a son. My grandfather was a more gentle soul, from the stories I've heard. I never knew him, as he died when my mother was just thirteen.

The lake was big, and it called to Anna, who swam at the YWCA pool regularly. She turned to her daughters and said, "Stay here and play on the beach, don't go anywhere, I'm going for a swim." In those days, it wasn't unreasonable to assume that they would do as they were told.

Mom, Anne, and Pat had been playing contentedly for some time when they realized their mother had been gone a long while. They looked up and tried to spot Anna, but didn't see her. What they did see was a crowd of people pointing out at the other side of the wide lake.

"Is that your mama?" one of the bystanders asked the girls. "I can barely see her; she's swum to the other side of the lake!"

The three sisters looked off across the lake and saw a small spot.

"I don't know," Mom said to the lady.

Sometime later, Anna walked back up the beach and sat down next to her daughters.

"Where did you go? Was that you in the lake?" they asked her.

"Yes," Anna replied.

"Why did you go all the way over there?"

"I just wanted to," she answered.

I've always assumed I simply chose to swim the Channel. But if my forty-seven years had taught me anything, it's that fate has a plan. When I heard this story again before I left for Dover, I understood a bit better where the swim and the Channel fit into my life, my history.

Fate had a plan, and I trusted it.

Chapter 33

2011—I Lied

The aftermath of my third failed attempt at the Channel was not fun.

The reactions from those around me, those close and those casual, varied greatly that September and the following fall.

Some were sympathetic, focusing on the role the weather had played. Many in this group tended also to focus on the extreme nature of the challenge. They assured me I had gotten a raw deal—either from nature or the pilot. That probably wasn't fair. I knew from conversations with my crew that the pilot had ignored input from them about what worked for me, but I was the one who climbed out of the water and stopped swimming, not him.

Some assumed I'd try again. Some went out of their way to say they hoped I'd try again.

My friend Mark, an accomplished Ironman triathlete, took me aside one day in the pool locker room and, adopting a serious and concerned look, gave me a long pep talk about persistence.

Some were silent unless asked. When I brought up the topic of trying again with Barb, she gently suggested that it might be beyond my reach. When I raised it with Dale, she told me quietly that she had other projects planned and wouldn't be able to train with me the following year. These were the most difficult conversations I had on the topic. I could see that those closest to me were distressed and frustrated: they'd believed I'd make it to France. They were disappointed in me, and I really couldn't blame them; I was, too. I'd managed to swim well into French waters and to the brink of hypothermic unconsciousness in 2008 . . . yet I'd stopped much earlier in 2010. People had invested time and emotional energy in me, and I'd let them down. They had shuffled their lives, spent their treasury, and delayed their plans to accommodate what I said I'd do—and I didn't do it.

Casual friends were generally positive, but throughout my life, I've always been very direct and unvarnished. I tend to call things as they are, warts and all. I am also a father and a veteran of corporate America—both of which tend to make one pretty good at detecting the truth. I knew that everyone was wondering if I'd bitten off more than I could chew.

Maybe I had.

I wallowed in self-disgust for a month or two, while pondering what to do. The obvious question was whether to go back and try again. While I set about forgiving myself for stopping my own swim, I went back to work, tended my kids, mowed my lawn, shopped for groceries, and did all the normal things. Amid all of it, though, I was troubled by the question at the back of my mind.

Should I go back to Dover?

It was through no fault of my friends and family that I felt alone with this question. I just didn't want to put them through the tedium of my deliberations. And more than that, I didn't want to ask them to invest in yet another endeavor that might end in failure. At least not for the moment.

The months post-Channel flipped past noiselessly and quickly. In October or November, I suddenly remembered Cliff Golding's challenges with the Channel—his six unsuccessful attempts before making it across. I wondered if he'd mind helping me think the situation through. We connected by phone one weekday morning, and instantly Cliff was like a brother-in-arms, helpful in a way that nobody else in my circle could be. He'd been where I was and had choices to offer about where I was going. He also told me some difficult truths and asked some hard questions about shame, embarrassment, loyalty, and persistence. I don't remember how long we talked, but I do remember canceling one work meeting after another to allow us more time. After we hung up, I felt relieved; I understood my particular challenge much better.

At the first opportunity, I contacted Mike Oram and booked a Channel swim for the next tide for which he had an available place, in 2013. We had a good conversation, and he beat me up good-naturedly about a few of my tactics. A couple of times, Angela Oram piped up loudly from across their shared office with some advice as well. It was all right, all true. Mostly, however, I noticed that Mike didn't seem focused on telling me what I'd done wrong. Rather, he talked about the unique challenge of piloting Mike Humphreys across the English Channel. I knew Mike O. was relentless and really appreciated his positive perspective.

When asked, I told some friends that I was going back "someday," and others, I told about my 2013 booking. That revelation could provoke complicated conversations that included questions such as, "What will you do differently?" Ultimately, I stopped talking about it. I knew that I had to start figuring out how to swim the Channel from scratch, how to absorb the challenge mentally; so while I understood the questions, I thought it more likely I'd learn what I needed to if I simply avoided them. I started planning interim swims between 2010 and 2013 to broaden my experience.

Jeffrey Hulett and I talked about a joint attempt across the Catalina Channel for 2012.

At the suggestion of both Cliff Golding and Mike Oram, I also made inquiries about swimming across the Straits of Gibraltar.

I was also dealing with the physical aftermath of my 2010 experiences. My shoulders felt destroyed, and my lower back muscles stayed seized almost through December, despite regular stretching, yoga, and physical therapy. I was in daily discomfort, my training routines fell by the wayside, and my swimming muscles seemed rapidly to melt away.

As my body shrank and tried to recover from the extreme stresses placed on it throughout my 2010 quest, my pen compensated, and I began to accelerate my writing. I wrote for magazines, for friends, for this book. I did interview after interview with Channel swimmers and personalities, while simultaneously planning other books, other challenges.

I'm monogamous by nature, though, and it was difficult to fully commit to my pen, or Gibraltar, or Catalina, or a mountain somewhere, while the Channel was still my first love.

I was thinking about that very thing on the day Mike Oram e-mailed me. It was January 2011. He'd had a cancellation for that September and wanted to know if I was interested in filling the slot. I opened his e-mail at work, read it, then sat back and exhaled deeply. I let the message settle on my screen while everything else receded into the background. Did I?

I went back to work, but I thought of little else all day and the next. Did I want to swim the Channel in 2011? What about my family, friends, work? Barb wanted to spend more time bicycling, I wanted to visit Evan in Tucson more often, and I wanted to take trips with Tyler and Connor as well. My shoulders were in lousy shape, and I knew I needed to rest and reconstruct my stroke to avoid future injuries. I didn't want to be fat anymore. Dale had plans for 2011 and wouldn't be able to train with me, so I'd have no regular boater.

There were a lot of reasons not to swim the Channel that year, and they were all true and important.

Then I thought—I could simply hide it. I could train under a veil of another challenge, and nobody else would suffer the emotional roller-coaster of another attempt so soon. Cliff and Mike had shown me that my biggest obstacle was cerebral, not physical, and I felt I could better overcome it in isolation anyway.

The truth was, I also didn't want to face the prospect of telling people I didn't make it again.

The next morning I reopened Mike's e-mail, typed three letters instead of two, and clicked "send."

I made the arrangements and recruited a very small group of people to help me. My first call was to Cliff, whom I asked to join the crew and stay silent about it—both of which he readily agreed to do. Mike agreed to stay mum as well. It wasn't the first time a swimmer had asked him for discretion. I told my boss at work so there would be no last-minute interference with my trip in September, and my doctor and physical therapists knew. I needed them to help rehabilitate my strained tendons and ligaments.

And then February dawned in Seattle.

On February 19, I drove to Lake Washington alone and stood and stared at the water. The lake was brutally cold, the sky was a foreboding gray, and my mind roiled with a thousand thoughts. The water was forty-five degrees Fahrenheit and very uninviting. I reflected, contemplated, and argued with myself. I wasn't sure I wanted to get into that water. My open-water training didn't need to start for a couple months yet, anyway, and the extreme cold meant that at best my swim would be relatively short.

I took a deep breath, tried to still the ceaseless debate in my head, and asked myself whether I wanted to swim the Channel or not. My family and friends had done their part in the past: followed my progress, trained with me, spent their time and treasure traveling to Dover. There were a lot of swimmers who had managed the feat in difficult circumstances, much more difficult than mine: Lisa Cummins, Tim Strange, Brent Hobbs, Cliff Golding, Sue Pepper, Ros Hardiman, Emma France, Jeffrey Hulett . . . and the list went on.

Did I plan on doing what I'd said . . . or not?

I did.

I stripped off my street clothes and walked down the beach into the cold water.

It began again.

Chapter 34

Dreams and Perspective

Training for my secret Channel swim went well, and I was able to manage the subterfuge relatively easily. Keeping my secret meant some very early morning swims while Barb was still sleeping, followed by little white lies about what time I'd started. I'd claim start times of 6:00 or 7:00 a.m. when I'd actually snuck out at 3:00, 4:00, or 5:00. I didn't enjoy lying but felt better about the deception as we coasted through summer and Barb was spared worries and allowed to enjoy the summer. Or at least as much summer as the Seattle rains allowed us.

The weeks and months of spring and summer flipped past like pages of a calendar on a breezy day, and soon late August arrived. I'd told family and friends I was going to Dover to work on this book and enjoy some swimming in Dover Harbor. I left for Dover on September 1 with my secret intact and arrived at Victoria House the next day, tired and somewhat haggard. After my normal settling in, I turned my attention to preparing for my attempt, buying supplies and touching base with Mike Oram about the upcoming weather.

Hurricanes require warm, moist air, temperatures of about eighty degrees Fahrenheit, high humidity, light winds, and very warm surface temperatures. In mid-August 2011, these conditions came together flawlessly just east of the Lesser Antilles, and Tropical Storm Irene began to form. It reached hurricane intensity shortly after striking Puerto Rico, and by August 20, the National Hurricane Center in the United States had issued an impending cyclone warning. Irene tracked north through Hispaniola and the Bahamas before she skimmed around the outer edges of Florida. On August 27, she made landfall in North Carolina and began to work her way up the US eastern seaboard. She bounced back out to sea to regain strength, and then made landfall again—twice. And she caused all of the damage and disturbance that such storms do. By the end of August, Irene had blown her worst at the United States and decided to make some waves in the United Kingdom. The jet stream obliged and carried what was left of the storm over the ocean at about the same time Delta was carrying me over.

By the time I arrived, the prospects for my 2011 Channel swim were already doomed. I spent a few days fitfully staring at weather websites and hoping for a break. It wasn't forthcoming.

On Monday, September 5, I woke slowly at Victoria House and stared up from my bed at the ornate ceiling in the Balcony Room. Decorative plaster circles adorned the ceiling around a crystal chandelier and lined the outer edges. A few ladybugs had taken up residence in the fixture and were buzzing around absentmindedly. I rubbed the sleep from my eyes and sighed, dejected, resigned. I'd awakened in the middle of the night in a panic that hadn't subsided with the dawn.

Both my shoulders were in pain. The left one had aching, lingering tendonitis in the bicep tendon, and the right had an inoperable rotator-cuff tear that often made it difficult to reach above shoulder level. In the mornings, I usually needed a few moments before I could get out of bed—before I knew which joints would complain most loudly that day. My muscles were strong, but the distress in my connective tissues regularly made simple things like carrying a briefcase problematic. My lower back was regularly in spasm, a result of running marathons plus overeager weightlifting in my twenties that had created a lifelong imbalance in my right hip. There was a painful bout of plantar fasciitis in my left foot stemming from too much cross-training to keep my fitness up for swimming. And on a regular basis, phantom nerve pain and burning sensations shot down my left thigh, a condition for which I'd been unable to even find a diagnosis.

I was just a journeyman swimmer. I'd managed a few good swims but wasn't of the caliber of Channel swimmers that I knew and called friends. I wasn't as fast as they were, and the lingering injuries meant I often couldn't match their training mileage. When I managed to show up fit and ready, self-doubt and fear toyed with my confidence, and I'd often been unable to overcome them.

I'd managed to prove three times that I wasn't capable of the focus and determination it took to accomplish the world's preeminent swim. I wasn't suited to stand among the men and women I'd hoped would be my peers someday. In conversations, most of them were understanding about my shortcomings in the Channel, but I felt like a poser, a pretender. At best, I was their chronicler, hoping to do some measure of justice to their stories through my writing. That was a privilege and a dream in itself, but it wasn't what I'd wanted from the English Channel. My dream had been to cross it in a swimsuit.

Dreams die painfully, whether they are meaningful dreams such as curing cancer, escaping poverty, or capturing someone's heart—or the dream of a father of three trying to swim across some rough water, mostly to satisfy his own vanity. All dreams die the same way—arduously.

I sat up and reached for the remote to flick on the Balcony Room's old TV. The news was on, and I started half-listening to the anchors as they outlined the world situation at the moment. In Syria, the government was brutally attacking and killing its own citizens in an attempt to retain power. There were similar actions underway in Libya. In Somalia, hundreds of thousands were starving from a drought-based food shortage, watching their children and elderly die as they marched across the desert in search of sustenance. Between news reports, the BBC was heavily advertising impending retrospectives of 9/11, the day in 2001 when three thousand innocent souls were brutally murdered. In Europe, several countries teetered on the brink of bankruptcy, and in the United States and United Kingdom, millions of people were still unemployed four years after a financial crisis caused a jarring contraction in the workforce.

The world was in a constant state of turmoil.

As I listened, my perspective on the Channel suddenly seemed very petty. My family was well-fed, and I had a steady income. There was a roof over our heads, water running from our faucets, and heat and electricity whenever we needed them. My loved ones were satisfied with life; their problems, such as which career to pursue and which body of water to swim across, were the problems of the privileged.

I reflected on all of this in the Balcony Room, and inevitably, I felt at peace. I had many blessings, and having "Channel Swimmer" in my eulogy wasn't an absolute requirement. It was a passion, not an obligation. I exhaled deeply, the kind of sigh that starts at the absolute bottom of your diaphragm and slowly squeezes its way through your lungs and open lips. It was time to put aside self-pity and pull myself together for a big Victoria House breakfast.

But first I had to call Mike Oram.

I waited while his phone made that funny British ringing sound that always makes me think of Winston Churchill in a bunker somewhere getting news of the D-Day invasion. I was soon rewarded with Mike's cheerful, "Hallo!" We exchanged pleasantries and began to talk about the weather.

"It's not good, I'm afraid," Mike said. "There's this system with the nasty winds, and then there are more systems lined up behind it on their way to our area after this mess leaves."

We talked at length, and finally Mike told me I should probably go home—it was over for the year.

I thought about that a moment. I thought about my seven years of training and thousands of miles of swimming. I thought about the friends I'd made in the Channel community. I thought about my sons and what I'd want them to teach their children, my grandchildren, about life and persistence. I wanted them to have the joy and comfort to do what they wanted to do, the confidence to follow whatever dream gave their lives meaning. For me, I knew in that moment that the most important things in life are being a father and a friend, a son and a brother, a partner and a good person to those that I've known for years as well as those I've just met.

My dream was to swim the English Channel.

The Channel might have decided to deny me even the chance to try in 2011, but it wasn't over and it wouldn't become over until I decided that's what I wanted, until I was absolutely convinced that I couldn't do it.

I'd come back in 2012, and in 2013, and each year until I walked out of the water into France.

I told Mike that, and he laughed and said, "Okay." I listened to him scratch my name down in his 2012 booking sheets for a possible swim if a place became available and reaffirm my 2013 booking. Then he paused and added, "What I don't understand is why you Channel swimmers do it."

It was a good question, and one I felt certain I'd be able to answer someday—the day I walked out of the water into France.

Chapter 35

St. Elmo's Fire

The iconic 1980s movie *St. Elmo's Fire* gets its title from a weather phenomenon in which electrical impulses appear to be airborne flames. This rare sight terrified sailors in the days of the great sailing ships—but in the film, one character uses it as a metaphor when talking to another character who is in distress at the moment; as a way to help her overcome her fears about her future. His point is that most fears are ephemeral if we can manage to see through them.

Over the years, I'd come to realize that fear was a contributor to my lack of success in the Channel. I reflected on this in mid-August 2012, as I settled into the Balcony Room at Victoria House for my fourth attempt to swim to France after I'd spent the year since my 2011 attempt in training and reflection. I was booked on three consecutive Channel tides with Mike Oram as my pilot. Even with St. Elmo's Fire in mind, though, my fears didn't seem ephemeral.

Swimming the Channel is difficult for anyone under any conditions, but as a returning Channel aspirant without a successful crossing to my name, I faced a unique challenge: I knew too much about what was to come without a sense of success to frame it, to put it into context. When we met for lunch at Chaplin's in 2009, Cliff Golding admitted to suffering the same fate.

I knew that at some point during my swim, I'd be struggling to find energy for five more minutes, despite the hours stretching out ahead. I'd be hungry and running low on energy, and my body would start to transition from burning ready glycogen to burning my ample fat stores. At that point, my swim would be in jeopardy. The transition would cause my mood to darken inexorably, and I'd find it hard to be upbeat about my chances. In my training, that jarring transition always took an hour or more, during which swimming was a slog—a death march of dragging one arm over the other.

I knew that at some point during my swim, I'd probably chafe. The Channel grease my crew applied to my body would wear away, and one body part would start to rub against another, to my skin's sorrow. If it happened when I was only halfway across, the saltwater would abrade my skin for another eight to ten hours, like wet sandpaper on an open wound.

I knew I'd vomit, because at some point I was likely to overfeed to the point where my stomach would rebel. Or I'd simply get seasick from the Channel's endlessly nauseating serenade of swells and chop, up and down, side to side. Or maybe I'd ingest too much saltwater and develop a swollen tongue, a horrible taste in my mouth, and nauseous heaving. One way or the other, I'd be getting sick—but I wouldn't be able to stop swimming. I'd probably end up vomiting into the water between breaths.

I knew I'd get stung. The jellyfish would be waiting in the Channel's separation zone, where ship traffic is thin enough that they don't get churned up by propellers. They might also be waiting off the coast of France, where they like the slightly warmer water. They'd be hanging in the water in a flotilla, and I'd have to simply stroke through as if thrusting my hands into buckets full of scorpions.

And I knew my shoulders would hurt. Those abused, maligned joints were well beyond the point where they deserved a year or two off from incessant swimming. In my left shoulder, either the lingering bicep tendonitis or the chronically inflamed rotator cuff would pinch, ache, or throb. My right shoulder would experience some bone-on-bone contact due to my arthritis and the swelling, soreness, and pain that entails.

As for the mental game—well, I didn't know if I had that buttoned down yet. I knew I'd start looking for plausible reasons to quit sometime a few hours after I started and probably not stop questioning myself until my crew signaled that I was close enough to land. Every one of my experiences in the Channel has involved stopping midway, and it was hard to believe I was fated for anything else.

I was afraid.

I was afraid I couldn't finish the swim, couldn't take everything the Channel would throw at me and persevere. I'd proven that three times.

I was afraid of more than that failure: I was afraid of the whole thing.

I was afraid of the lack of control that comes from being entirely in the hands of my crew, despite my confidence in them. I had never really given up total control in any situation, on any issue, at any time—perhaps ever.

I was afraid of the pain.

I was afraid of a swim and a day that would go on endlessly, filled with relentless water and waves and pain and more pain laid out ahead of me like Sisyphus's boulder and mountain. Afraid of looking back toward the White Cliffs of Dover after ten hours to see how far I'd come, only to realize that I still had more miles and hours ahead of me than behind.

And I was afraid of the cold—the unremitting, unrelenting, inexhaustible cold water that would declare war on me the moment I stepped into the Channel and maintain its assault until the moment I walked out in France. I knew I was trained and acclimated to handle it, but that didn't appease me. My hypothermia in 2008 had taught me that the cold could stop me dead in my tracks.

So why go ahead?

There were things that outweighed my anxieties. There was my passion and obsession for rising to this challenge, and there was my confidence that I could. There was an understanding that the Channel and I were going to reach a fork in the road at some point and part forever. I'd have to put swimming it behind me and move on, for better or worse.

And there was my pride.

Those things didn't outweigh my fear comprehensively—they merely overshadowed it ever so slightly.

I was getting in the water, no matter what.

But I was scared, and I knew I should be.

Chapter 36

The Fourth

On August 17, 2012, I was on the end of Prince of Wales pier, looking back toward the Dover waterfront. The pier, one of the interior seawalls of Dover Harbor, juts out about three quarters of a mile from Dover Beach on the south end. It hosts a promenade, a café, and a lighthouse perched at its easternmost extremity. From the lighthouse, you can see France on a clear day. The pier is a great place for people-watching, and that day was no exception.

There was a group of teenage boys fishing, while two girls sunbathed among them on the deck and chatted. I'm guessing the girls were waiting for the guys to catch something so they could all leave. The boys were preoccupied with giving one another good-natured grief about their lack of fishing skills, so it might take awhile. Just past the kids, a tall man and a dark-haired woman in exercise tights walked briskly down the promenade and chatted in English laced with a European accent I couldn't immediately place. She was about the age of my oldest son and was qualified to wear the tights; he was about as gray as I, built like a Channel swimmer, and was definitely not. Farther down the pier, two heavily bearded fishermen dressed in stained white togs were working the water for a catch. One of them was casting anew, while the other stared intently down into the harbor at his lure. Beyond the teenagers and the Hemingway brothers, fishermen stretched as far as the eye could see, all the way back to shore. Most of them had carried chairs, coolers, beer, and bait down the pier and looked settled in for the day.

Despite the appeal of character-watching, I walked out to the end of the pier to look at France in the distance and shake my fist at it. That elicited strange looks and the hasty departure of an elderly couple standing nearby. Next, I turned to gaze back on the town I love, drinking in a view I'll remember until well after I can't remember what I had for breakfast.

August 17 was a warm day, and eight years of cold-water training had left me with a diminished tolerance for heat, so I leaned against the railing for a moment to cool off, keeping my eyes trained toward England. About a quarter mile to my left, in the cruise ship berths of the marina, were the *Ocean Princess* and the *Saga Sapphire*, in port for the day. In between the seagulls' laughing screeches, I could just hear snippets of the announcements being made on deck for the benefit of those passengers who hadn't scurried off to see Canterbury Cathedral or other local sights.

To my right, about three miles away and seated majestically on a generous piece of leafy countryside, sat Dover Castle—still the quiet, impassive master of all it surveyed that it had been since the Romans were here. Having brought three crews to Dover for earlier Channel attempts, I have a lot of memories from in and around the Castle. I've toured its grounds with my sons, sat on Henry VIII's throne, explored the underground tunnels with Barb and others, and had my swim stroke critiqued by my friend Dale after she stood on the Castle's terrace watching me swim in Dover Harbor hundreds of feet below.

I turned straight ahead and was rewarded with a fine view of Dover. Arrayed before me were the stately white apartment and business blocks of the south end of the beach and the gritty, gray apartment block to the north that looks as if it were designed by a Soviet architect. Across the street from the buildings, smack-dab on the south end of the beach, was the new Dover Water Sports Center, which we don't use because, I'm told, it's a bit overpriced and overorganized. Business didn't seem to be suffering, though. Their rental racks of sailboats had emptied onto the water, and there were people sailing languidly all around the harbor. There were no Channel swimmers in the harbor at that moment, so the sailors had the water all to themselves. The beach was covered with sunbathers watching the horizon, squirting on sunblock, or gingerly making their way to the water across the pebbled surface. Nearby, on the promenade, Sue's Seafood Shack was doing a brisk turnover at its waterside tables. I'd been tempted by Sue's fare in the past but had never succumbed; when I'm in Dover, I'm usually too worried about upsetting a Channel swim to eat fresh seafood that's been sitting in the sun, albeit on ice.

Serving as the backdrop for everything was the glorious water itself—the cause of my frustration and the inspiration for my persistence. Reflecting the cloudless sky, the water was as brilliantly blue as a Caribbean postcard, calm and only as rippled as a Pringles chip. At sixty-four degrees Fahrenheit, it was warm enough that my upcoming swim might include a few more jellyfish than I'd prefer, but I'd coexisted with them in training.

Having finally cooled off, I started my walk back to Dover proper and the pub that would provide the calories I needed for my Channel attempt. It looked as if my swim might not happen immediately due to a revised weather forecast, so I'd possibly have a day or two extra to load up.

Over the next few days, however, I started to suffer the ravages of a flu I'd picked up sometime during the preceding week. The weather in the Channel wasn't conducive to an attempt anyway, but sitting in bed with a fever was the last thing I wanted to be doing when a good weather day came along, so it was stressing me out. I conferred with Mike Oram by phone, and he advised me to wait until I felt fully up to the swim. He also said that the weather looked cooperative for the twenty-third or possibly the twenty-fourth, six or seven days away

After a couple nights' sleep, I felt better the morning of the twenty-second but was still worried I wasn't fit enough. I sat around after breakfast trying to gauge my health while surfing BBC's impressive morning lineup: *Fall Guy* reruns and the Kardashians. To clear my head, I headed to Shakespeare

Beach, where Channel swims begin—a place I'd been so many times over the years. As I walked, I got mad at myself for seeking perfect circumstances for a crossing. Maybe I was being a perfectionist. I forced myself to think about the Channel the way I'd conditioned myself to do it: confidently. It was simply a very long swim that mirrored those I'd done in training for years. More intimidating, perhaps, but just a swim. Bolstered by this meditation and not suffering unduly from flu symptoms, I called Mike and told him I would be ready to go the following day if the weather held.

In my experience, there are few things more detrimental to a good night's sleep than the prospect of swimming from England to France the next day, but I tried to settle in on Wednesday night and make the best of it. Come Thursday morning, my eyes blinked open and stared up at the roundel imprinted into the ceiling plaster of the Balcony Room in Victoria House. A Dover mosquito danced delicately across the plaster as I exhaled slowly from the bottom of my diaphragm all the way up through the top of my lungs and thought, *Whew. The Channel.*

My crew and I met Mike and his boat crew and headed out of Dover Harbor on the *Gallivant* at just after ten thirty. It took a half hour to putter around the south seawall to Shakespeare Beach for my start, and we saw other swimmers preparing to leave at the same time. The day was brilliantly sunny, with bare wisps of clouds, and the water was calm for the Channel. Mike's crew pulled the boat up expertly alongside the beach, and I jumped in for the short swim onto land for my start. A blare of Mike's boat horn and I was off—comfortable in my medium. The water was a creamy light green that hid all of the histories and mysteries of the Channel except those floating within about eighteen inches of my eyes. The *Gallivant*, a blue and white thirty-six-foot cabin cruiser, with a low portside doorway from which Mike could watch and talk to his swimmers, was chugging reassuringly alongside me as I swam.

For the first time in my Channel swimming experiences, I'd given complete control over feeds and logistics to my crew. That move was really counter to my personality, but I'd prepared myself and was comfortable with the idea. In any case, there was nothing to worry about because Cliff and Bryan (and, of course, Mike) were more on top of things than I could have been. They could view the situation objectively—which was the whole point. They said my first feed would be an hour into the swim, and I followed their instructions, took my feed on schedule, and continued along. Thirty minutes later, I took my second feed.

I was still feeling strong when my tenth feed came along. I'm told I'd been averaging about 1.5 knots overall but was slowing a bit, which is to be expected as the adrenaline of the swim start wears off. After feed ten, I put my head back in the water and my face felt cold, as if it had not touched the water until that moment. I processed that for a few moments and then continued. The water was about sixty-three degrees, above the water temperatures I'd trained in for years. By the time my next feed came along, my arms had started getting cold too, and the chill was moving slowly from my wrists to my shoulders, as if cold molasses was being poured down them. But I was accustomed to handling cold arms while swimming. In Seattle, it's often cold and raining above the surface and relatively calm underneath it. So I chalked it up to the rigors of the Channel and got on with it. I should have shared these issues with my crew, but it didn't occur to me because I'd gotten past them in training.

I swam on for one more feed, and then my last feed of the day came along—just as it had on my last three attempts. I don't clearly remember seeing the signal from Bryan or Cliff that indicated my feed would be in five minutes, but I remember things starting to unravel underwater. I couldn't get my arms to stroke their normal path, and I was breathing heavily. Chugging steadily alongside, the boat actually seemed to me to be veering from parallel to perpendicular and back again. I looked over at it and then floated around to the back and hung there, asking for one of my crew. Sadly, the crew member I asked for was Lynne Smith—who had accompanied me on my 2008 attempt. At the moment, she was probably at home in Northern Virginia. In retrospect, I guess I wanted her to fish me out as she had done on that swim, when I had been in a similar state.

Ten minutes later, I was on the *Gallivant,* and it was steaming back toward Dover Harbor. I was heaving and defeated for the fourth time by the English Channel. Mike Oram held me upright to make sure I stayed lucid and conscious, while the crew dissected what had happened. I sat and listened in shame and frustration.

"Perhaps the Channel is not the place for you, Mike," Oram said to me after I'd stopped shivering and heaving.

I thought he might be right.

Chapter 37

The Mountain

I woke the following morning and spent time on the phone autopsying my swim with Mike and Cliff. Both were very illuminating. Both had experience, introspection, intellectual curiosity, and importantly, world-class abilities to talk. Cliff provided a rundown of the swim, which was helpful to me in filling in things I didn't know or remember. Mike provided impressions and queried me about my own, after which he shared thoughts on what it would take for me to get across successfully.

Later, Marcy MacDonald called me. Marcy is an accomplished Channel swimmer from New York. With eleven crossings under her belt, she's working her way toward the US record for most Channel crossings. She started our conversation by saying, "We'll get to the bottom of this together when you get home." I was still reeling from my experiences, but a "we" from Marcy meant a lot to me.

Everyone's support was gratifying, but I just couldn't get my head into the right place for making another attempt that year, as I had said I would do if necessary. I wasn't convinced that simply waiting for my resurgent flu to abate and the weather to cooperate would carry me to a better result. So I made plans to go back home to Seattle.

Later that afternoon, I walked through Dover, making my way up the White Cliffs trail along the coast. I sat and watched the busy port process ferries, inbound ships, cars, and tourists. It started raining lightly, so I headed back along the narrow footpath edged by grass and bushes down to sea level. I was stopped by a young European couple just leaving the port on foot, in need of directions to the beach and a good restaurant. Given how well I knew the town, that was easily handled, and I continued on my walkabout.

I went past Swimmer's Beach and onward downtown to Pencester Gardens, the park between High Street and the River Dour, from which Dover takes its name. The rain had stopped, and I sat on a red bench to watch the town enjoy the evening. I knew a lot of people in Dover and yet actually knew very few. All my friends were related to Channel swimming, but the vibrant local community around me didn't really know me at all. It didn't matter; having enjoyed years in their midst, I felt I was among friends. I got up and walked to High Street and turned left, passing mainstays of my years in Dover, including the Eight Bells Pub. I'd tried every ale on tap at the Eight Bells and enjoyed watching locals sampling too many of the same from time to time. I turned off High Street onto a small footpath that runs through the church grounds that adjoin both High Street and Pencester Gardens. The church grounds had a number of old headstones, many of them askance. Seated on a couple of tombs were four men talking and laughing, beers in hand. Taken by surprise, I looked at them for a moment; they stopped to return my look.

One of them stood and wished me a good evening with a grin, while the others nodded amiably, smiling.

"How are you?" I responded.

"I'm wantin' a cushion on these stones," he replied, "but 'at's awright."

Behind me, I heard a footstep and turned to see a well-dressed and heavily made-up woman coming down the footpath throwing dirty looks at the men. I could understand her dismay about drinking in public, but these guys seemed harmless enough and they somehow fit the scene. She passed by in a cloud of perfume with a "hrmmph" and continued away.

I turned back to the men with a grin and said, "Well, she seems to be having a bad day!"

The standing man smiled broadly, revealing gaps where teeth used to be, and asked, "Offa you a drink, mate?"

"I'd better not, but thanks," I said, adding, "I love this town."

He looked at me for a moment and said, "Yeah," before returning his attention to his friends.

I walked about fifteen yards and looked back at the men one last time before turning the corner. The gap-toothed man held up his beer in salute. I waved and left.

Perhaps the town knew me after all.

I walked back to Victoria House, my home away from home, the long way, digesting everything. Would I go back? I probably would—but I knew I'd need to start over in order to figure out why I kept shutting down in the Channel. Even in the grip of dark frustrations and still stinging from my fourth dejected ride back to Dover by pilot boat, I realized there must be something worthwhile in my persistence and something possible about my ambition if so many qualified people were confident enough to help again.

I knew the challenge for me was not the Channel, or the training, or the injuries, or even the cold water. The challenge was within. The challenge was me. I'd honed my Channel tactics over the years and had tried everything at least once—with similar results. To be sure, there were things to improve on in my training and during the swim—but when I looked at the situation in the harsh light of day, I was forced to admit for the first time that I was the common denominator in my results. The mountain ahead of me was not to find the perfect training, conditions, or feeds, but to find a way to defeat the aspects of myself that were shutting down when I was in that cold, salty stretch of water between Dover and France. How could I conquer my own approaches, biases, reactions, and personality when I've spent a lifetime developing them? In this, I was on my own. It would be completely on me to conquer my fears and unleash my ability to keep swimming no matter what.

I spent my flight to Seattle reflecting, and soon my plane cleared the Cascade mountain range bordering Puget Sound and began its circle over Lake Washington before landing. It was evening, and the sunset glittered on the Seattle waters as I looked down and thought about what I wanted to do. I still longed to be in the water, but for the moment, I wanted to swim in my home waters, simply for the joy of it.

The next morning I woke early, pulled on my swimsuit and warm-ups, and ten minutes later I was at the waterfront. Before I'd left for the beach, I'd scanned my smartphone and found e-mails from many of the Channel veterans I've talked about in this book, offering support. I thought about those friends and the journey I'd been on with them. My challenges in crossing the Channel were something that, ultimately, nobody but I could overcome because they were founded in my own weaknesses in the endeavor. But I had made these friends in the Channel community and they could help if I'd let them—if I went back. I had only to outwit myself and my own instincts to achieve my goal. It was a daunting prospect and, in some ways, the ultimate challenge, but it seemed a mountain worth climbing—but that wasn't why I was swimming that day. My swim that day was because I loved being in the water and doing what I was meant to do.

I walked into the water and began swimming southeast toward the sun rising over Lake Washington—and toward the future.

Chapter 38

Going to Dover

Whether you're interested in making an attempt at swimming the Channel or simply interested in visiting to take in the sights, Dover is a very accessible town.

Getting There

Getting to Dover is easy. As a major port town, it's served by all the major London airports, and there are very good roadways into town. Gatwick is the easiest airport if you intend to rent a car and drive yourself. That airport is about seventy miles from Dover, and it's a relatively straight shot. You leave Gatwick on the M23 and go north to the M25 about 10 miles. Take the M25 east about fifteen miles and look for signs to take the M20 south. Once you're on the M20, it will take you about another hour to reach Dover. In the last few minutes of your drive, you'll be rewarded with a wonderful view of the Channel—and France in the distance, if it's a clear day.

Heathrow is more troublesome by car, mostly because you're forced to spend much more time on the M25 motorway, affectionately known as the "world's largest car park" for its horrendous traffic. To reach Dover from Heathrow, you leave the airport on the M4 going toward the M25. When you reach the M25, take the east ramp and then follow the M25 until you see signs for the M20 south. The M20 will take you right into Dover. It's a bit more than a hundred mile drive.

If you plan to rely on the British rail system, both Heathrow and Gatwick are good options. To get to Dover from either, take a train to London and then catch an appropriate train to Dover Priory at Victoria Station. After arriving at Heathrow or Gatwick, you simply take the Heathrow Express or Gatwick Express, respectively, to get into central London. Those trains run approximately every fifteen minutes and take you nonstop to Paddington Station and Victoria Station, respectively. If you're on a budget and arriving at Heathrow, you can opt for the London Underground into Central London, but that will take about twice as long due to multiple stops. You'll also have to drag your luggage around more and fight the crowds on the tube for a seat. If you're traveling in tourist-choked summertime, the Express train is more than worth the premium.

Lodging

Dover offers lots of bed-and-breakfasts, with some hotels sprinkled in. There are a number of soulless traveler's inns alongside the motorways into Dover and in Dover itself, but why not stay in one of the colorful B&Bs? Other than staying in Deal (15 miles north) once, I've mostly stayed with Bill and Audrey at their wonderful Victoria House, and I would highly recommend it, but they have since retired and are no longer taking in guests, unfortunately. Many other swimmers find comfort and hospitality at the following lodgings, which also cater to Channel swimmers:

- Varn Ridge Channel Swim Park, 145 Old Dover Road, Capel Le Ferne
  - o + 44 1303 251765
  - o E-mail: info@varneridge.co.uk
- Sandown Guest House, 229 Old Folkestone Road, Dover, Kent, Ct179SL
  - o + 44 1304 226807
  - o E-mail: stay@sandownguesthouse.com
- Hubert House, 9 Castle Hill Road, Dover, Kent, CT161QW
  - o + 44 1304 202253
  - o E-mail: stay@huberthouse.co.uk

What to Do and See

Within an hour's radius of Dover Harbor, there are some notable sites to check out. Here are just a few:

- Dover Castle—I've been to Dover Castle many times and could probably do a passable job of writing a guidebook entirely dedicated to it. I won't do that; I'll just provide a few highlights. The castle is a multilayered tourist attraction spanning multiple generations of the history you might have learned in grade school. There are remnants of a Roman lighthouse on the property that are about a thousand years old. There's a whole raft of history in the walls and floorboard related to Henry VIII's time on the throne. And to round it out closer to our own time, there's a massive tunnel system in the White Cliffs under the castle that was carved out by the British Army for use during World War II. All of these historical points, and more, can be experienced through tours and time spent walking around the grounds. Bring your kids and budget a day for the event.

- Canterbury and Canterbury Cathedral—Home to the Church of England and the stunning Canterbury Cathedral, Canterbury is a medieval town you can tour easily on foot. You can bring the kids on this excursion, too, as there are plenty of shops, restaurants, and other attractions to keep energetic minds occupied.

- Deal Castle—One of the castles commissioned by Henry VIII through funds appropriated from priories and monasteries across England, Deal Castle was a working defense castle in Henry's time. It's a particularly accessible castle for a walk and exploration, and it's very kid-friendly. My son Connor played with the foam swords we bought him at the Deal Castle gift shop for years and years.

- Samphire Hoe—Located about five miles south of Dover, Samphire Hoe offers hiking, a wildlife preserve, great fishing, and other outdoor activities in a green park situated on the top of the land where the Chunnel leaves the English coast. Simply drive out of Dover toward the M20 and watch for the signs on your left-hand side.

Chapter 39

Acknowledgments, Truths, and Biases

My Channel swimming journey took much longer than planned, and I had a lot of help along the way with both the swim and the book in your hands. The story wouldn't be complete and accurate without taking some time to acknowledge those who helped graciously, mention the biases I developed that colored my perception of English Channel-swimming, and disclose the truths about licenses I took in the production of this story.

Acknowledgments

- The crews on my English Channel attempts went well above and beyond the call of family and friendship, and I owe them sincere thanks. They included my older sons Tyler and Evan (my youngest son, Connor, was too young to go out on the Channel pilot boats), Lynne Smith, Bryan Wilkinson, Brent Hobbs, Ros Hardiman, and my partner Barb Hinnaland. In addition to thanks, I owe these people an apology for my unsuccessful swims. Swimming the Channel is a tough task and success isn't always in the swimmer's control, but I didn't always give the task everything it demanded. In the course of that error of omission, I put these people through a lot of effort, turmoil, and cost, and I owe them an abject apology.

- I also owe Dale McKinnon, who crewed for me multiple times and trained with me for years and years and years, a debt of gratitude I can never repay. Thank you, Dale.

- Bill and Audrey Hamblin were extraordinarily hospitable every time I stayed at Victoria House. They're like a second family that it took Channel swimming to discover, and I'm thankful and humbled to call them friends.

- It's difficult to believe I had to assemble a medical "team" to coax my body through the adventure, but it was absolutely necessary. It included Dr. Timothy Locknane, my sports generalist, who offered me guidance and a sympathetic ear over the years. My chiropractors regularly kept me straight and functional: Drs. Tim Clanton, Karen Sheppard, and Caedin Pettigrew. Jewell Smith and Sonam Metse at the Jade Spring Wellness Center in Kirkland were invaluable with acupuncture and massage. And my physical therapist, Sara Chisholm, deserves special mention for her freakishly strong hands and invaluable advice as a fellow swimmer.

- The esteemed Chairman of the CS&PF, Mike Oram, was an extremely helpful source of information about the topic and generous with advice to a fault, particularly through his many e-mail missives through the years. Thank you, Mike.

- I took the facts about Channel swimmers' times, places, dates, and so on from the swimmers themselves and confirmed them through a database maintained by Julian Critchlow, a Channel swimmer who also advises the CS&PF committee. The database can be found at http://home.btconnect.com/critchlow/index.htm. Thank you, Julian, for your hard and unpaid work on the database.

- Freda Streeter, Emma France, Michelle Tuptalo, and Barrie and Irene Wakeham have selflessly helped me and many, many others on Swimmer's Beach for years; thank you very, very much.

- There were numerous friends who crewed for me with rowboats, kayaks, or speedboats, or just by watching carefully from a beach. Many of these swims took place during training, many during rough or difficult conditions. Those who helped me included Dale McKinnon, of course, and Tim Duerr, Brian Madison, Glen Ader, Chip Lang, Arne Anderson, and my partner Barb. Thank you for your sacrifice on my behalf. Arne—I'm sorry about your iPod on the bottom of Lake Washington.

- I'd be remiss if I didn't thank the team that helped me edit and rewrite this book multiple times. Those include my editor, Laura Ross, and my great friend in publishing, Liz Leiba.

- Finally, my thanks go out to everyone whom I interviewed or who talked to me for this book. I couldn't have written this without you, and I actually wrote it *for* you. I apologize for any inadvertent errors in transcription and sincerely hope you enjoy reading this as much as I enjoy our talks and your friendship. I also apologize sincerely that I could not fit everyone that talked to me into the book. Unfortunately, the dictates of the time line and the story arc meant that some swimmers' stories were left on the cutting-room floor.

Truths and Other Details

Everything in this book happened as described, but there are a couple of disclaimers.

First, I'm a known cynic and love sarcastically tinged humor. I often wonder if that's why I've dragged out my Channel adventure—to spend more time in England, the homeland for dry, sarcastic humor. Watch *Little Britain* sometime, and you'll see what I mean. (And apropos of that—did you know that its star, David Williams, swam the Channel?) As a sarcastic cynic, my attitude and memory *might* have slightly colored my recollection of some events and discussions. It's all basically true, though—including the McDonald's episode in which the weights-and-measures police shut down my order of two quarter-pounders. Could I have made that up?

Second, while everything happened as described, the book required multiple rewrites because my English Channel adventure has taken more years than I'd hoped. In the interest of presenting a readable time line while including stories from previous years, I've shuffled some of the interviews and events in cases where the timing didn't impact the story. Ros Hardiman, for example, was interviewed in 2008 and 2009, while I talked to Mike Oram most extensively in early 2011, after I'd already failed in the Channel three times. Another example was my shoulder problem in 2010: While that happened exactly as and when described, I didn't actually ask the Channel community for their tales of similar issues until I was finishing up this book, in 2011. Other interviews were scattered around the years, but I worked them into the book as best I could because I respect the accomplishments of the people involved so much. In the cases where I moved timing of interviews and such, none of the pertinent details of my own swimming or the swims of those interviewed were changed—those are timed as they happened.

A last example of this timing issue is the reference to Pacific Northwest swimmers in Chapter 22, Opening Day in Bellingham Bay. Some of those swims actually happened in the year I finished this book, so I was not reflecting on as many of them as I mentioned in 2010; in 2011, I rewrote the chapter to work them in out of respect for their achievements. These are the actual details of those swims:

Solo Swimmers

- Tim Cespedes—2007
- David Livengood—2010
- Michelle Macy—2007, 2009

Relay Swimmers

Oregon Ducks—2010—Joni Young, Tim Cespedes, Jim Teisher, Natalie Groat, Andrew Shaar, and Mirjana Prather

Karen Gaffney relays—2001—Two six-person relays, including Karen Gaffney, Kathryn Haslach, Tim Haslach, Gail McCormick, Sara Quan Nelson, Tom Landis, Mike Tennant, Joe Tennant, Marc Bowen, Kelsey Bowen, Laura Schob, Lindy Mount

Third, I'd like to comment on the art of piloting: I tried to represent my experiences carefully and accurately in this book. Those include candid commentary about my first Channel pilot, and I'd like to be clear. It's a poor workman that blames his tools, and a swimmer blaming his or her pilot for a failed attempt has been a relatively regular tradition in English Channel swimming, it's sad to say. So, to be clear—I don't blame my first Channel pilot for my unsuccessful attempts, and I take full responsibility for my swim in 2010. It was I who stopped putting one arm in front of the other and quit swimming, not my pilot. I was the one who abandoned the swim, and the failure was my responsibility.

That said, it is my opinion, developed over many years of research for this book, that there was more Chris Osmond could have done in 2010. That may very well be because I'm simply a marginal swimmer when it comes to the Channel, and as a result, I need a pilot with specific skills, someone with the intensity and passion to go beyond the norm to help me succeed. Okay, I'll accept that and my responsibility. But in the interest of other marginal swimmers who might attempt the Channel, I feel compelled to be candid. There are many fine pilots, but my research and experience indicated that Mike Oram was probably that pilot for me, and I'm forever respectful of his passion and dedication to the sport of English Channel swimming and to the swimmers whom he pilots.

Finally, readers may notice that I did not include profiles or interviews of record holders or more elite swimmers in this book. That was by design, as I wanted to profile the more "average" Channel swimmers, to whom I believe most readers can better relate. My premise was that if these swimmers and friends of mine can do the Channel—and readers find they want to—then with proper training, they can do it too. Throughout the years that I ran and cycled competitively, through my triathlon years, and finally for the eight years before the completion of this book, it's always particularly struck me that endurance sports are very democratic pursuits. You merely have to choose to participate, and you only have to endure to finish. In the early days of my running "career," the average marathoner would finish in less than four hours—yet today, due to the rapid expansion of regular runners taking up the 26.2-mile challenge, 80 percent of marathoners finish in *over* four hours. Given determination, dedication, and persistence, virtually anyone can do these types of events. It would be very difficult to persuade me otherwise, and I tried to focus on swimmers in this book who would illustrate that point.

Biases

CS&PF vs. CSA—I made my Channel swim attempts with the cooperation of the CS&PF (Channel Swimmer's & Pilots Federation). The other sanctioning body is the CSA (Channel Swimming Association). In recent years, the CS&PF has become by far the larger organization in terms of the number of swims it oversees. The CSA is, however, the older and more traditional sanctioning body. Most of my friends and the people profiled in this book swam with the CS&PF, and the volunteer crew on Swimmer's Beach was much more closely affiliated with that body. As a result, most of the characters in this book are CS&PF-affiliated. I mean no disrespect to the CSA by this; they are a very well-established organization, with good Channel pilots and plenty of experience.

About the Author

Mike Humphreys spent most of the first decade of the third millennium training for the world's top open water swim: the English Channel. When he isn't in Dover, Mike splits his time between Seattle, Washington, and Atlanta, Georgia. A father of three and a Microsoft manager in Xbox gaming when he's not out in open water, Mike has been swimming, running and cycling obsessively for 35 of his 50 years and has the scars, aches and pains to prove it.

Mike is currently training for his fifth attempt at swimming the English Channel, scheduled for summer of 2015. He's also working on his next book—about Mount Kilimanjaro.

CPSIA information can be obtained at www.ICGtesting.com
Printed in the USA
LVOW06s0240101013

356291LV00001B/55/P

9 781481 757386